The Future of International Law Enforcement
New Scenarios — New Law?

Veröffentlichungen des Instituts für Internationales Recht an der Universität Kiel

Herausgegeben von

Jost Delbrück und Rüdiger Wolfrum

Institut für Internationales Recht an der Universität Kiel

115

The Future of International Law Enforcement New Scenarios – New Law?

Proceedings of an International Symposium of the Kiel Institute of International Law March 25 to 27, 1992

Edited by

Jost Delbrück

Assistant Editor:
Ursula E. Heinz

Duncker & Humblot · Berlin

Die Deutsche Bibliothek – CIP-Einheitsaufnahme

The future of international law enforcement : new scenarios – new law? ; Proceedings of an international symposium of the Kiel Institute of International Law. March 25 to 27, 1992 / ed. by Jost Delbrück. — Berlin: Duncker und Humblot, 1993
(Veröffentlichungen des Instituts für Internationales Recht an der Universität Kiel ; Bd. 115)
ISBN 3-428-07643-5
NE: Delbrück, Jost [Hrsg.]; Institut für Internationales Recht ⟨Kiel⟩: Veröffentlichungen des Instituts . . .

Fremddatenübernahme: Berliner Buchdruckerei Union GmbH, Berlin 61
Druck: Color-Druck Dorfi GmbH, Berlin 49
Printed in Germany

ISSN 0720-7263
ISBN 3-428-07643-5

Foreword

From the time of its inception, the Institute of International Law at the University of Kiel has concerned itself with the role and functions of law in maintaining international peace and security. This tradition was established under the guidance of *Theodor Niemeyer* — the founder of the Institute. It was forcefully carried on by *Walther Schücking* — the far-sighted protagonist of international organization as a means of maintaining peace and security in a conflict-ridden world. And it was taken up again after World War II by the first postwar director of the Institute, *Hermann von Mangoldt,* and his successor *Eberhard Menzel,* who not only contributed far-sighted ideas about a future European Security System in international legal and political terms, but also initiated the now established tradition of making the Institute a regular meeting ground for international legal scholars and representatives of national and international administrations. Problems of international security and peace have figured prominently in the agendas of the series of conferences of which the recent colloquium on the "Future of International Law Enforcement" is a part. The present volume, published under the auspices of the Kiel Institute, contains the papers and comments presented and the proceedings of this colloquium held from March 25-27, 1992 in the Senate Conference Room of the Christian Albrechts University at Kiel.

The end of the Cold War and the ensuing chances of the United Nations to live up to its role as it was envisaged by the United Nations Charter, i.e. to act as a central authority in the international efforts to maintain international peace and security, have once again focussed international interest on the perplexing problem of international law enforcement. In particular, the collective effort of the coalition forces, authorized by the United Nations Security Council, to fight the Iraqi aggression against Kuwait and restore peace and security in the Gulf area, has raised many questions as to the scope and limits of the authority of the United Nations to enforce international law. The critical signs of a destabilized post-Cold War international system and the renaissance of nationalisms in the wake of this dismemberment of the Soviet Union and Yugoslavia attributed a special sense of urgency to finding answers to these questions. It was the purpose of the Kiel colloquium to examine and discuss the prospects of a revitalized United Nations law enforcement authority — and possibly of regional arrangements to be charged with a similar authority — in the light of likely future conflict scenarios.

In the past, there has been concern about a growing divergence of views between the international law communities in the United States and in Europe with regard to the function and role of international law in international relations, particularly with regard to the use of force in international law enforcement. As it is the firm conviction of the organizers of the Kiel colloquium that a transatlantic consensus with regard to these vital issues is indispensible, they believed that it was highly desirable to convene the conference under active participation of international legal scholars from both the European and the American side. The result of the exchanges during the conference has been encouraging, and there is agreement that this dialogue shall be continued in the future.

No colloquium can be successfully held without adequate funding. The Kiel Institute gratefully recognizes the substantial financial support granted by the Stiftung Volkswagenwerk, by the State of Schleswig-Holstein, and the Christian Albrechts University as well.

Kiel, September 1992 *Jost Delbrück*

Contents

Abbreviations

AJIL	=	American Journal of International Law
ASEAN	=	Association of Southeast Asian Nations
CIA	=	Central Intelligence Agency
CSCE	=	Conference on Security and Cooperation in Europe
EC	=	European Communities
ECOMOG	=	Economic Community of West African States (ECOWAS) Cease-Fire Monitoring Group
ECOSOC	=	Economic and Social Council
EEC	=	European Economic Community
EPIL	=	Encyclopedia of Public International Law
GA	=	General Assembly
GAOR	=	Official Records of the General Assembly
GATT	=	General Agreement on Tariffs and Trade
IAEA	=	International Atomic Energy Agency
ICJ	=	International Court of Justice
ILC	=	International Law Commission
IMF	=	International Monetary Fund
Inter-Am.C.H.R.	=	Inter American Commission on Human Rights
NATO	=	North Atlantic Treaty Organization
OAS	=	Organization of American States
OEO	=	obligations erga omnes
OAU	=	Organization of African Unity
OECD	=	Organization for Economic Cooperation and Development
para(s).	=	paragraph(s)
Res.	=	Resolution
SC	=	Security Council
Supp.	=	Supplement
UNEF	=	United Nations Emergency Force
UNHCR	=	United Nations High Commissioner for Refugees
UNTAC	=	United Nations Transitional Authority in Cambodia
v.	=	versus
WEU	=	Western European Union
ZaöRV	=	Zeitschrift für ausländisches öffentliches Recht und Völkerrecht

Opening Address

Jost Delbrück*

Ladies and Gentlemen, Dear Colleagues:

It is a great honor and a pleasure to welcome you on behalf of the Institute of International Law to this symposium which is part of the series of regular biannual symposia which we are holding in Kiel since 1964. Due to financial problems, this symposium, which was to be held at the traditional date in late November, had to be postponed to this late March 1992 date. Now we can gratefully recognize the financial support granted by the Volkswagen-Stiftung (VW Foundation) and by the Government of the State of Schleswig-Holstein. We are now able to have this symposium as usual, that is, we can extend to you the kind of hospitality which is, in a way, essential for a fruitful scholarly exchange and for which the Kiel symposia seem to have become notorious over the years.

We thank you very much that you have so readily accepted our invitations. Except for *Louis Henkin,* who was not able to cancel his commitments in New York and as a member of our Board of Advisers very much regrets not to be with us, all participants invited have made to Kiel. We gladly want to welcome the members of the Board who could attend. As a representative of the Board members we like to extend an especially warm welcome to *Sir Arthur Watts* who not only has become a frequent participant in our symposia but who has also served brilliantly as the President of the Phillip C. Jessup Moot Court during the German national rounds here in Kiel only a few weeks ago. We heartily welcome our colleagues from the United States who by their participation help us to achieve one of the main aims of this symposium, namely to engage in a much needed thorough dialogue between international lawyers from Europe / Germany and from abroad. At this point, I like to say a very personal "thank you" to Professor *Mary Ellen O'Connell* for her advice in drawing up the program for our symposium and who also helped in persuading our American participants to attend. We also warmly welcome our friends from the neighbouring countries (Austria, France and Switzerland) and from Germany — most of them "old hands" in participating in these symposia. Thanks to all of you for joining us! At this point, a first "thank you" goes to the Institute's staff who made it possible that we are now assembled around this nice "round table," literally speaking.

* Prof. Dr. *Jost Delbrück,* Director of the Institute of International Law at the University of Kiel; Professor at the Indiana University.

The symposium is devoted to a challenging topic as you may have seen and this may be one of the reasons that you have made your way to Kiel. To be serious now, the issues that we are confronting after the dramatic changes in the international system are highly complex and ask for our full attention as international lawyers. After the fall of the Berlin wall many people, particularly the Germans, thought that "eternal peace had broken out." But then, within weeks of the first all-German federal elections, the Gulf crisis escalated into a military conflict. It found us unprepared. It took weeks before the German public realized that they were witnessing, for the first time, military enforcement of international law, i.e. the prohibition of aggression, by the organized international community of states, the United Nations. It was realized that the military action taken by the coalition forces was not yet another instance of lonely decisions of some governments to engage in the use of force, but rather an action authorized by the UN Security Council, and that this could very well be the beginning of a new era of the international community living up to the responsibility for international peace and security as it was written into the UN Charter in 1945. Although the German public ultimately approved of the action taken against Iraq by a similar percentage as in other European countries, the very idea that the United Nations might react in the same way in future confrontations raised a controversial debate here and elsewhere.

Would membership in the United Nations oblige members other than the Great Powers to active participation in peace-*making* operations? What would the scenarios be like which would induce the Security Council to decide in favor of military enforcement action in the future? If the response given to the Iraqi aggression really was the result of a renewed commitment to the enforcement of fundamental international legal principles such as the prohibition of the use of force, what would the reaction of the community of states be if the Security Council would be stalemated again? Was there an obligation of individual states or a given group of states to act outside the United Nations on behalf of the international community? And finally, would we have to react only to military threats *strictu sensu* or would other threats such as grave violations of human rights in a given state, or would major instance of willful destruction of the environment like burning oil wells or poisoning of water courses threatening international peace and security ask for collective — possibly forcible — reactions by the community of states? These were the kind of questions asked publicly and which started to be discussed among international lawyers. And these were the questions which persuaded us to look into the matter of international authority to enforce international law under the changed conditions of the international system at this symposium. The agenda of the symposium is one which asks us to face up to qualitatively different challenges from those posed during the Cold War. The challenges are qualitatively new ones, and they ask for innovative answers.

But there is more to the task we have set ourselves for this symposium. We want discuss the problems put in front of us with our American colleagues. We all know that time and again there has been a divergence of views and approaches between European and American international lawyers with regard to the question of what the proper role of international law is to be in international relations. In times of a rapid destabilization of the international system as we are witnessing it today, close cooperation and mutual understanding between the United States of America and Europe is essential at all levels. To contribute to this cooperation and to the promotion of mutual understanding is a major reponsibility also of international lawyers. It is our hope that our meeting will establish a sound basis for fulfilling this task and for future exchanges.

In this spirit I welcome you to Kiel again. Let us hope for a rewarding exchange of ideas so that you will find it worth your while to have attended this symposium.

Now I should like to ask Professor *Wolfrum* to chair today's sessions.

Opening Address

Rüdiger Wolfrum*

Thank you, Jost! As indicated I would like, on behalf of the rectorate of the University, to extend a very warm welcome to every participant in this symposium. The rectorate is indeed very pleased about this high ranking participation. It is an honor for the University to host so many distinguished scholars from the United States as well as from Germany. Speaking in my capacity as a co-director of the Institute of International Law, I hope that we will have a fruitful and very extensive discussion, and that this is not just two days of business but that we can establish a permanent dialogue across the ocean.

Having the floor, I would like to provide some information about the University for those who have not visited Kiel on a previous occasion. The University of Kiel was founded in 1665 and thus belongs to what we refer to as the third wave of university foundations in Europe. In this period a couple of universities in northern Europe were founded, such as the University of Lund, Tallin, and Rostock, for example. The founding of universities in this period was a reaction to the Thirty Years War and the devastation brought about through it. This is the reason why this university has in its coat of arms the motto "pax optima rerum." I believe that this is a motto which may properly be applied to this symposium, too. As to whether this university is accordant with this motto — I will not go into detail, but at least we try hard. The University of Kiel now has nearly 20,000 students, and this figure is constantly increasing. As the size of the staff has not changed since the early seventies, when Kiel had 12,000 students, I will admit that we are totally overcrowded. For example, the law faculty has a little bit more than 2,500 students with a staff designed for about 1,200. Last winter the faculty had to accept more than 800 new students, while having a capacity of merely 350. There are classes with more than 700 students, this being the rule rather than the exception for first and second year students. I leave it to you to decide whether this can be regarded as an effective form of training. However, an enlargement of the faculty is not to be expected.

Thank you again for coming, thank you again for participating and showing your confidence that we are able to host an interesting conference!

---

* Prof. Dr. *Rüdiger Wolfrum*, Director of the Institute of International Law at the University of Kiel; Vice-Rector of the Kiel University.

New Scenarios of Threats to International Peace and Security: Developing Legal Capacities for Adequate Responses

W. Michael Reisman*

A priority for communities, whether acting individually or in concert, is to provide for their security. Security is often calculated in terms of power and military assets but a moment's reflection should make clear that any community's structures and capacities for decision — the fundamental institutions and procedures for making essential decisions — are prerequisite to knowing what assets to acquire and how to use them. How can lawyers and other policy planners assess the institutional adequacy of the international legal and political community for responding to the range of most probable threats to inclusive security in the next decade?

The question is neither theoretical nor moot. Addressing it is an exercise that must precede rational institution building, amendment and change. The drafters of the United Nations Charter in 1944 and 1945 went through it, as did the framers of the NATO and Warsaw Pacts in their day. In each instance, the institutional processes the drafters proceeded to establish expressed their responses to the security problems they anticipated. Given their resources and the political context in which they operated, they felt that these institutional arrangements were the best they could achieve.

World events in the last three years have given this type of exercise, in eclipse, as a practical matter, for four decades, renewed timeliness. The United Nations Security Council instructed the Secretary-General on January 31, 1992

> to prepare ... his analysis and recommendations on ways of strengthening and making more efficient within the framework and provisions of the Charter the capacity of the United Nations for preventive diplomacy, for peacemaking and for peace-keeping.
>
> The Secretary-General's analysis and recommendations could cover the role of the United Nations in identifying potential crises and areas of instability as well as the contribution to be made by regional organizations in accordance with Chapter VIII

---

* *W. Michael Reisman,* Wesley Newcomb Hohfeld Professor of Jurisprudence, Yale Law School. This paper is part of a larger project on the use of future images in international legal planning. My colleagues *Myres S. McDougal* and *Andrew R. Willard* made many useful comments and suggestions.

of the United Nations Charter in helping the work of the Council. They could also cover the need for adequate resources, both material and financial.[1]

The Security Council's mandate focuses on the role of public international organizations. That specific focus may be appropriate for an official of an international organization. But to make the question raised at the outset relevant for the assessment and mobilization of the *aggregate* resources of the international political system as a whole and not merely to the organized and official parts of it, the scholar must expand the focus further to include possible non-governmental and individual state participation in "preventive diplomacy, peace-making and peace-keeping."

I. Conceptions of Security

If this exercise is to be relevant, the word "security" must be given a realistic and contemporary meaning, lest the planner construct elaborate Maginot lines for threats from the past which the threats of the future can neatly circumvent. Even the word "contemporary" in this connection must be given an expansive and future-oriented meaning. Because of the fluidity of the international political system at the moment and the constantly evolving character of the strategic and, in particular, the coercive modalities of a science-based civilization, it would be imprudent to assign to the word "security" a meaning restricted to an institutional capacity to respond to one type of threat, for example, a conventional military thrust by one state into the territory of another. A military action of that sort may indeed continue to be one category of security threat to which some degree of probability may be assigned but there may be other novel yet plausible security threats as well. Hence the advantages of a functional, contextually responsive and futures-sensitive understanding of the concept of security.

Security must be conceived of as more than immediate or short-term self-defense. By "security" we will mean the maintenance of minimum international order through a period of time. This can include the capacity to respond to the full range of conventional threats insofar as they continue to loom as possibilities, but it must also include the capacity to sustain and if necessary, improve those processes of production and distribution of valued outcomes at a level sufficient to maintain public order within and between the components of the industrial and science-based civilization that constitutes the infrastructure of the world community.

"Threat" and "security" can be very subjective terms, whose content depends on the viewpoint of the person using them. In terms of the definition proposed here, every act of violence or destruction somewhere will not necessarily equal a threat to security. A possibly reversible event such as global warming may

[1] UN Doc. S/23500, 31 January 1992, 3-4.

precipitate gains and losses among communities and even seriously harm some; it may have drastic epidemiological consequences. Yet it may not be an inclusive security threat. This does not mean that it should not stimulate inclusive decision responses to protect the values that are threatened. Nor does it imply that those values are unimportant or less important. Security, as a minimum concept, does not extend to the achievement of many other political goals and aspirations of the international system. It merely recognizes that their achievement presupposes the maintenance of minimum order and that the diversion of adequate resources for that purpose is necessary.

The line between minimum and optimum order is not static. Insofar as something characterized as optimum proves to be related to a minimum concern, it will have to be treated henceforth with an appropriate urgency. The point is that in a consideration of how to design and appraise methods for the maintenance of inclusive security, one must distinguish between maintenance of minimum order and achievement of optimum order, i.e., the highest aspirations of the international system.

II. The Need for International Arrangements

We may take two points for granted. The first is the continuing need for institutionalized *international* arrangements. In certain states and political circles, the hoary totems of sovereignty continue to be venerated. Moreover, much of formal politics and political ritual continues to seep through the bureaucratic dermis of the nation-state. But nationalistic rhetoric notwithstanding, the social and economic systems of our modern industrial and science-based civilization are thoroughly and inextricably integrated into many different types of transnational arrangements. As a result, political and legal programs in any so-called "national" unit must, at least, take account of policies and conditions in other units. More often, the national programs now require active and ongoing collaboration with coordinate parts of other governments. The cross-boundary cooperations that have come to comprise so much of modern international law, as imperfect as many of them may be, are not options. They are imperatives.

III. Proaction and Prosponse

A critical dimension of the contemporary imperative of these cross-boundary arrangements is collaborative planning to *forestall or to respond adequately* to categories of events that are not necessarily expected to occur but are expected, if they should occur, to cause a degree of injury that is deemed unacceptable because it is irreparable or because the injury would entail extremely heavy political, social or economic costs. The anticipation of and provision for events of this sort is sometimes referred to as "contingency planning." The very extent to which terms such as "scenarios" and contingency planning have become clichés is itself indicative of a basic shift in thinking. Given the fragility of certain struts of modern industrial and science-based systems, we now consider advance planning for contingencies that seriously threaten them to be indispensable.

This means that modern decision-making systems must be and, to a remarkable extent, are engaged in an ongoing process of developing capacities for "proacting" or "prosponding" rather than "reacting" or "responding." The notion of proaction is used in social science literature to designate with precision one actor's purposive behavior that has been initiated in large part *in anticipation* of the behavior of another actor; the first actor believes that if the other's behavior eventuates, it will produce some unacceptable results. Proaction has, as will become clear, distinctive strategic, legal and moral implications.

I propose to use the word "prosponding" to designate the planning and preparation of a range of possible responses to security-threatening actions that another actor is expected, with a relatively high degree of probability, to initiate. Because prosponsive plans can, if they are known to an adversary, deter it from proceeding with its own plans or enable it to evade the channeling or blocking effects the prosponse was designed to achieve, prosponsive capacities always involve calculations about secrecy: how much should the prosponder allow the target to know about capacities and plans? This question also poses strategic, legal and moral dilemmas.

Contemporary international politics involves the ongoing selection and adaptation of particular proactive or prosponsive strategies in the very design, construction and modification of fundamental decision processes. Failure to develop an appropriate proactive or prosponsive capacity and strategy is not necessarily fatal but the failure may later entail the investment of greater resources and the shouldering of greater costs in averting a particular, unanticipated threat or repairing the injury it caused. That may be acceptable to certain decision-makers (i) if they believe the additional costs will be imposed on others, whether they are internal or external adversaries; or (ii) even if the costs will fall on the community for which the decision-makers have temporary custody, because they can be deferred from "their watch" to that of their own successors.

IV. Some Moral Implications

Shifting the emphasis from a reactive and responsive to a proactive and prosponsive model of security involves moral and legal challenges to the values of our civilization. The essential model of criminal justice in the liberal democratic state presupposes that both the provisional characterization of criminal behavior and the application of sanctions will only take place if the offending behavior was normatively characterized as criminal at the time it occurred. Criminal justice must be reactive, for one of the distinctive concerns of a liberal democracy is the maintenance of a private sphere that allows multiple opportunities for the individual to experiment with living styles. The primary limitation on individuals is that they not "break the law," i.e., not violate some preexisting norm. But the invitation to this process of individuation through an active and possibly experimental creation of and participation in private spheres requires that what is prohibited by law be clear and pre-announced; hence the maxims *nullum crimen sine lege* and *nulla poena sine crimine*.

Proactive and prosponsive orientations can put considerable stress on these policies, for their incorporation as part of the strategic arsenal of a democracy carries with it the implication that official normative expectations may not always be pre-announced. The prospect that behavior that is currently lawful may be viewed, retrospectively, as unlawful and an appropriate target of community sanctions can restrict and chill the private sphere. I believe that liberal democracies can accommodate the need to develop proactive and prosponsive strategic planning with the values of liberalism and human dignity but it will require significant adjustments in domestic processes.

V. Future Constructs

Our civilization has developed many complex conceptions of time for political and economic purposes. Routinely, we speak about and appear to be basing plans and current behavior on "the future." But there are, at any moment, many possible futures.

To cite a very simple and mundane example: Smith, like many other people in his social and economic situation, diverts a certain portion of his current income from consumption to a pension fund. This current behavior is premised on a future in which he continues to live beyond an age at which he can or wishes to work. Smith also diverts a certain portion of current income from immediate consumption to make payments on a life insurance policy. This current behavior is premised on a future in which he will have died long before the future his previous plan anticipates eventuates. The second future concerns plans for dependents who survive Smith and for whose welfare he would like to provide.

Smith has thus created two incompatible futures, assigned probabilities to them, and made provision, through the investment of current resources, for the eventuation of either. Smith's constructive futures are not static or impervious to influence by his current behavior. Smith can increase or decrease the probability of one or the other of those futures' eventuation by adjustments in his current behavior, whether in health care, exercise, diet, vocational and recreational risk avoidance and other choices. All of Smith's calculations are based on information that becomes available to him about the consequences of different current options for the eventuation of different futures.

If Smith or those to whom he delegates these planning tasks are sophisticated, they will appreciate that his plans involve assumptions about the continuing viability of various political, legal and economic institutions and processes: the insurance industry, its regulatory agencies, an economy that continues to be productive within a political framework that continues to honor private and public arrangements such as his, a stable ecology, a network of supportive international relationships for his state and so forth. Smith, acting alone, or in concert with others, may be able in varying degrees, to influence how some of these elements of his constructive futures develop.

Like many other people in our civilization, Smith routinely projects a number of different futures and makes provision for their eventuation, while assuming, within certain limits, that the eventuation of any of them depends in part on what many other human actors do. Smith may have developed other futures but assigned them a low probability of eventuation or, at least, a probability of eventuation so low that the diversion of current resources is not warranted. For example, Smith may fantasize that he will receive a bequest from an unknown relative, marry an heiress, or win the national lottery and hence no longer have to divert current income for constructive futures. But if he does not quit his job or draw out his pension fund the moment he buys the lottery ticket, it is clear that he has assigned these futures, however desirable he finds them, a very low degree of probability.

A disengaged observer would judge Smith as rational if the various futures for which he was diverting current resources were probable and correlated to Smith's key values. But if Smith over-estimates improbable futures or diverts an exorbitant proportion of current resources to prepare for their eventuation, the observer would conclude that Smith is behaving irrationally, whether on the basis of wish fulfillment, obsessional neurosis, paranoia or stupidity.

Political and legal planning in our civilization builds on the sorts of assumptions that are common to Smith and hundreds of millions of others. It tries to develop means to imagine and then generate a range of possible futures or what *Harold Lasswell* called "future constructs."[2] These constructed futures are perforce exercises in disciplined fantasy. They may range from utopias or desirable futures through to dystopias or the most undesirable futures. For each future, probabilities of eventuation must be estimated and assigned.

---

[2] *Harold D. Lasswell,* The Garrison State and Specialists on Violence, in: American Journal of Sociology 46 (1951), 455-468; see also *William Ascher,* Forecasting: An Appraisal for Policy-makers and Planners, Baltimore 1978.

Political and legal planners and their governments may be as irrational as Smith might be. They may cavalierly ignore threats to key values that an observer would perceive or massively exaggerate dangers that the observer would appraise as highly improbable or, if probable, posing a minimum danger. A common pathology in such planning is the so-called "National Security Doctrine"[3] which may result in what *Lasswell* characterized as the "garrison state."[4] Sometimes cunning calculation rather than misperception may enter into these "pathologies." The garrison state justifies control by the garrison. Precisely because certain futures enhance the power position of certain planners, intellectual honesty as well as the usual techniques of disciplined self-scrutiny that are recommended to anyone engaging in social or legal decision are necessary.[5]

VI. Constructing Threatening Futures

Any number of futures may be constructed. When the purpose of the exercise is planning for security, all but inclusively threatening futures may be excluded. The selection of contingent futures posing inclusive security threats need not be random if it is based on estimates on axes of

— social vulnerability;

— threat magnitude; and

— threat probability.

Vulnerability and threat are, by their nature, relational in the sense that the degree of threat and vulnerability of, let us say, two states with regard to each other changes according to the relative power balances and interdependences between them. Vulnerability and threat vary in another sense as well: they are determined, for various current and projected contexts, by estimates of the relative technology, available knowledge and political environment of the various entities that influence and potentially threaten one another.

Because vulnerability and threat may be constantly changing in light of variations in power relations, technology and knowledge, the construction of alternative futures is perforce an ongoing intellectual task. While some political and cultural values of relatively stable communities may impart a degree of consistency to the most preferred constructive futures of those communities, the features and dynamics of dystopic constructive futures may be subject to rapid change.

3 See *Jorge Tapia-Valdes*, Estrategocracia: el gobiernò de los generales, Santiago de Chile 1986; *W. Michael Reisman*, Private Armies in a Global War System: Prologue for Decision, in: Virginia Journal of International Law 14 (1973), 1-55.

4 *Lasswell* (note 2).

5 On self-scrutiny, see *W. Michael Reisman*, The Tormented Conscience: Applying and Appraising Unauthorized Coercion, in: Emory Law Journal 32 (1983), 499-544.

Futures deemed most significant, either because of the likelihood of their eventuation or because of the scope and intensity of damage to critical social values if they do eventuate, must be elaborated further if they are to be used as a way of testing the capacity and adequacy of existing institutional arrangements to respond to them in ways that protect public order. If existing arrangements appear to be incapable of doing that, this method indicates where new institutional arrangements are required and provides an imaginative framework for testing hypothetical novel arrangements.

VII. Using Futures to Generate Prospective Strategies

The intellectual function of the threat in each future construct is to provoke consideration of possible strategic proactions and prosponses. Analytically these various types of prospective strategies can be characterized in five different ways:

a. "preclusive" proactions and prosponses seek to make the eventuation of the constructive future less likely; Israel's destruction of the Iraqi Tammuz reactor in 1981[6] is an example of a vividly preclusive proaction; a regime of non-proliferation and export control agreements would seek a preclusive prosponse by use of legal instruments;

b. "circumventive" prosponses anticipate allowing the eventuation of the constructive future but seek to minimize the threats it would pose by some anticipatory action, e.g., when heretofore critical oil supplies are threatened, shifting from petroleum to another form of energy, or developing alternative sources of petroleum;

c. "accommodative" proactions or prosponses calculate the relative costs of allowing the constructive future to eventuate and then seeking accommodations with it. If, for example, one constructs a future in which a latter-day Saddam is poised to seize Saudi oil-fields, an accommodative prosponse is the calculation of how much the dictator will actually be able to charge for petroleum once he controls it and whether the planner's community can bear the freight;

d. "anticipatory defensive" proactions or prosponses involve assessing the costs of allowing the threat hypothesized to eventuate, estimating the costs involved in making the threat ineffective and then taking appropriate proaction, e.g. if an aggressor is permitted to improve his geo-military position, anticipatory defensive proactions could include new mutual defense and assistance agreements, forward location of new military bases, new armaments, credible threats, etc.;

e. "integrative" proactions involve actions in which common interests are reclarified in ways in which motives for and perceptions of threatening behavior

[6] Israeli Jets Destroy Iraqi Atomic Reactor, New York Times, 9 June 1981, A1: 6.

are obviated: all "win." *Jean Monnet*'s European Coal and Steel Community is an example of a successful integrative proaction. *Ronald Reagan*'s proposal to develop a "Strategic Defense Initiative" which would then be made inclusively available is a less plausible example of an integrative prosponse.

The aggregate costs of each of these strategies can be considered prospectively in terms of whether they are effected in overt or covert form, whether by threats or actual military action and so on. Aggregate costs also include the probable responses of the target of the various proactive and prosponsive constructive strategies. Only integrative strategies are likely to curtail adversarial responses by, at least in that relationship, transforming the adversary into a partner. Israel's destruction of the Tammuz reactor, while eliminating an immediate threat, could be expected to drive *Saddam* to redouble his efforts to acquire nuclear weapons while shielding the project from the same sort of preclusive proactions.

Creating a constructive cascade of proactions and reactions permits the planner to assess the long-term utility of a particular proactive or prosponsive strategy, before investments in or applications of it have been made.

VIII. Contextualizing Constructive Futures

Constructive futures are not still-shots taken with a 35 millimeter camera. If they are to be useful, they must be full-fledged motion pictures, replete with rounded characters and plots that develop dynamically and stochastically. The construction of alternative futures may be accomplished by use of the phase and value analysis techniques which have been elaborated by the New Haven School.[7] Briefly, information is gathered and organized for any process in terms of (i) the participants or actors; (ii) their perspectives, including identifications, demands and matter-of-fact expectations of past and future; (iii) the situations in which interactions will take place; (iv) the resources the various participants will be able to draw upon; (v) the strategic modalities by which they will manipulate those resources; and (vi) the outcomes of the process, described in terms of production and distribution of values, e.g. power, wealth, enlightenment, skill, well-being, affection, respect, and rectitude.

Decision-making in any process is described in terms of its constitutive structures, including the performance of seven decision functions: intelligence gathering, promotion of new policies, prescription of policy as law, invocation of provisional violations of law, the application of law to violations, termination of established law and appraisal of the aggregate performance of the decision

---

7 See generally, *Harold D. Lasswell / Myres S. McDougal,* Jurisprudence for a Free Society: Studies in Law, Science and Policy, Dordrecht / Boston 1992; for a more abbreviated statement, see *W. Michael Reisman,* Law from the Policy Perspective, in: *Myres S. McDougal / W. Michael Reisman,* International Law Essays: A Supplement to International Law in Contemporary Perspective, Mineola, N.Y. 1981, 1-14.

process. A method such as this for gathering and organizing information, whether derived from the past or projected for the future, also permits the scholar and planner to incorporate the efforts of others in collaborative activity and to avoid the pitfalls of pure guesswork.

The New Haven School is acutely concerned with precision about the intellectual task that an observer is performing: the clarification of social and political goals, the gathering of data about decision trends with regard to the achievement of those goals, the conditions that affected those trends, likely future efforts and their degree of success and the invention of alternatives which are more likely to achieve the projected goals. All of these are important and legitimate intellectual tasks for the legal scholar and practitioner. But it is important that the scholar or practitioner engaging in any one of these tasks be careful to identify which task is being performed and not to collapse one into the other.

IX. An Example: The Hemorrhaging of Soviet Military Industrial Skills

If constructive futures, as an intellectual device, "work," they should lead the scholar to consideration of matters that might not have been initially contemplated. The point can be illustrated by a rather obvious example. Imagine a future in which the political and economic collapse of the Russian Federation leads to a brain drain into certain developing countries of erstwhile Soviet scientists and technicians who had theretofore worked in Soviet nuclear, chemical and biological weapons development. Once this future is constructed, it presents in dramatic fashion a range of events-congeries that may constitute a threat for the planner's community. Each event-congeries, in turn, generates "down the line" a cascade of other events.

Those constructive events are meaningful to the planner only if they are assessed in terms of a set of social and political goals with which they converge or diverge. In assessing which arrangements produced goal convergence and which did not, the planner can benefit from the richness of historical perspective by researching the past for events comparable to those hypothesized in the constructive future. He can imaginatively project further developments of the future construct and, finally, may use the insights gleaned from the exercise to generate alternative proactive or prosponsive strategies, whether preclusive, accommodative, circumventive, anticipatorily defensive or integrative.

In a constructive future concerning proliferation of former Russian nuclear, chemical and biological skills, a canvass of the pertinent past might provide useful perspective. At the time of the collapse of the Third Reich, top scientists in different sectors of Nazi military research were seized by the victorious powers in an operation called, in the West, "Paperclip."[8] Less well-known and possibly less talented researchers and technicians, operating on the principle of *sauve qui peut,* made their own arrangements with the governments of various developing countries. What were the consequences of this dispersal and proliferation of weapons-production skills for world public order at the time? What factors conditioned those consequences? What steps did the international organizations and national leaders who then viewed themselves as custodians of world public order take? With what consequences?

The information gained from this sort of inquiry may indicate the utility of various prosponsive options. On the other hand, it may reveal that the context of conditions of the future construct is so different from the past that the past is not instructive. Yet even that information is of value.

The legal planner using the technique of future constructs must assemble a spectrum of prosponsive options. For the future construct we have hypothesized, one strategic option might be preclusive, i.e., international efforts to forestall or contain a transfer of technology of this sort. Possible methods of implementing this prophylactic objective might range from propping up or helping to reconstruct the central control system of Russia which would then restrict emigration as well as weapons sales, to accepting the disintegration of the Russian Federation and concentrating on the creation of non-proliferation regimes, inspection regimes, export control regimes, etc., to undertaking to "outbid" those governments in the market for these weapons productions specialists and so on.

Each of these strategic options has a configuration of immediate costs and advantages as well as secondary and tertiary consequences which themselves have costs and advantages. For example, a strategy of propping up Russia (which was, I believe, considered favorably and pursued with regard to the Soviet Union by the United States, France and the United Kingdom until it proved unfeasible) might, as one consequence, create a power balance in Europe to the disadvantage of Germany, a consequence some other European states might view as favorable. But since the strategy would have to rest on support of the secret police and the military, key muscle sinews of the old empire, it could generate other security problems in the future, if and when Russia succeeded in repairing itself. And even in the short term, it would have negative human rights implications within the Russian territory. Each of the other strategies would have a different configuration of costs and advantages.

A second level of consideration in this future construct would have to assume that, efforts to the contrary notwithstanding, varying degrees of partial diffusion of those skills to governments whose control of them would be considered threatening will occur. Methods of proacting or prosponding to this level of

[8] See generally, *Christopher Simpson,* Blowback, America's Recruitment of Nazis and Its Effects on the Cold War, New York, N.Y. 1988, 35.

threat might include sanctions, blockades, covert action, yielding to those claims of the new possessors that are stimulating its quest for the weapons and that might obviate their need and so on. The prospective adequacy of each of these prosponsive options in terms of minimum security needs and other pertinent public order goals permits the planner to reconsider the urgency of a preclusive or circumventive option.

The options generated at this level of consideration would in turn provoke another set of consequences which would form a new context and which might require further planning. Note, however, that one does not proceed blithely from level to level. Strategic challenges presented by secondary and tertiary consequences and the costs of responding to them may force reconsideration of proactive or prosponsive options in the previous levels. In retrospect, one may conclude that certain possible consequences are simply so threatening that one cannot responsibly allow for their eventuation.

Future constructs thus serve as a type of ongoing "imaging" of desirable and undesirable futures that allow present strategic and tactical options to be adjusted so that they increase the probability of the eventuation of the desirable future and minimize the probability of the eventuation of the most undesirable future. To borrow a spatial metaphor, much as a bat navigating space without an ocular apparatus emits sounds which bounce off objects before it and thus allow it to adjust course to secure or avoid a convergence with particular objects, the policy planner consciously creates images of different futures with which the likelihood of convergence or avoidance, whichever may be desired, can be increased or decreased by adjustments in current strategic behavior.

X. Six Constructs of Threats to International Peace and Security

Our assignment today is the construction of alternative futures that test the adequacy of the international legal and political system to respond in ways that maintain its security. By its nature, this is a gloomy task, for security planning must create dystopias in which there are genuine threats to inclusive security and that are not improbable or remote. The threats we will elaborate are those that elites are expected to characterize as inclusive. If their perspectives are parochial or short-sighted, they may not characterize certain events as inclusive threats, even though a dispassionate observer would.

One of the particularly disagreeable aspects of this exercise is that from the perspective of elites many terrible events simply do not constitute inclusive security threats. Elites and their constituencies may feel urgent moral or political reasons for dealing with them but they do not view them as threatening inclusive security. The carnage in the south of Somalia may have accelerated the outflow of refugees from that tragic country and may increase stress on the social infrastructure of surrounding states that have acted as absorption points, but its consequences for world security are apparently perceived as minimal.[9] A war that grinds on in Afghanistan but no longer engages the Superpowers is on the same order. A brutally despotic successor to *Saddam* who does not or cannot harbor aggressive ambitions is not a security threat.

Sometimes matters that some states try to characterize and treat as inclusive threats simply recede. In June, 1991, the Assembly of the Organization of American States issued the Santiago Declaration in which it characterized the military overthrow of freely elected civilian governments as a common threat and established an Inter-American organizational procedure to respond.[10] The intensity of commitment to the Santiago Declaration was tested shortly thereafter when President *Jean Bertrand Aristide* was overthrown in Haiti. A sanctions program was mounted. It proved to have the double disadvantage of being both economically destructive in Haiti and politically unsuccessful. *Aristide* is still in exile. The inclusive threat to the hemisphere was apparently insufficient to warrant a hemispheric reaction that would have succeeded.

With the brevity necessary for this presentation, I propose to develop six future constructs which do present what will be perceived as inclusive security threats and then to use them as a means for examining the adequacy of current international organizational arrangements and legal formulations. Insofar as these artifacts appear inadequate to the challenges, proactive and prosponsive political and legal changes may be recommended. I shall exclude a number of rather obvious futures, for they have been considered in detail elsewhere. Thus, a future construct of a recrudescence of the Cold War between the U.S. and Russia will not be examined.

XI. First Future Construct: International Institutional Capacity to Respond to Manifest Inclusive Threats

Chapter VII of the United Nations Charter assigns to the Security Council the competence to respond forcefully, if necessary, to threats to the peace, breaches of the peace or acts of aggression. A right of unilateral coercive action under

---

9 A sad indication of this was provided by Under-Secretary-General *James O. C. Jonah* who, frustrated by repeated efforts to secure a cease-fire in Somalia so that relief for 250,000 starving civilians could be introduced, said, "It should not be taken for granted that the international community, in the face of such behavior, will continue to exert all efforts to bring food to Mogadishu when there are equally competing demands in other parts of the world," see, *Perlez*, UN Halted by Somalia Shelling, Says Food Relief Could End, New York Times, 7 March 1992, A4: 1-4.

10 The Santiago Commitment to Democracy and the Renewal of the Inter-American System, OEA / Ser.P AG / doc.2734/91, 4 June 1991.

the rubric of self-defense for some of the same contingencies is allowed in Article 51 of the Charter. It has been argued that there is an inverse relationship between these two competences: the more effective the Security Council's discharge of its function, the less the necessity and justification for a unilateral right. During the Cold War, when the Security Council was effectively blocked by the veto, Article 51 competences were, under the theory of inverse relationship, necessary to fill the gap left by the Council's paralysis. With the end of the Cold War, it has been suggested that a radical reduction in Article 51 unilateral competences is called for.

That proposition can be tested by the use of a future construct that poses a serious inclusive threat: the problem of maintaining a continuing supply of hydrocarbons to the industrial world. The proposition might also be applied to less inclusive threats, breaches of the peace or acts of aggression, e.g. the seizure by one state of part of the territory of another. While such actions violate key norms of the international legal system, it is not certain that they are viewed as precipitating an inclusive crisis of the magnitude of a threat to the supply of oil. I will treat this aspect in a different future construct later.

Those parts of the planet that are integrated into an advanced industrial and science-based civilization are intensely energy dependent. But the distribution of hydrocarbons, which are, at the moment, believed to be the most economical form of energy available, does not coincide with the areas of most intensive consumption. Substantial deposits are found outside of Western Europe, North America and Japan. As a result, key struts in the international political system of this century were designed by the most powerful states to ensure their continuing access to and security for flows of hydrocarbons.

Saddam Hussein's seizure of Kuwait posed a significant threat to this ongoing supply. If *Saddam* had pressed on into Saudi Arabia, he would have controlled a significant part of world energy resources. Even if *Saddam* had not advanced but had confined himself to consolidating his new base in Kuwait, the fact that he was unchallenged there would have changed the power balance in the rest of the Arabian Peninsula and put increased pressure on Saudi Arabia to accommodate its energy and other policies to the wishes of the new regional hegemon.

What are the international institutional responses available for such threats or actions? With the end of the Cold War confrontation between the Superpowers, the United Nations Charter's security system would appear, at first glance, to have revived and now to be adequate for conventional reactive purposes. But can this initial impression sustain closer analysis? The Superpower rivalry has ended yet the genetic blocking mechanism of the Charter, the power of any one of its five Permanent Council Members to veto a Council action, is still available to each of them. Any of the five Permanent Members interested in striking a private agreement with a state posing an inclusive resource deprivation threat and thus using the threat to advance its own special interests has two options.

It may try to use its veto option as a bargaining chip with the threatener or as a bargaining lever against the other Permanent Members who wish to use the international machinery to repel the threat. If one looks to trend data, one finds that this strategic dynamic was not entirely absent in the recent Gulf War.

The lever of the veto option is efficacious only if it is agreed beforehand that no one but an international organization may respond lawfully to a military threat to the world's oil supply. But if this is agreed, then in many constructive futures, the continuing availability of the veto power of the Permanent Members means that the United Nations system can be paralyzed or diverted to the special interests of one Permanent Member. Abolition of the veto would be so stoutly resisted as to be impossible now.

Ironically, the chances of the UN security system working in the post-Cold War period might be improved, if unilateral, extra-organizational coercive options were to remain available to members under Article 51 for the contingencies contemplated there. The possibility that any state or states might simply take the matter out of the hands of the international organization and, lawfully, press a campaign on their own on the basis of a right of collective or individual self-defense, would then put pressure on more reluctant or potentially blocking members of the Security Council to reach an accommodation about a collective response. If they did not, they would still see a *de facto* collective response mounted but because it would be extra-organizational, they would lose all influence over it.

Hence the maintenance of conventional organizational reactive competences for the first future construct we have essayed appears to require the continuing availability, as an international legal matter, of unilateral state competence to engage in uses of force in circumstances like these. This future construct suggests, counter-intuitively, that the continuing availability of that unilateral competence may actually be necessary for the operation of the United Nations security system in some projected contexts.

Of course, this unattractive option would be obviated if preclusive or circumventive strategies could be devised to minimize the consequences of a threat to inclusive security. What preclusive strategies are available to the international community for this future construct? Insofar as the threat is likely to take shape through the use of military power, various arms control and export control regimes may limit the ability of probable resource deprivation threateners from acquiring the arsenal necessary to accomplish their objectives. The current capacities of international organizations, acting with exporting states, to restrain nuclear, chemical and biological proliferation or even to restrain the transfer of conventional weapons appear to be less than adequate for the task. Hence, if a preclusive strategy is to be developed for this construct, substantial gains must be made in international organizational capacities to control the movement of critical weapons systems.

What circumventive strategies are available? Certainly, a method that could achieve a radical reduction of the unit cost of alternative energy forms would obviate the threat, at least for those advanced industrial states that could rapidly readapt and use another energy form. But poorer states that lacked a sufficiently adaptable industrial infrastructure might find themselves locked into hydrocarbons, even though they would have become a comparatively primitive form of energy. This dependence would still give the resource deprivation threatener substantial control over other parts of the planet which, in turn, could be factored against the advanced industrial states. Conservation methods could also act as a partial circumventive strategy, though they would amount to an alleviation of rather than a solution to the problem.

In our general discussion, we considered the possibility of accommodative strategies for this type of future. In this future construct, they would involve anticipatory calculation of how much the state now in control of the resource would actually be able to exact and whether its maximum price or conditions would be bearable or tolerable to others.

Anticipatory defensive strategies might involve substantial stockpiling or activation of other petroleum sources. The anticipatory defensive proaction would not be available, however, to weaker or shakier political economies.

Because the various prospective options for this future all seem inadequate, it would appear that one lesson of the first future construct is that the international community must maintain a form of lawful unilateral reactive capacity. But this would require, assuming current circumstances continue, tolerating highly coercive unilateral actions as a way of keeping pressure on international organizational processes. This presents other difficulties.

XII. Second Future Construct: Nuclear Proliferation and Limited Nuclear War

Though many commentators continue to emphasize the importance of nuclear non-proliferation, proliferation is already a fact. About 10 % of the states of the world appear to have acquired some nuclear weapons capacity. Others are in the process of doing so. Still others do not have the industrial infrastructure to nuclearize their arsenals but, thanks to their valuable natural resources, they have the money available to purchase nuclear packages. With the disintegration of the Soviet Union, the possibility of acquiring such packages in the international market, with or without the specialists necessary to adapt them, is greatly increased.

While possession of a weapon is a prerequisite to its use, mere possession does not necessarily mean that the weapon will be used. But many of the governments that have or may acquire nuclear weapons do not have the types of command-control systems that reduce impulsive uses of the weapon. Hence, even as the probability of global nuclear war between the Superpowers decreases, the probability of limited nuclear war between much smaller nuclear states increases. Let us consider, first, a construct in which a small, now nuclear state threatens to use its weapon against a state with which it has what it conceives to be an important conflict of interest and, then, a second, "evolved" future construct in which such weapons are actually used. Are the institutional capacities of the international system sufficient to respond to both events?

The process of proliferation may have accelerated somewhat with the breakdown of the Soviet Union but it was already well under way. As long as the Cold War continued, the nuclear parity of the Superpowers and their common interest in avoiding nuclear war meant that each had an urgent interest in controlling nuclear mavericks in its respective sphere of influence from engaging in nuclear mischief against any other small state. This was a relatively stable system of control but it did not entirely rule out the option of using nuclear weapons. If a protegé of one Superpower had fired on a protegé of the other, each protector might have found itself under acute pressure to respond as a way of maintaining its credibility in its own sphere. With the end of the Cold War, the peril of the former control system is, in some ways, reversed.

If a new nuclear state threatens a non-nuclear state, Superpowers with capacities to deliver nuclear weapons anywhere on the planet would be able to deter the nuclear initiative, *if* they had committed themselves beforehand to counter-strike. Of course, deterrence, by its nature, requires a prior and public commitment. But this type of deterrent system would require at least one of the Superpowers, if not both, to retain a nuclear capacity adaptable to such situations. If both nuclear Superpowers conclude that the only threat posed to each is the nuclear arsenal of the other and agree to draw down and disassemble them reciprocally, a potential restraint on other states that already have or will nuclearize in the future evaporates. But continuing the Superpower nuclear restraint, in turn, would extend their hegemony. Superpowers, by virtue of their arsenals and delivery capacities, would be the *ultima ratio* of international law and politics.

Neither Superpower is likely to engage in total unilateral disarmament. But it is far from certain that the Superpowers, though still endowed with substantial nuclear assets, will be willing to undertake a deterrent role in every bilateral conflict. Issuing threats is not without cost. A threat to deter puts the general credibility of an international actor on the line. A failure to follow through — for example, because the costs are deemed to outweigh gains in a particular case — can seriously erode that credibility, with consequences in many other arenas. Hence a rational actor is parsimonious in making such commitments.

Who will benefit from this uncertain regime? If a nuclear North Korea were to threaten Japan, one might assume that the United States would direct clear and credible deterrent communications to North Korea. In this case, one would assume a high probability of following through. If North Korea were to threaten South Korea after United States forces had quit the peninsula, or if one Central Asian state in the area formerly governed by the Soviet Union were to threaten a proximate state, would the United States or Russia commit themselves to a deterrent role and then, if necessary, act?

If the answers to hypothetical questions such as these are uncertain if not clearly negative in some cases and combinations of cases, international institutional responses must be developed in anticipation. With regard to the proliferation of chemical and biological weapons, I suggested in a paper delivered at the American Society of International Law, that if all of the Permanent Members terminate their chemical and biological weapons capacity, one unintended consequence will be to enhance the ability of international cheaters to use such weapons in bilateral conflicts. The Permanent Members of the Security Council may have to retain an arsenal sufficient, either to supply or to respond on behalf of a victim of a chemical or biological weapons attack.[11]

If the same reasoning applies to a future construct of nuclear proliferation, two lessons, both counter-intuitive, emerge. Permanent Members of the Security Council who have a nuclear capacity should retain it. The prospect of nuclear Superpowers is no occasion for joy, but since these states are already designated by the Charter of the United Nations as part of the core of custodians responsible for international security, they should be permitted to perform that assignment effectively. Until now their nuclear arsenals have been designed largely out of the concern to check each other. Now they must perform an additional task. This construct would suggest that Permanent Members should develop a protocol under which it is agreed that one or all will respond promptly and in an appropriately punitive way to a nuclear attack by any other state on any third state. This will, hopefully, deter such adventures.

In the absence of the maintenance of such a capacity and the creation of such an authoritative commitment, let us construct a future in which nuclear weapons have been used in a certain arena. To what extent can international institutions, as currently structured, respond to this sort of calamity? Given the scale of damage, the available resources and normative arrangements necessary for international disaster relief, current structures would be pathetically inadequate. Moreover, current disaster relief presupposes an operating governmental apparatus in the state in which the disaster has occurred. It is through that state apparatus that aid is expected to be channeled and distributed to victims. But virtually all infrastructure may be destroyed in a limited nuclear attack. Moreover, the fallout may make it impossible for local authorities to respond.

---

[11] *W. Michael Reisman*, Chemical Weapons: Designing Operable Systems for Enforcing Restraint, in: Proceedings of the 83rd Annual Meeting of the American Society of International Law (April 5-8, 1989), 468-482.

This dismal future construct would suggest the need for the development of a new type of international trusteeship, under the supervision of an international organization rather than a state acting on behalf of an international organization. Its function, of course, would be the same: to engage in long-term rehabilitation and reconstruction for devastations, whether wrought by nuclear war or some other form of folly.

XIII. Third Future Construct: Conventional Aggression

The first future construct we essayed presented an inclusive threat precipitated by a conventional act of aggression. Though the act was against a single state, the effects were so widely felt that they stimulated an inclusive response. All bilateral acts of aggression are characterized, by international legal definition, as threats to the entire community, yet, definitions notwithstanding, in concrete cases, certain acts of aggression are either denied that characterization or ignored or international responses to them are limited to symbolic gestures.

Consider, for example, China's entry into Tibet, India's entry into the Portuguese enclaves, Indonesian entry into East Timor. The international community did not respond with any intentional effectiveness to any of these acts of aggression. When Indonesia seized West Irian and The Netherlands made clear that it would respond in force and when Argentina seized the Falkland Islands and the United Kingdom indicated it would respond, international legal attention did focus. In the case of West Irian, a symbolic solution which essentially accommodated the aggression was cobbled together. In the Falklands / Malvinas crisis, the United Kingdom vindicated its alleged right of self-defense without substantial assistance from the international security system. Would the United Nations have acted as it did in response to the Iraqi aggression in Kuwait if the United States had not characterized the situation as intolerable to the security of the political economy of the alliance which it leads? Would the United States consider becoming engaged in an attack threatened by Iraq against the survival of Israel? Would it become engaged in a conflict threatened by Uganda's invasion and absorption of part of Ruanda?

The question is whether the inclusive international security system of the United Nations is geared to respond to all bilateral infractions that could be characterized as breaches of the peace or as acts of aggression, but which do not threaten the major interests of the Permanent Members of the Security Council or larger regional powers? The evidence one might marshall to answer this question is troubling. Because the answer is sufficiently unclear for a large number of states, they have concluded, the expansive language of the Charter notwithstanding, that they cannot depend on the United Nations security system. The conclusion is not altogether irrational. Hence they repair to their own devices, establishing bilateral and multilateral security pacts and developing arsenals they believe adequate for the threats they anticipate to their security. Reliance on mutual defense treaties has substantial costs for the international system but may provide some deterrence. Reliance on more *ad hoc* arrangements for collective self-defense is uncertain. But if there is a possibility that the Permanent Members of the Security Council — or only one — will conclude that a particular act of aggression does not warrant an organizational response or their engagement, who else will undertake a meaningful collective self-defense on behalf of a particular victim?

Given the correlative, developing and obsolescing feature of modern weaponry, this future construct indicates a continuing arms race with increasing proliferation, diversion of sorely needed economic resources for national arsenals, calculations of when an adversary may be growing stronger and the initiation of pre-emptive actions may become "defensive" and so on. At the political-legal level, it leads to a search for limited mutual defense systems which, in turn, are often viewed by others as latent war communities. In short, the United Nations' ineffectiveness in dealing with bilateral aggressions that do not pose systemic threats stimulates trends within the uncertain international system which entail risks we wish to avoid.[12]

An appropriate organizational response to such conventional aggressions would require enhancing the capacity for action of the United Nations under Chapter VII of the Charter. There is, however, little indication of enthusiasm for activation of the Military Staff Committee. The offer by President *Mitterand* of providing up to 2,000 soldiers within a week hardly addresses the issue. Yet the uncertainty that would reign without an effective United Nations is less than optimum.

One economic but at best short-term method of dealing with the problem exposed by this future construct would be the installation of a routinized procedure for delegation by an international organization to a regional or functional organization or to a particular state or group of states of the authority to respond militarily to a conventional act of aggression. The North Atlantic Treaty Organization, for example, could be "deputized" for certain actions in designated geographical zones and for purposes consistent with its Charter. As other organizations, emerging from the debris of the Cold War, take more coherent form, they,

---

12 Ironically, when the UN system seeks to respond to a bilateral conventional aggression, its partial ineffectiveness may actually exacerbate the situation. For several decades, one contingent military strategy discussed in war colleges in many small countries involved rapid advance into an adversary's territory, followed immediately by an application to the Security Council for a cease-fire. Although the Council could be expected to insist upon the withdrawal of all parties to their positions prior to the eruption of the incident, the immediate effect of the cease-fire would be to freeze the aggressor in its position and give it an incentive to drag out Council deliberations as long as possible. When the veto by one of the two Superpowers, then ranged against each other, could be counted upon to paralyze the Council, this strategy could pervert the apparatus of the Security Council and let it actually protect aggression.

too, could be deputized for appropriate action. A general delegation by the Security Council now to certain organizations would obviate a veto problem when a threat materialized. Obviously, the same care currently used in the selection of peace-keeping forces in particular missions will also have to be used in organizational selection. Where an individual state is selected, it might be possible to compensate the state so authorized for the costs it incurs in the mission.

Some tentative movement toward this type of practice may be indicated by the Secretary-General's reported willingness to allow Eritrea to secure the port and airport in Mogadishu so that international aid might continue to be brought into that beleaguered city. The ECOMOG force in Liberia has been effectively a Nigerian force and has operated without Security Council authorization. Yet it has not been criticized internationally.

Were the Security Council to establish a protocol under which the Secretary-General would be authorized to "deputize" particular parties to respond in *ad hoc* collective self-defense to a conventional act of aggression, the relative simplicity of the operation might make it more plausible to potential aggressors and, in itself, act to deter some aggressions that would otherwise be consummated.

XIV. Fourth Future Construct: The Breakdown of the United Nations System

Too many simultaneous conflicts, none of which is, in itself, inclusively threatening — but each of which may be of concern to critical constituents of the international system — could so tax the resources of the United Nations as to render it ineffective or lead to its breakdown. At the moment, there are peace-keeping operations in Lebanon, the Golan Heights, the Sinai, Cyprus, El Salvador, Iraq and Kuwait, Angola, and India and Pakistan. One thousand, three-hundred and eighty people are already deployed in Cambodia, where a transitional authority is expected to expand to 22,000 people. Almost 400 military personnel are deployed in Yugoslavia, where a force is expected to expand to 14,000 people. There are 300 people in Western Sahara where the future deployment is expected to expand to 2,700 people. Funding for many of these operations has yet to be secured. The cost of the Cambodian operation alone will be almost US$ 2 billion. The cost of the Yugoslav action is expected to top US$ 600 million.

Let us imagine a future in which fissiparous pressures in Central and Eastern Europe, in Central Asia and in the Balkans lead to more claims of self-determination, more secessions leaving substantial irridenta in the new units which, in turn, cause the outbreak of conflict in those regions. Since one consequence may be massive refugee movement towards Western Europe, the European Community may be expected to press for international engagement in order to secure cessation of the conflict and to staunch the refugee flow. The resources of the

United Nations simply could not meet so many conflicts. In March, 1992, when the lives of 250,000 starving civilians in Somalia were in peril and the UN was unable to arrange even a minimally durable cease-fire between the warring factions that would permit introduction of relief supplies, *Bryan Wannop,* the head of the United Nations Development Program in Nairobi observed that "a cease-fire agreement doesn't mean anything to factions in Somalia." The New York Times reported:

> Mr. Wannop said members of the peacekeeping mission in Somalia this week had concluded that the only way to solve the situation was through outside force. "But the world is not ready for it," he said.[13]

Prospective actions might involve the expansion of parts of the United Nations system to the point where they would be adequate for these challenges. At the moment, the willingness of major contributors to the United Nations to shoulder this additional burden is in doubt. Other actions that might seek to limit the armaments flowing into these regions could reduce the severity of the conflict but, as we saw in other future constructs, the effectiveness of these programs has not been high enough to be encouraging.

One option would be to undertake to protect the international system, such as it is, by trying to "internalize" conflicts of this sort by reinforcing an international norm in favor of existing boundaries. The international legal system has long distinguished between events of international concern and events within domestic jurisdiction. One purpose of this distinction was to protect the autonomy of governments from international intervention, whether genuine or disguising the intervention of Great Powers using the international organizations as their instruments of diplomacy. But a systemic consequence of the distinction was to remove from international responsibility a significant proportion of violent events that were occurring almost entirely within national boundaries and would otherwise be of international concern. The distinction barred international organizations as well as other states from involving themselves in so-called "domestic" conflict.

This distinction certainly has many negative features but it could become a strategic device, were the Security Council and the General Assembly to adopt a preferential norm in favor of the maintenance of existing boundaries. The systemic advantages of some sort of doctrine of *uti possidetis* have been appreciated by elites in Latin America and more recently in Africa. It was essentially adopted, in 1964, by the Heads of State of the Organization of African Unity[14] and endorsed in 1986 by a Chamber of the International Court in the *Burkina Faso* v. *Mali* case.[15] It has been applied, in general terms, in the Helsinki Accords.[16]

---

[13] *Perlez* (note 9).

[14] AGH / Res. 16(I), July 1964.

[15] *Case Concerning the Frontier Dispute (Burkina Faso / Republic of Mali),* ICJ Reports 1986, 554-663.

If such a doctrine were adopted *erga omnes*, it would act to restrain the fractionation of existing states and while it would not terminate a conflict between various language and ethnic groups within existing units, it would render the conflict domestic rather than international; the primary function of the UN would be to keep outsiders out. The international human rights program would have to be expanded to address violations of human rights *within* those states and the law of armed conflict would have to be generalized to apply to any conflict, whether international or internal, as a way of reducing the severity of the conflict.[17] This device would come under intense stress if the conflicts involved irridenta of proximate states.

Expansion of the notion of internalization is hardly an optimum solution but, over the short term, it may recommend itself because of its relative economy.

XV. Fifth Future Construct: Low-Intensity Warfare

The term "low-intensity conflict" is used in a comparative and relative sense to distinguish conflicts in which the types of armaments and intensity of destruction are relatively confined. What is often involved are probing actions, short-term penetrations, support of sabotage within the target state etc., all initiated and directed from the security of another state. These actions are designed to maintain pressure on the target government but they are kept at a level which is supposed to preclude justifying a coercive response on the part of the target. I have argued elsewhere[18] that a series of international legal innovations, beginning with efforts by the General Assembly to define aggression and culminating in the Merits Judgment in the *Nicaragua* v. *United States* case[19] before the International Court, have been counter-productive, indeed "nomogenic" in that, while seeking to limit aggression, they have made it easier for participants bent on this sort of mischief to conduct low-intensity conflict.

Article 3 (g) of the Definition of Aggression characterized "any of the following acts ... as an act of aggression ..."

> the sending by or on behalf of a State of armed bands, groups, irregulars or mercenaries, which carry out acts of armed force against another State of such gravity as to amount to the acts listed above, or its substantial involvement therein.

---

16 Digest of United States' Practice in International Law 1975.

17 *W. Michael Reisman*, Toward an Integrated International Law of Armed Conflict, in: Proceedings of the 85th Annual Meeting of the American Society of International Law (forthcoming, 1992).

18 *W. Michael Reisman*, No Man's Land: International Legal Regulation of Coercive Responses to Protracted and Low Level Conflict, in: Houston Journal of International Law 11 (1989), 317-330.

19 *Case Concerning Military and Paramilitary Activities in and against Nicaragua (Nicaragua* v. *United States of America)*, ICJ Reports 1986, 14-546 (103).

In the Merits Judgment in the *Nicaragua* case, the Court characterized the General Assembly's definition as constituting customary international law.[20]

The Court held that a military action will not constitute an "armed attack" and hence stimulate a right of self-defense on the part of the target unless it "occurs on a significant scale."[21] In addition, the Court excluded from the category of armed attack, "assistance to rebels in the form of the provision of weapons or logistical support."[22] The Court did not say that such actions were lawful. It allowed that such assistance might qualify as a threat or use of force or amount to an intervention, for which recourse to the Security Council would be possible. Recourse to the Security Council encounters all of the difficulties considered above and is often unlikely to be effective. Resort by the target state to unilateral self-defense or participation by another state in collective self-defense against the initiator of low-intensity conflict would not be permitted.

The Court's theory would work on one factual assumption. Were the Security Council transformed into an effective agency for response to a wide-range of low-intensity challenges, it could deal with the threats posed in this construct. But as discussed in the previous future construct, that transformation is unlikely, for the conduct required of significant actors is unlikely to be forthcoming. As it is, the theory elaborated by the Court encourages a strategy of low-intensity conflict precisely because it precludes coercive responses by the target. Instead, it directs the target exclusively to the Security Council where the probability of an effective remedy is remote. In consequence, this tolerance for low-intensity action is likely to increase the predilection of target states to use covert forms of response to counter the low-intensity conflict. They will try to conceal their authorship of the actions involved because they have become definitionally unlawful. International law, with regard to this aspect of the use of force, as it has been shaped in the past ten years, does not contribute to the maintenance of minimum order.

Short of a desirable but improbable institutional change in the Security Council's operation in the near future, the situation could be ameliorated if international law reverted to the customary law norm under which low-intensity conflict would be deemed to be an "armed attack," entailing the right of self-defense on the part of the target. The very possibility of a lawful response under the rubric of self-defense could then serve to deter states otherwise disposed to use low-intensity conflict from engaging in what would be a much riskier adventure.

---

20 *Loc. cit.*, 103.

21 *Loc. cit.*, 104.

22 *Loc. cit.*, 104.

XVI. Sixth Future Construct: Non-State Terror

State-sponsored terrorism is part of the phenomenon of low-intensity conflict and has been considered in the previous future construct. It is also useful to consider a future in which groups whose political objectives have been thwarted in non-violent settings or who are motivated by nihilistic objectives resort to various forms of terror. The growth of a communications grid about the planet has made it easier for non-state groups to use selective violence against civilian targets anywhere on the planet. This new form of unconventional coercion is generally referred to as terrorism.

The capacity of irregular groups to disrupt international commerce and travel links by hijackings or bombings of airlines has been deemed sufficiently threatening to generate special treaty regimes but one cannot say that any of the activities targeted in those treaties have posed a major threat to inclusive world order. Assume, however, that terrorists of the future equip themselves with nuclear or chemical and biological weapons or, after the mapping of the genome, terrorists design bacteriological weapons that are able to target particular ethnic or racial groups. What are the resources and institutional capacities of the international system for responding to threats of this type?

International cooperative agreements between police may make the sharing and use of information more efficient, but the interdiction of terrorists and the neutralization of their "weapons" will ultimately depend upon the state or states in whose territory they are operating. Terrorist operations have often been conducted in states that were supportive, internally disrupted or where governments were too weak to exercise control. With the increasing probability of disruption within states in many parts of the world, there should be no shortage of venues for terrorist bases in the future.

A likely method of response will be covert action by those advanced industrial states which feel particularly threatened by these activities. Since these actions will be conducted in the territories of weaker states, they will put considerable stress on norms of non-intervention. Insofar as the threats themselves materialize, however, there may be no other alternative for neutralizing them. Hence, one option entails the development of criteria for assessing the lawfulness of such covert actions as some measure of introducing law to them. This is, as one can imagine, a most perilous exercise.[23]

Conclusion

The range of future constructs we have generated suggests that, at least for these futures, the political structures and legal capacities of the international

---

23 For some suggestions, see *Reisman* (note 5).

system are not sufficient for the maintenance of security. The problem could be exacerbated in the future by the growing lack of congruence between the Permanent Membership of the Security Council and the effective power process. The Security Council's core is the victorious alliance of the Second World War but even the presence of the People's Republic of China in the "Chinese" seat reduces the historical cohesion of that force. Plainly the United Nations will have to adapt to reality or it will find that other effective arenas have superseded it. Unhappily, the behavior of some aspirants to an enhanced role in the Council during the Gulf crisis — widely perceived as an inclusive threat — did not show a correlation between power and responsibility.

One trend in world order that currently seems to be strengthening is a cause for some encouragement. There is a growing body of historical data indicating that enlightened democratic governments are less likely to engage in military adventures. Thus the international human rights program may yield substantial unanticipated dividends in the maintenance of minimum security.

Two general recommendations emerge from this exercise. Intelligence about current and prospective trends is more urgent than ever. The United Nations and the major actors in the international system must develop better methods of keeping themselves and each other informed. The information gleaned must be incorporated in new future constructs that can indicate where further information is required and stimulate the invention of appropriate alternative strategies. Scholarly conferences, such as this one, incorporating people from different countries, can be particularly helpful in tempering parochial concerns and helping to establish a clear focus on the common interest.

More generally, we need to develop and use methods of constructing futures as a regular part of decision-making. It is a commonplace that we must survive the present to have a future. Less obvious is the fact that we need futures if we are to survive the present.

The Future of International Law Enforcement under Chapter VII: Is There Room for "New Scenarios"?

Tom Farer*

I. From the outset I have seen my mandate shrouded in ambiguity. The invocation of Chapter VII of the UN Charter implies concern with collective security at the global level of decision-making. The implications of the question "Is There Room for New Scenarios?" are rather more uncertain.

Was I intended to brood over the issue of whether, without transgressing the conventions of legal positivism, it is possible to push beyond traditional notions of what contingencies constitute a "threat to the peace"? Presumably not, since in fulfilling their mandates the other reporters will pick most of the meat off of that bone. Alternatively, I could examine the prospect for Security Council authorization of coercive measures of one sort or another to enforce the main principles and purposes enumerated in the Charter. That would involve anticipating the leading states' evolving conceptions of self-interest, an essay in political rather than strictly legal analysis (a distinction, to be sure, which may not recommend itself to my good friend Professor *Reisman*[1] and which I, myself, often find problematical.[2]

A third alternative was to concentrate not so much on what UN member states are likely to authorize or at least tolerate in the near future, as on what they ought to do in light of the threats to international order. We can reasonably anticipate, in short, an essay in *de lege ferenda*. That alternative leads as well to meditation on what is the nature of the order to be defended. Is it the one built out of the rubble of World War II in which the overriding value has been preservation of the formal independence and territorial integrity of states? Or is something new slouching toward Bethlehem to be born?

In this connection I should note that one new goal for the great powers would be nothing more (nor less) than consistent enforcement of the inherited normative dispensation. Iraq's invasion of Kuwait was hardly the first challenge to the

---

* *Tom Farer*, Professor of Law and Director of the Joint-Degree Program in Law and International Relations at The American University in Washington, D.C.

1 See, e.g., Professor *Reisman*'s introduction to *W. Michael Reisman / Andrew R. Willard* (eds.), International Incidents: The Law That Counts in World Politics, Princeton 1988, 3-24.

2 See, e.g., my editorial comment Human Rights in Law's Empire: The Jurisprudence War, in: American Journal of International Law (AJIL) 85 (1991), 117-127.

Security Council in its role as steward of the political independence and territorial integrity of sovereign entities. To mention only the more flagrant cases, in recent years Indonesia has swallowed the former Portuguese colony of East Timor, Israel steamrolled its way into Beirut and continues to run a puppet state in a fraction of Lebanon while Syria makes itself comfortable in much of the rest of the country, and Iraq had previously invaded Iran. None of these delinquencies aroused the Security Council to hurl the thunderbolt of enforcement measures.

A fourth alternative was to focus not only on the norms and policies identifying the appropriate occasions and limiting conditions of collective coercion, but also on the institutional setting for their application. I think here of such conventional issues as the size, membership, and mandate of the Security Council and of its relationship to the General Assembly, to regional organizations, and to individual states invoking a right to self-help. In this category of concerns we might also include the question of whether the prospective challenges to a minimally satisfactory order exceed the adaptive capacity of the UN structure and thereby necessitate construction of a separate global security directorate and / or more sub-global security arrangements together, perhaps, with looser restraints on self-help.

II. I propose not so much to choose as to forage among these issues, in the first place by considering the various ways in which the Security Council can perform its function of maintaining international peace and security.

One way is to organize and deploy armed forces under its command in those instances where military pressure appears necessary to prevent or to terminate a breach of the peace. It was long thought that the capacity to command troops depended on prior implementation of the military staff committee arrangement envisioned in Articles 45-47 of the Charter, on negotiation of agreements with individual UN members "governing the numbers and types of forces [they would provide], their degree of readiness and the[ir] location, and on the earmarking of national units for service under UN command."[3]

---

[3] Articles 43 and 45. At least some Permanent Members of the Council seem ready to evade those conditions by slipping along the route of armed peace-keeping and humanitarian relief, what the British officer-scholar *John Mackinlay* would call "Chapter Six-and-three-quarters, see *id.*, UN Military Action in the Nineties: Toward Chapter Six-and-three-quarters, in: *Leon Gordenker / Thomas Weiss* (eds.), Collective Security in a Changing World, Boulder 1993. On 10 August 1992, according to an article in the Washington Post, 11 August 1992, A1, The U.S., Britain, and France "reached agreement on a UN Security Council resolution that would authorize use of military force in Bosnia in the event Serb militia forces oppose international deliveries of humanitarian aid to Sarajevo ..." The resolution reportedly "calls on the international community to 'take all measures necessary ... in coordination with the United Nations' to facilitate the delivery by humanitarian agencies of relief 'to Sarajevo and wherever needed in other parts of Bosnia-Hercegovina.'" According to the Washington Post, "France and Britain had favored language calling for a build-up of the UN peace-keeping force in Croatia," while "U.S. negotiators supported a scaled-down Persian Gulf War-Style operation in which the UN sanctioned use of force but left control of the troops to the member nations most directly involved in the military effort." One obvious precedent for a UN-

As an alternative to applying force directly through troops under its command, can the Security Council authorize member states to employ force on behalf of Council ends? Since this is exactly how it proceeded in effecting the expulsion of Iraq from Kuwait[4] and since it did so essentially without legal challenge, Council authority to adopt this course of action may now be indisputable.

There is, I suppose, a little room for doubt on that score. Iraq's invasion of Kuwait being a naked case of aggression, the Security Council's role could have been seen as coordinating and monitoring the acts of collective self-defense, which Kuwait and its allies were at liberty to initiate without Council authorization. Thus, although the Council purported to draw on its broader powers to deal not simply with aggression but with all acts threatening international peace and security, the invocation was arguably gratuitous, analogous to dicta in a judicial opinion, and hence not a precedent for authorizing the use of force in cases where the precipitating events would not trigger rights of self-help under Article 51.

The weakness of this argument stems from the breadth of the actions ultimately authorized by the Council. Self-defense seems a slender justification for wiping out Iraq's capacity to produce or deploy in the foreseeable future nuclear, chemical, and bacteriological weapons systems[5] and for carving a Kurdish haven out of Iraqi territory.[6] These actions are far more easily justified as prophylactic measures to eliminate a threat to international peace and security. Hence the broad support these measures have enjoyed does evidence consensus about the Council's authority to legitimate action which would not be justifiable as self-defense under Article 51.

Although the ambiguous language of Chapter VII has not in practice restrained the Council from authorizing military measures, the implications of that ambiguity for the Council's authority, to *compel* cooperation in military operations have yet to be tested. Article 42 states that

> [s]hould the Security Council consider that [political and economic] measures would be inadequate or have proved to be inadequate, it may take such action by air, sea, or land forces as may be necessary to maintain or restore international peace and security. Such actions may include demonstrations, blockade, and other operations by air, sea, or land forces of Members of the United Nations.

By itself, that language implies that the Council may demand military action and that member states have assumed an obligation to comply. The tone of unqualified obligation appears elsewhere in Chapter VII: In Article 48, for in-

commanded military operation against insurgents (in Bosnia, the local ethnic Serb militia purports to be acting autonomously rather than as an arm of Serbia) is the UN-commanded force that subdued the Kantangese Gendarmerie during Zaire's post-independence civil war.

4 SC Res. 678, 29 November 1990.

5 SC Res. 687, 3 April 1991.

6 SC Res. 688, 5 April 1991.

stance, which provides that "[t]he action required to carry out the decisions of the Security Council for the maintenance of international peace and security shall be taken by all the Members of the United Nations . . . [and] [s]uch decisions shall be carried out by the Members . . ." And in Article 49's statement that the members "shall join in affording mutual assistance in carrying out the measures decided upon by the Security Council."

But Article 43 introduces a note of conditionality which sounds again in Articles 45 through 47. It may be helpful to recall Article 43's exact language:

> 1. All Members of the United Nations, in order to contribute to the maintenance of international peace and security, undertake to make available to the Security Council, on its call *and* in accordance with a special agreement or agreements, armed forces, assistance, and facilities, including rights of passage, necessary for the purpose of maintaining international peace and security [emphasis added].
>
> 2. Such agreement or agreements shall govern the numbers and types of forces, their degree of readiness and general location, and the nature of the facilities and assistance to be provided.
>
> 3. The agreement or agreements shall be negotiated as soon as possible on the initiative of the Security Council. They shall be concluded between the Security Council and Members or between the Security Council and groups of Members and shall be subject to ratification by the signatory states in accordance with their respective constitutional processes.

The obligation to perform and the anticipation of negotiated agreements defining at least the dimensions of each country's obligation converge in the body of Article 45. Its opening sentence — "In order to enable the United Nations to take urgent military measures, Members shall hold immediately available national air-force contingents for combined international enforcement action" — has the flatness of Article 42. But its second sentence — "The strength and degree of readiness of these contingents and plans for their combined action shall be determined, within the limits laid down in the special agreement or agreements referred to in Article 43, by the Security Council with the assistance of the Military Staff Committee" — picks up the reference to agreement as a possible condition for activating the obligation and adds another in the form of the "Military Staff Committee."

As they spell out the character and functions of the Committee, Articles 46 and 47 strengthen the impression that the Committee is an essential element in the enforcement process. It "shall be established . . ." It shall "advise and assist the Security Council on all questions relating to the Security Council's military requirements for the maintenance of international peace and security [and] the employment and command of forces placed at its disposal . . ." It "shall be responsible under the Security Council for the strategic direction of any armed forces placed at the disposal of the Security Council."

The language of Chapter VII is thus susceptible to conflicting conclusions about the obligations of member states. At one extreme it might be argued, in light of Article 43's last paragraph, that they assumed no initial obligation other than to enter into negotiations in good faith concerning the obligations they might assume if, pursuant to their constitutional processes for the ratification of international agreements, they chose finally to accept an obligation to assist in carrying out enforcement measures. On this view of Chapter VII, by ratifying the Charter a member commits itself to implement enforcement measures of a non-military character, but retains discretion about participating in military operations. It might, however, cede that discretion by means of a collateral agreement.

This interpretation of Chapter VII would make it symmetrical with Western Hemisphere regional security arrangements. Article 8 of the Inter-American Treaty of Reciprocal Assistance provides that in case of aggression within the Hemisphere, the members may vote to adopt enumerated measures which include partial or complete interruption of economic relations and "use of armed force." A two-thirds vote in favor of such measures is binding on all signatory states, "with the sole exception that no State shall be required to use armed force without its consent." One could, of course, claim that the very explicitness of the Inter-American arrangement cuts against the narrowest view of Charter obligations; for it suggests both that important UN members were sensitive to the distinction between military and other sorts of enforcement measures and that where they wished to limit their obligations, they knew how to do so unambiguously.

Article 43's subjection of agreements negotiated between the Council and member states to ratification in accordance with national constitutional processes certainly need not be construed as an oblique way of preserving national discretion. For the requirement of ratification may have been intended simply to assure that such agreements were embedded in national consciousness and internal law. On this view, a state's obligation was not conditional on ratification; instead ratification was an additional obligation.

Even assuming one nevertheless adopts the view that any obligation to participate in a military operation *controlled and directed* by the Security Council is conditioned on ratification *and* the establishment by the Permanent Members of a Military Staff Committee, it does not necessarily follow that the failure of those conditions deprives the Council of authority to require states to employ military measures. For states frequently draw a very bright line between military cooperation and the subordination of their respective armed forces to the strategic much less the tactical direction of foreign commanders. Only after suffering horrible losses in part as a result of sloppy articulation between their respective efforts and under the most desperate circumstances in the latter part of World War I could the French and British agree on an integrated command structure topped by a French general.[7] The issue of who should command troops returned

---

7 See *Theodore Ropp*, War in the Modern World, New York 1962, 239-274 (266). See also *Archer Jones*, The Art of War in the Western World, Oxford 1989, 434-488 (476/7).

to plague Anglo-American cooperation in the early stages of World War II.[8] While remaining committed to the defense of the West, *Charles de Gaulle* withdrew France from NATO's integrated structure rather than subordinate French forces to the direction of a U.S. Supreme Commander. And lest it appears that Europeans have a peculiar sensitivity on this issue, one should note the evident determination of the *Bush* Administration as it prepared for war in the Persian Gulf to retain operation control over the forces it was deploying there.

Nor is the reluctance of one state to subordinate its forces to the direction of another simply a matter of pride or chauvinism. The command and control and the logistics of military operations are immensely complicated under all circumstances. Where officers speak different languages and units have different traditions, training, and experience, complexity is compounded.[9] Moreover, the ends of allied states may be similar without being identical. Decisions about how to conduct the war affect political outcomes. In addition, different tactics and strategies imply different casualty rates. Commanders and political leaders may well disagree about the rates they find endurable. For all these reasons, the blank-check acceptance of foreign command is a far more remarkable step than accepting an obligation to join with other states in coordinating military measures.

At the present moment in international relations, perhaps at any conceivable moment, the issue of whether the Council has the authority only to authorize rather than to demand military measures by individual states or groups of them may seem of purely theoretical interest. For the states most likely to be called upon to enforce Security Council decisions are Permanent Members able to veto Security Council actions they find uncongenial. But the issue does in fact have practical relevance. Forces responding on behalf of the Security Council to a threat to the peace may well require facilities, supplies, landing and over-flight rights from other UN members. Some, like Jordan during the Gulf War, may prefer neutrality. Jordan nominally accepted its undoubted obligation to impose economic sanctions against Iraq. Could it also have been required to allow use of its air bases or space by the coalition forces? Neither the language nor history of the Charter appears to offer an incontestable answer.

In addition to authorizing coercive measures by willing states (and thereafter monitoring their behavior to assure compliance with the limits of their mandate and principles of customary international law) the Council could authorize regional and other sub-global organizations to act on its behalf. Or it could choose simply to acquiesce in actions they initiate. With respect to these final alternatives, perhaps it would not be ungracious to recall that, during the Cold War, Washington sought to obliterate the distinction between authorization and acquiescence by

---

[8] See generally *John Keegan*, The Second World War, New York 1990.

[9] See *Mackinlay* (note 3).

treating the latter as conclusive evidence of the former within the terms of Article 53 of the Charter.[10]

III. Bearing in mind these alternative routes open to the Security Council, let us consider from the perspective of the liberal democracies the occasions on which enforcement measures might well appear desirable. I have identified ten of them bunched into four categories. The first category I would label "traditional national security concerns" or "nationally focused security threats." The second I call "ideological concerns." The third I would summarize as "diffuse security threats to the international community" and the fourth as "non-military threats to global security."

Category one contains four contingencies:

1. There is an armed attack or the threat thereof by a state or paramilitary forces operating with the support or acquiescence of some public authority against another state's territory, its political independence, its policy autonomy, its troops abroad or in the global commons, its official personnel or its private citizens especially where the attack on them is systematic and / or extensive.

2. The aggressor, having injured its target, terminates or suspends its illicit acts and plausibly declares its intention not to begin again in the immediate future.

3. A group of states conspire to monopolize a critical good or service and use their monopoly power in ways that threaten the political independence, territorial integrity, or public health, safety and order of consuming states.

4. Private groups operating in states unable to suppress them conspire to violate the public law of other states in ways threatening grave injury to public health and safety.

The closest approximation of the third contingency was the short-lived Arab oil boycott following the 1967 Middle East war. Shortly after the boycott, as you will recall, U.S. Secretary of State *Henry Kissinger* declared that if the boycott were renewed and if it endangered social order in the West, the main consuming states would be justified in treating it as aggression. Neither the boycott nor the threat was renewed.

Since time is limited and the contingency is remote, I will limit myself to two observations. The first is that with this single exception, the Western democracies have consistently rejected the view episodically championed by Third World Countries that, for purposes of defining aggression, economic force be equated

---

10 See *Tom Farer,* The Role of Regional Collective Security Arrangements, in: *Gordenker / Weiss* (eds.) (note 3). See also *Abram Chayes,* Law and the Quarantine of Cuba, in: Foreign Affairs 41 (1963), 550-557; *Leonard Meeker,* The Dominican Situation in the Perspective of International Law, in: Department of State Bulletin LIII, July 12, 1965, 60, 62.

with the military form.[11] *Kissinger*'s position was, in other words, aberrant. Secondly, if economic leverage is employed primarily to influence the *foreign* policy of another state, a powerful presumption operates in favor of its legitimacy.

The drug lords of Colombia exemplify my fourth contingency. While American Presidents have identified drugs as a grave threat to the health and safety of United States society, they have consistently disclaimed any intention of employing force against the drug mafia other than in cooperation with host governments. On the other hand, the administration of President *Bush* has asserted a right to enter other countries and seize persons subject to prosecution under U.S. law.[12]

It appears that the U.S. has acted on that claim only once, namely when arranging with Mexican nationals for the kidnapping of a Mexican doctor indicted in the United States for involvement in the torture-murder of a U.S. drug agent.[13] Perhaps the U.S. invasion of Panama could be cited as a second example. But its precedental relevance is attenuated by U.S. reliance on other justifications, primarily an alleged threat to the safety of U.S. citizens residing in Panama and to the operation of the Canal, the latter threat activating rights under subsisting treaties between the U.S. and Panama.[14] Moreover, Panama is not representative of category four in that through the medium of its de facto head of state, General *Manuel Noriega*, it was officially complicit in the drug trade.

In upholding the constitutional jurisdiction of U.S. courts to try the Mexican national in question, the Supreme Court seemed to concede that, at least under the circumstances of the instant case, the kidnapping violated customary international law.[15] While that concession is unexceptionable, it has only marginal relevance to the paradigm case of a major criminal undertaking operating with impunity. Given the geographic and financial dimensions of organized crime and its evident capacity to penetrate and intimidate civil society and public institutions even in a country as large and powerful as Italy, it is evident that it already constitutes a threat to international peace and security within the terms of Chapter VII.

---

[11] In negotiations at the UN over a definition of aggression (see GA Res. 3314 (XXIX), in: GAOR 29th Sess., Supp. 21), proposals to include economic modalities were rejected. See *Bengt Broms*, The Definition of Aggression, in: Recueil des Cours 154 (1977-I), 299-400 (386).

[12] The claim seems implicit in the Administration's decision to defend federal criminal jurisdiction over a Mexican national forcibly kidnapped from his home by persons working under contract with the U.S. Drug Enforcement Administration (DEA) and flown by private plane to Texas where he was arrested for participation in the kidnapping and torture-murder of a DEA agent and the agent's pilot. The Administration's position was upheld by the Supreme Court in *United States* v. *Alvarez-Machain*, 112 Sup. Ct. 2188 (1992).

[13] *Ibid.*

[14] See *Anthony D'Amato / Tom Farer / Ved Nanda*, Agora: U.S. Forces in Panama: Defenders, Aggressors or Human Rights Activists, in: AJIL 84 (1990), 488-515.

[15] *Supra*, note 12.

For purposes of this symposium, I want to concentrate on the first two contingencies where discourse is most developed. United States scholars broadly agree that self-help in almost all the circumstances enumerated in "1" is either a preexisting right left unaffected by the Charter or a right that may be exercised pursuant to Article 51.[16] Only armed intervention for the rescue of citizens can fairly be regarded as contested ground.[17] I am nevertheless prepared to argue that it is reasonably well established by a demonstrable pattern of verbal claims, acts and acquiescences, at least where the threat to them is systematic and / or extensive. Of course there are notoriously controversial applications, instances like Panama where the threat was susceptible to termination by means short of force (tolerating *Noriega*'s regime or unequivocally threatening to use force in the event of future incidents),[18] or Grenada where the threat seemed fabricated and compliance with the principles of necessity and proportionality was at best doubtful.[19] But in the abstract the claim of right to defend citizens against an imminent threat to their physical security is now hard to dispute persuasively.

Self-help against the enumerated acts being legitimate, if the aggrieved party and its allies require no assistance, the Council's appropriate functions are (a) to confirm that the alleged delinquency has in fact occurred and that the measures of self-help being employed are necessary and proportional and (b) independently to explore all diplomatic avenues to the restoration of peaceful relations between the aggressor and its intended victim. If the target of aggression wishes assistance or if the Council concludes that a request for assistance is inhibited by pressure from the aggressor, then obviously the Council itself should organize coercive measures designed to vindicate the rights of the aggrieved party and the international community's interest in protecting the threatened values and in deterring additional violations of its norms.

Under the circumstances enumerated in category "2", the aggrieved party may wish to obtain reparations, or to avenge itself and to deter future violations of its rights; it may wish, that is, to take reprisals. Scholars and governments have

---

16 *Tom Farer* and *Christopher C. Joyner* survey main-stream views in: The United States and the Use of Force: Looking Back to See Ahead, in: Transnational Law and Contemporary Problems 1 (1991), 15. See also *Oscar Schachter,* In Defense of International Rules on the Use of Force, in: University of Chicago Law Review 53 (1986), 113.

17 The contest is not, in fact, very spirited any more. Opponents of or at least profound skeptics about any such exception to the inhibitions of Article 2, paragraph 4, have come largely from the ranks of Third World Governments. See *Tom J. Farer,* Law and War, in: *Cyril Black / Richard A. Falk* (eds.), The Future of the International Legal Order, Vol III, Princeton 1971, 15-78 (55, note 151).

18 See *Tom Farer,* Panama: Beyond the Charter Paradigm, in: AJIL 84 (1990), 503-515.

19 See *David Forsythe,* The Politics of International Law. Boulder 1990, 63-87. See also *Scott Davidson,* Grenada: A Study in Politics and the Limits of International Law, Brookfield, Vt. 1986.

for decades jousted over the legitimacy of reprisals other than those authorized by the Security Council.[20] And if they are authorized, the responsive measures are not strictly reprisals, since their legitimacy does not depend on the illegality of the provoking acts: they are, rather, Chapter VII enforcement measures. As suggested above, the Council can act affirmatively in pursuance of its mandate to maintain international peace and security. But is its discretion to do so plenary?

For scholars of the classical school (or, if you prefer, legal positivists),[21] the answer must be "No." The sharp difference between the language chosen by the Charter drafters to identify the conditions requisite for the Council's non-coercive initiatives to effect pacific settlement under Chapter VI ("a dispute, the continuance of which is likely to endanger the maintenance of international peace and security") and the language spelling out the conditions of Council actions under Chapter VII ("a threat to the peace, breach of the peace, or act of aggression") bespeaks a clear intention to limit the Council's coercive jurisdiction. Those like myself who would endow the Council with broad discretion to undertake prophylactic measures must discount the significance of original intent. Doing so moves one out of the classical school.

In other words, adherence to full-blown legal positivism must incline one to conclude that in order to authorize or require coercive measures against a state that has terminated its aggressive activities, the requisite Council majority must reasonably believe that the measures are required to alter the will or cripple the means for renewing aggression in the immediate future. I, myself, would recognize a Council mandate to authorize punitive measures against a previous aggressor in order to inhibit other potential aggressors; in the idiom of the criminal law the measures would be for general rather than specific deterrence.

The sanctions currently being applied to Iraq constitute one of the very few instances of what might loosely be called Security-Council-authorized reprisals. Far more common in the Charter era have been instances of reprisals in the strict sense. Certain commentators, Professor *Reisman* among them as his remarks at this symposium make clear, refuse to entertain doubt about the continuing legality of the customary law of reprisal.[22] Neither the negative implications of the Charter

---

[20] Scholars finding reprisals as such impermissible include *Louis Henkin*, Use of Force: Law and U.S. Policy, in: *Louis Henkin et al.*, Right v. Might, New York / London 1991, 37-69 (41-42); *Ian Brownlie*, Principles of Public International Law, 2nd ed., Oxford 1973, 452; *Georg Schwarzenberger*, A Manual of International Law, 5th ed., London 1967, 185/6. Scholars concluding that the right survives the UN Charter's coming into force include (in addition to *Michael Reisman), Robert Tucker*, Reprisals and Self-Defense: The Customary Law, in: AJIL 66 (1972), 586-595; *Julius Stone*, Aggression and World Order, Sydney 1958, 94-98 and *Derek Bowett*, Reprisals Involving Recourse to Armed Force, in: AJIL 66 (1972), 1-36.

[21] On the distinction between classicists and The New Haven School, see *Farer* (note 2).

[22] See *supra*, note 20.

text nor the language of Security Council resolutions explicitly rejecting reprisals as a means of law enforcement[23] nor the risk to order of unilateral recourse to force for purposes other than immediate self-defense have managed to shake their conviction.

The case for reprisals can be rested both on an interpretation of state practice under the Charter and of the Charter itself. With respect to practice, it seems fair to say that while the Council occasionally anathematizes reprisals, it often ignores them; and on those occasions when it does debate their propriety, its discourse often centers on questions of responsibility for the precipitating act, necessity and proportionality,[24] criteria for appraisal built into the pre-Charter law. With respect to the Charter text, defenders of reprisal argue, it seems to me, in terms of implied condition and what amounts to *rebus sic stantibus*. The arguments run roughly as follows: When ratifying the Charter, states agreed to limit recourse to self-help on condition that the Council effectively performed its collective security tasks; so once it became apparent that, as a consequence of the antagonistic relationship between its dominant members, the Council was paralyzed and thus the condition could not be satisfied, preexisting rights to self-help were restored. The *rebus sic stantibus* argument assumes that the Council's paralysis was a contingency not foreseen by the original parties to the Charter which fundamentally alters the character of the obligations they assumed.

The end of the Cold War and the recent demonstration in the Gulf of Security Council efficacy could be held to vitiate the defense of reprisals. To be sure, no reasonable person will find in Desert Storm a great power consensus in favor of vigorous, even-handed policing of the globe. But one could hardly argue that the founding parties ever imagined an absolutely impartial and omnicompetent Council.[25] Whatever the problematical merits of available positivist arguments in favor of the traditional law of reprisal, the more import question is the *de lege ferenda* one, namely whether order in the post bipolar world would be best served by a requirement that reprisal be authorized by the Council or, subject to its review, by regional or other sorts of treaty organizations in cases involving their members.

---

23 See, e.g., the resolution adopted by the Security Council in connection with the Harib Fort Incident (the U.K., nominally acting on behalf of the South-Arab Federation, had bombed a fort in Yemen which, it alleged, was a center "for aggressive action against the Federation.") SC Res. 188, 9 April 1964.

24 See *Bowett* (note 20), 7, 33-36.

25 Well before the end of World War II, important participants in the U.S. foreign policy establishment had concluded that the postwar relationship with the U.S.S.R. was likely to be tense, in part because *Stalin* would seek agressively to exert Soviet influence beyond his country's borders. Hence they could not have been surprised by the immediate lack of cooperation in the Security Council between the wartime allies. See generally *J. L. Gaddis,* Strategies of Containment, New York 1982, 10-15.

The second category, "ideological concerns," also incorporates two contingencies. One (contingency 3 in our outline) is where a government is committing, or unwilling or unable to prevent private groups from committing, gross violations of non-derogable human rights: The rights to life, to family, and to protection from slavery, physical abuse, arbitrary detention, and discrimination on the basis of race, ethnicity and other ascriptive characteristics in the enjoyment of all recognized rights. The other is where a democratic regime is threatened or violently displaced by internal groups or where insurgents arc struggling to establish or restore democratic governments.

Like reprisals, humanitarian intervention is contested territory. Even measures short of military operations may raise serious legal issues. For instance, a unilateral ban on imports from an alleged delinquent has to be reconciled with provisions of the GATT. Other measures may conflict with the concrete provisions of bilateral and regional commercial agreements. For purposes of this paper, I will put those issues aside and concentrate on the military instrument.

What position should the OECD states take with respect to massacres. Should they insist that massive violations of non-derogable rights are in all cases threatening to international security and hence satisfy the conditions for Security Council enforcement measures? Should they also recognize a right of unilateral intervention when the Council either cannot act or shows no sign of acting in time to prevent grave abuses? Suppose the Council acts by adopting means that fail to prevent or immediately to terminate terrible abuses as it has done in the case of Bosnia-Herzegovina. Should ineffective action nevertheless block unilateral action?

The risks associated with unilateral intervention probably could be reduced by linking it in various ways to the UN and regional organizations. For instance, the *prima facie* legitimacy of an intervention should be conditioned at least on a requirement that the intervenor immediately report the intervention to the Security Council and request Council review of the claim of gross violations. Where the intervening state claims that the risk of renewed human rights abuses prevents an immediate withdrawal, it must offer to place occupying forces under UN supervision and allow the UN to substitute forces from other countries. Where the intervening state and the alleged delinquent are members of a common security organization, whether or not organized on the basis of its members regional propinquity, the organization's political organs might substitute for those of the UN subject, of course, to the latter's ultimate authority.

Whatever normative regime seems most appropriate for instances of massive violation of rights to personal security, does it require adjustment when the endangered right is that of representative government,[26] the fourth contingency on my agenda of threats to international peace and security?

---

[26] Article 25 of the International Covenant on Civil and Political Rights.

One major obstacle to a regime of mutual guarantees is the distinct possibility of its protection being claimed in circumstances where the guarantors cannot agree on the democratic credentials of the claimants. Assume that all participants accept the *Schumpeter*ian rule of recognition: A democracy is that institutional arrangement where the power to decide is determined by a competition for the people's votes.[27] When it comes to applying that rule to concrete cases, the opportunities for dissensus are as rich as they are diverse.

Observers may disagree about the fairness of the competition. As contemporary political life in the United States illustrates, the playing field in capitalist democracies almost invariably tilts towards incumbents and the rich. The result is a continuum of legitimacy, one without a bright line immediately beyond which all observers will suddenly agree that the tilt of the field invalidates the result of the competition. Observers may also disagree over whether elections bestow a sufficient power to decide. Unelected groups, most commonly military or paramilitary in character,[28] or constitutional restraints imposed by unelected groups as a condition of relinquishing power to democratic forces,[29] may sharply narrow the policy options of elected officials. Guatemala is but one case in point. Finally, democracy can rot from within; elected officials exercising the power to decide may, in the name of national security, suspend constitutional guarantees in order to enhance their power or longevity. Then, when faced with rebellion, they may call for assistance.

Where guarantors cannot agree, inaction is the appropriate result. But as Dr. *Johnson* once remarked, the fact of twilight does not prevent us telling day from night. The fact that some cases will be unclear does not force the conclusion that the democracies should be supine whenever one of their number is assaulted.[30]

Among democratic states, the impulse to protect and promote democracy does not arise exclusively from sympathetic identification with the repressed. The rewards to be won through democracy's spread are not merely psychic. They are also available in the hard currency of national security.

Studies of the historical record tend to confirm the intuition that mutual possession of democratic institutions makes states improbable opponents in an armed conflict. Some scholars claim that authentic democracies have never fought

27 *Joseph A. Schumpeter*, Capitalism, Socialism, and Democracy, 2nd ed., New York 1947, 269.

28 As in Guatemala.

29 I think, for example, of the various constitutional restraints imposed by General *Pinochet* of Chile as conditions for exposing himself to electoral competition and then relinquishing the Presidency after his defeat.

30 For the sketch of a treaty organization that would guarantee the democratic regimes of the Caribbean's Anglophonic states, see *Tom Farer*, The United States as Guarantor of Democracy in the Caribbean Basin: Is There a Legal Way?, in: Human Rights Quarterly 10 (1988), 157.

each other. Others, employing somewhat different definitions of democracy or fighting, find a few exceptions.[31]

It is true, of course, that the sample available for empirical inquiry is quite small. Democratic government did not achieve an unchallenged hegemony in the West until after World War II. As late as 1914, two of the five great powers — Russia and Austria-Hungary — were autocracies. And a third, Germany, was only partially democraticized: Its elected parliament could reject budgets, but it did not control the appointment or removal of ministers and thus had virtually no capacity to initiate policy and only a limited power to obstruct it. The exceedingly narrow scope of the parliament's power to decide convinces me that the Kaiser's Germany should not be seen as having been a democracy. (A contrary conclusion would, of course, give us a rather pronounced disconfirming case of our theory.) Peace and democracy have, to be sure, coincided in the North Atlantic area since the end of World War II, and its former foes now act as if they could not imagine each other as future antagonists. But nuclear weapons and the bipolar structure of post-War international relations offer a credible alternative explanation for this phenomenon.[32]

While the empirical evidence is inconclusive, the deductive proof is strong. By their nature, democracies are far more transparent than autocracies. They can observe each other's budgets, military production, training and deployment, political debates and popular sentiments. Transparency eases the security dilemma of participants in an anarchic political system. Authentic democracies, moreover, have political institutions surrounded by an aura of legitimacy and shaped to the purpose of accomodating the competing demands of diverse social forces. Two consequences flow from these features. One is that democracies generally have fewer incentives to promote the sort of belligerent hyper-nationalism that demonizes other states and serves to enhance the legitimacy of unelected rulers in a secular and skeptical age. The other is the existence of ideological barriers to aggression. For democratic governments owe their legitimacy to the principle of popular self-determination. Hence, when one attempts to impose its will on another, it acts against the moral basis of its existence.[33]

So when a democratic government in a region where such governments are the norm is overthrown, the other regional governments may reasonably find a

---

[31] For a crisp review of the literature, see *Randall L. Schweller,* Domestic Structure and Preventive War: Are Democracies more Pacific?, in: World Politics 44 (1992), 235-269. See also *Stephen Chan,* Mirror, Mirror on the Wall ... Are the Freer Countries More Pacific?, in: Journal of Conflict Resolution 28 (1984), 617-647.

[32] See *John Mearsheimer,* Back to the Future: Instability in Europe After the Cold War, in: International Security 15, No. 1 (Summer 1990), 5-56.

[33] See *Michael Doyle*'s trilogy: Kant, Liberal Legacies and Foreign Affairs: Parts I and II, in: Philosophy and Public Affairs 12, Nos. 3 and 4 (Summer and Fall 1983), and Liberalism and World Politics, in: American Political Science Review 80 (December 1986), No. 4.

threat to peace and security.[34] Whether the same claim can be made globally is subject to doubt. For although democracies rarely, if ever, fight each other, the data suggests that they are as likely as other types of polities to become involved in armed conflicts.[35]

In any event, I find it hard to envisage a Security Council in which China occupies a seat legitimating pro-democracy interventions.[36] Nor is China the only obstacle. The Saudi Arabian King recently proclaimed democracy incompatible with Islamic principles.[37] And members of ASEAN have evinced distaste for any effort to promote democracy in their part of the globe.[38]

IV. With respect to categories three and four, discussion of norms and means is at an early stage. On this occasion I propose only to clarify the contingencies falling within these categories and to underscore the need for discussion to proceed.

As I indicated above, category three consists of diffuse military threats to the global community. Its first contingency is where a state seriously violates an arms control or disarmament pact concerning the development, deployment, or

---

34 During the twenty-first regular session of the General Assembly of the Organization of American States, held in Santiago, Chile in June 1991, the assembled Ministers of Foreign Affairs and Heads of Delegation announced their "decision to adopt efficacious, timely, and expeditious procedures to ensure the promotion and defense of representative democracy." The decision is formally entitled the "Santiago Commitment to Democracy and the Renewal of the International System." (AG / RES.1079 (XXI-O/91)) Thereafter, at the same meeting, the members adopted one of the foreshadowed procedures by resolving as follows: 1. To instruct the Secretary General to call for the immediate convocation of a meeting of the Permanent Council in the event of any occurrences giving rise to the sudden or irregular interruption of the democratic political institutional process or of the legitimate exercise of power by the democratically elected government in any of the Organization's member states, in order, within the framework of the Charter, to examine the situation, decide on and convene an ad hoc meeting of the Ministers of Foreign Affairs, or a special session of the General Assembly, all of which must take place within a ten-day period. 2. To state that the purpose of the ad hoc meeting of Ministers of Foreign Affairs or the special session of the General Assembly shall be to look into the events collectively and adopt any decisions deemed appropriate, in accordance with the Charter and international law (AG / RES.1080 (XXI-O/91)). In a Whereas clause stating the rationale for these operative paragraphs, the member states invoked the Preamble to the Charter of the Organization as establishing the premise "that representative democracy is an indispensable condition for the stability, peace and development of the region" and affirmed the necessity, in light of the "widespread existence of democratic governments in the Hemisphere," to make the Charter premise "operative."

35 See sources cited *supra*, note 31.

36 In a statement to the 1992 Heads-of-State Meeting of the Security Council, Chinese Premier *Li Peng* rejected democracy as a universal paradigm of the good society and particularly rejected its relevance for assessing China's regime (UN Doc. S / PV.3046, 92-93 (31 January 1992)).

37 Royal Decree No. A/90 (Sha'ban 27, 1412 A.H. and Royal Decree No. A/91 (Sha'ban 27, 1412 A.H.). See New York Times, 2 March 1992, 1.

38 Washington Post, 28 January 1992, A18.

transfer of weapons of mass destruction or their associated delivery systems. The provocative character of such violations and the concomitant rise in the temperature of interstate relations will almost invariably generate a threat to international peace and security.

Recent developments hold uncertain promise for the direction and pace of nuclear weapons proliferation. On the one hand, despite their claims and denials, governments manifest acceptance of the proposition that proliferation — of chemical and biological and nuclear weapons and of ballistic delivery vehicles — is not only a matter of international concern but is also presumptively bad. Acceptance represents a dramatic change in the community's view of a nation-state's rights. Discretion in the choice of means for protecting political independence and territorial integrity used to be at the very core of what people meant when they spoke of national sovereignty.

I am not suggesting that the practice of states has already generated a hard normative ban on transfer or acquisition. The principle of the formal equality of states probably precludes emergence of a hard-law global prohibition that would leave earlier entrants to the weapons-of-mass-destruction club free to continue deployment. But though we have here a form of normative restraint too soft for the label law, restraint there certainly is. Will it endure, however, in the face of developments calculated to feed the desire for and to reduce the material costs of entering the club?

Israel — a First World State in terms of meritocracy, technology, social cohesion, general education, and managerial competence — has in its wars with coalitions of Arab states consistently demonstrated the qualitative operational gap between the conventional force of First and Third World powers even when there is a superficial similarity in the quality of planes, tanks, artillery, and small arms they deploy. The Gulf War reconfirmed this fact of contemporary life. The lesson will not have been lost on Third World regimes that can envision future collisions between their interests and those of the United States.

There is an old Texas saying: "God made some men big and others small; and Mr. Colt made the .45 to even things out." The weapon of mass destruction is today's Colt .45.

Other recent developments — the end of the Soviet Empire and of the Cold War — have loosened national control over a legion of nuclear-weapons scientists and technicians and over relevant materiel. The attendant implosion of the Soviet economy, the stagnation in the World economy, and the general decline of public-sector capacity to supervise the transnational movement of people, goods and services eases the supply-side problems of states tempted by weapons systems that might deter opponents they could not hope to match at the conventional level.

The second contingency in category three is where a state either assists — whether positively or through friendly acquiescence — private groups attempting to obtain, store, manufacture or deploy weapons of mass destruction or is unable to prevent such groups from operating out of its territory. I am confident that militarily capable governments that imagine themselves as possible targets of such groups will claim a right to self-help wherever acquisition seems likely to occur. They will, in other words, treat that prospect as triggering a right to preempt that goes well beyond *The Caroline* Case's requirement that "the necessity of self-defense [be] instant, overwhelming, leaving no choice of means, and no moment of deliberation."[39]

I turn finally to the fourth category — non-military threats to global security which, like the third, contains two contingencies (with no doubt many factual variations). The first contingency is where public or private entities act in the global commons — high seas, Antarctica, outer space — in ways threatening grave and irreparable damage to the commons. Dumping toxic wastes is but one among a vast number of possible examples.

The various treaties and UN declarations governing these areas, together with broad principles of state responsibility, establish a reasonably developed network of substantive norms capable, it seems, of continuing refinement. What remains problematical is agreement on norms and institutions for enforcement. On the high seas, the sanctity of national registry, strongly reaffirmed in the 1982 Law of the Sea Convention,[40] inhibits the world's naval powers from policing on behalf of the global community. Since delinquencies are likely to be small but numerous, often committed by private operatives of uncertain national provenance, the conditions for resort to the Security Council will probably have to be triggered, if at all, by states threatening or initiating unilateral enforcement in *prima facie* violation of existing normative restraints. As the closest thing we now have to an international security directorate, the Security Council should begin stretching its jurisdiction under the peaceful settlement provisions of Chapter VI of the Charter to encourage negotiations looking to improved means for identifying, capturing, and punishing polluters of the commons.

The second contingency — tenth overall in my taxonomy — is where a state performs or tolerates performance of acts constituting a gross threat to the health and safety of persons in other states. An example would be a state which, despite being warned, continues to operate a nuclear power plant of a type banned in other countries on safety grounds and employing safety measures inconsistent with minimum standards enforced in other states. Analogous cases are certain to proliferate in the years ahead. In responding to them, the international commu-

39 Letter dated 6 August 1842 from U.S. Secretary of State *Daniel Webster* to *Lord Asburton*, in: *John Bassett Moore*, A Digest of International Law, Vol. II, Washington 1906, 409-414 (412).

40 International Legal Materials 21 (1982), 1261; see, in particular, Articles 91 ("Nationality of Ships"), 94 ("Duties of the Flag State") and 110 ("Right to Visit").

nity is likely to find that positive incentives in the form of economic and technical assistance are likely to prove at least as efficient as negative sanctions.

Unfortunately, no global institution exists with unambiguous authority to marshal and deploy prophylactively such incentives or their negative correlatives to mitigate my tenth or any of the other challenges the international community faces. The IMF, the World Bank, the regional development banks, national aid programs, and trade regulations collectively constitute an enormously powerful armory of non-violent law-enforcement instruments. Few things could so enhance the future prospect as an agreement among the leading producers of goods, services, and capital to establish a mechanism by means of which their immense economic power could be deployed to enforce the law of nations.

Comment

Alfred P. Rubin*

First of all, I want to thank our hosts and the sponsors very much. The hospitality has been wonderful, and the conference, so far, sparkling. I should mention that I could not review either Prof. *Reisman*'s or Prof. *Farer*'s paper before arriving in Kiel, so my comments must be based on a very quick scanning and notes taken as they were speaking. As you will see, I did do some non-commentator-like preparation on my own.

Hearing both Prof. *Reisman* and Prof. *Farer* speak, I am reminded of a book that was very popular about a generation ago called, "1066 and All That." It is a "memorable" history of England; history as remembered by British school children without regard to what actually happened in history or what, in fact, they were taught. It ends saying that the United States then became top nation, and "History came to a." Lest anyone think I am being humorous in this, I will mention that right now in the United States there is a certain enthusiasm for a book which has been written in expansion of an article by *Francis Fukuyama,* formerly of the State Department Policy Planning Staff, called "The End of History." His argument is that with the dominance of liberal democracy as the favored political system throughout what the author regards as the world, the interesting parts of history have simply ceased to exist; the struggles are over; the good guys have won. And yet, having heard what Professors *Reisman* and *Farer* were saying, it did occur to me that history might not yet have ended. Perhaps the future will be considerably less rosy in many ways than what many of us had thought we could anticipate from the end of the Cold War. Finally, in these preliminary remarks, I must say that in his paper Prof. *Reisman* according to his usual practice inserted a Greek-rooted word that nobody outside of Yale or Greece can understand; at least I cannot understand it. In his oral presentation he skipped the word. The word is "*iatrogenic*." I challenge you to look it up in a dictionary and, if that does not help, to do what I did: to ask him what it means. He will tell you that it actually has a distinctive meaning.

Prof. *Reisman* points out that the quest for alternative worlds, the search for a scenario to which we ought to react, rests upon a knowledge of the current distribution of authority and an extrapolation from where we are to the challenges

* *Alfred P. Rubin,* Distinguished Professor of International Law at the Fletcher School of Law and Diplomacy, Tufts University.

that we expect. Ought we to meet those challenges by trying to redistribute authority in the world; to change the Westphalian constitution? That would not be easy and the issues get confused when we speak in terms of rights and entitlements rather than authority distributions.

As Prof. *Reisman,* the Wesley Hohfeld Professor of Law at Yale University, knows better than anybody else, because *Wesley Hohfeld* wrote the book, the question of What is law, and What is a legal relationship, What is a jural relationship, is essential to an understanding of how the legal order really works. *Hohfeld,* you may remember, concludes that there are only four fundamental jural relationships which, on a little further analysis, can be reduced actually to one jural conception: Authority; legal power; the ability to change legal relationships. Rights can be reduced to a question of Who determines What; what organization, group or individual has the authority to determine if an entitlement exists and to react to that determination.

If one looks at the international legal order this way, the questions with regard to each of the scenarios that Prof. *Reisman* poses are, Who determines the rule of law? Who determines if there has been a violation of it? and Who determines exactly what, if anything, should be done about it? Under the current distribution of authority, apparently the Security Council of the United Nations determines if there has been a violation of law. But that appearance is deceptive. The Security Council certainly determines what, if anything, should be done about threats to the peace, although that determination is not exclusive. The Security Council has no power to determine rules of law; it is not a legal organ.

The International Court of Justice, of course, is the judicial organ of the United Nations. But it is a reactive organ; it does not determine rules of law in the abstract, only in response to cases or requests for opinions presented to it. And even then, occasionally it determines rather peculiar rules of law that may or may not be law properly so called.

Under the current distribution of authority in the international legal order it is not at all clear what role is played by the rules of substantive law. Instead political decisions are made as to national and organizational responses to real situations regardless of law; what Prof. *Reisman* calls "proacting" and "prosponding." To insert a legal dimension into this paradigm we would have to consider the authority of each actor to determine the substance of the rule and its authority to consider the perceived rule as a factor in its decision to act or not.

The result is certainly realistic in the modern world and very depressing. What it means from a great power point of view is the assertion of authority to determine only for oneself, or to "autointerpret," as *Leo Gross* put it, what the rules of law are, and what the legal order authorizes you to do in response to perceived violations of those rules. Great powers can do this and would be extremely reluctant to yield in any degree their authority to make those interpretations of law.

From the point of view of non-great powers, the situation is rather different. Some might enjoy being protected states with low defense budgets, having great powers assume a security role for them. On the other hand, even protected states ought to be at least very nervous about being subject to the protection of a great power. The obvious example on everybody's mind right now is Israel. A shift in great power policy means a security threat so severe for such a small, semi-protected state that it must reconsider its fundamental relationships. No state can let its security depend ultimately on political decisions made by other people elsewhere without real regard to the people whose actual lives and treasure are in danger; no state. The many victims of great power interventions must be unhappy with this distribution of authority.

Prof. *Reisman* mentioned the current situation with regard to Libya and the Security Council's embargo replacing what he apparently regards as possibly legitimate covert activity to kidnap two Libyan agents accused by the United States and United Kingdom of complicity in the Lockerbie atrocity. If I understand him correctly, he would see such a kidnapping as a counteraction to Libya's refusal to extradite the two. I find his underlying assumptions extremely disturbing. It seems to me that Libya, possibly wrong in its policies, is in this case right in the law. Libya is not legally obliged to extradite or hand over the two accused persons; the Security Council resolution does not legally require Libya to do so. The 1971 Montreal Convention actually foresaw precisely the current situation. The Libyan reaction to the British-American extradition demand is legally correct if the Convention sets out the governing law. Moreover, the Security Council did not require Libya to extradite the two accused officials. The Security Council merely "urged" Libya to "respond fully and effectively" to a very carefully worded resolution. I do not think that the United States interpretation of the resolution would have been adopted by the Security Council had it been presented to it in the words the United States now uses. We must bear in mind that the United States has as yet, as far as I know, not accused Libya of direct involvement in the incidents, but has only accused two Libyan individuals of complicity in the atrocity at Lockerbie. Had the United States accused Libya of responsibility for the atrocity, the legal result would not have been to authorize kidnapping two individuals, but rather a claim against Libya in whatever form is appropriate; possibly involving reprisal and possibly merely money damages. Whether reprisal would have been justified in law raises other questions which we will come to.

Would the world as envisaged by Prof. *Reisman* actually help to maintain the peace, or would it promote "small" wars? I suspect the latter, which I find a very depressing conclusion, although I have difficulty confuting it. Would it promote democracy? I doubt it. It has been proposed that great powers should intervene in the internal affairs of smaller states to support democracy. Prof. *Farer* has correctly pointed out that whatever they ought to do, in fact they do not; they intervene for other reasons. They may argue that they are protecting democracy, but, in fact, there are very few instances where support of democracy can be demonstrated to be even a significant reason for the intervention, much less the dominant reason. In fact, great powers, particularly the United States, tend to intervene not really to promote democracy, but to support their own perceived national interests. Our national interests are much more complex than having democratic neighbors. They include economic interests, long-range political interests, security interests, the general interest of all regional powers that their neighbors not be too strong, and even short-term domestic propaganda interests.

I deeply mistrust the notion that democracies can be properly supported by external intervention. It is very hard to teach democracy to people who, if they permit their government to fall into the hands of a radical clique or "mafia," feel that somebody from outside ought to come in and handle the matter for them, rather than learn to handle the matter themselves.

Is there any way out of this sad prospect? The objections that I have raised are not objections to Prof. *Reisman*'s analysis, with which I basically agree. The objections are to the conclusions to which it leads him. Perhaps the only way out is to change the Westphalian system; but that is unrealistic.

Or is it? As an alternative to Prof. *Reisman*'s idea of empowering at law great powers to intervene as their political calculations and moral principles dictate, what about a wider federation?

The United States is a federal state in which thirteen smaller states joined, yielding their capacity to go to war with each other in return for the benefits of a qualified union and a central government whose total authority over these states was not fully determined. The biggest crisis the Union faced was in a civil war in 1861-65 not by states fighting against states, but by a confederation of states fighting the rump of the Union over the legal issue of the reach of federal legal authority in that union to ameliorate the moral abomination of chattel slavery. The final chapter of the movement towards centralized authority, and state-based resistance to that movement, in the United States has yet to be written.

Europe seems to be moving slowly in the same direction now. It is not at all clear how far Europe will go. Starting with a Coal and Steel Community, then a partial economic union, there is now a movement towards monetary union and other coordination that implies a still broader community that could modify the Westphalian system in Europe in ways sufficient to make war in Europe unthinkable. This was not the path foreseen by *Mitrany* 60 years ago. He expected functional organizations operating between states in a continuing Westphalian order to make cooperation among states in matters *not* involving high policy so much a part of the international system that war would become unthinkable. What we see now is states joining at the top in a union so nearly political and involving matters so close to the heart of public policy that it becomes difficult to categorize many vital activities as internal or external to the states. War in Europe has become, as a practical matter, not impossible, but so chancy and so disruptive for members of the Community that it ceases to be a rational response to almost any challenge. But ethnic and the remnant of "national" interests are so strong that irrational responses might well prove strong enough to break the ties now so painfully being built.

Aside from the persistence of ethnicity as a politically significant fact, the problem with projecting this sort of redistribution of authority to include non-European powers is that regional powers and the one remaining great power, the United States, would have great difficulty in joining in a greater union with anybody in a way that might derogate from the capacity of those powers to take unilateral action to meet what each perceives as a threat to its interests. It must be remembered that today those powers, including the United States, are not cabals of small elites however they might appear from the outside, but true democracies following a representative form of government. American interventions in Panama and Grenada, possibly even in Nicaragua, were overwhelmingly popular with the American people while they were going on. They were even more popular after they stopped with what appeared to be a great success by United States military forces. Now that it is not clear that General *Noriega* will be convicted or, if convicted, that the conviction will be upheld on appeal in the American courts, or, if upheld, that scholars of law and history will in retrospect be proud of the American action, I am not sure how popular that intervention, and the others, will be to our children.

Democracies learn lessons very slowly and sometimes one fears that they never learn lessons at all. In the United States, we throw the ruling rogues out every four years and replace them with another batch of rogues who have to start at the bottom and learn all the same lessons. As soon as the lessons are learned, we throw these rogues out and replace them with yet another batch. Lest anybody think I am unduly cynical, I should point out that every time our current President modifies a position in light of recent experience, he is hit from his right wing, which seems to get about thirty per cent of the Republican vote in every Republican primary election. The presence of what appears to be a solid ideological fringe of about 15 per cent at each end of the political spectrum in the United States is probably typical of a lively democracy and represents a political force that cannot be ignored. This leads to a fairly pessimistic conclusion; the same one Prof. *Reisman* implied in his analysis positing the continued importance of military force in a world in which ideological fanaticism occasionally dominates the policies of important and powerful countries.

Prof. *Farer* gave us a rather different approach; one that strikes me as equally insightful, equally challenging and equally difficult to comment on. He does consider the possibility of an alteration of the Westphalian order; in this case the possibility of supplementing the weaknesses of the Security Council as structured under the UN Charter, with a more active OECD. The world's major economic powers, he argues, could step in where the Security Council is blocked by its voting procedures to authorize and pay for humanitarian intervention, perhaps, or other interventions in the interest of world stability and harmony, ecological survival, and so on. I have some problems with this proposal.

First of all, and quite apart from the political problem of getting a consensus procedure established in the OECD or similar organization that would somehow avoid the political problems of achieving consensus on the same matters in the Security Council, there is the question of money. Nobody likes to pay for anything. Even for the popular Gulf War, the United States had to stretch its persuasive and bargaining powers to the utmost. It apparently was so successful that more money was actually promised than the War cost; but that "victory" will surely make the next effort infinitely more difficult.

Then there is the question of intermediate level policy. It is one thing to decide to use force in what appears to be an emergency situation. It is another to decide when to stop using force; what represents "victory," or the achievement of a goal worth the first cost but not worth further expense in lives or treasure. The obvious example today is the outcry in the United States and elsewhere about the end of the Gulf War with *Saddam Hussein* still in power in Iraq. But no other policy was politically possible at the time, either in the United States or in Europe. There are always people who urge extreme or unrealistic policies, and they will always argue after the event that they were the only ones who had been "right" in their policy proposals. Their arguments carry political weight in the retrospective analysis of policy that affects elections. The leaders of different countries weigh differently the pressures coming from their fanatic constituencies and the impact of various possible courses on the next election. Consensus among those leaders in any international forum is therefore rare and costly for those most anxious for a consensus-based policy.

Prof. *Farer* suggests that individual state action in "reprisal" can be expanded; that the UN Charter does not actually forbid reprisals despite Article 2, paragraph 4. I frankly disagree with this analysis, although I agree with Prof. *Farer*'s conclusion on a slightly different basis. He argues that the restraints on reprisal that might be seen in Article 2, paragraph 4 have to be deleted from our reading of the Charter in light of changed circumstances since 1945: *rebus sic stantibus*. In my opinion the circumstances have not changed radically enough since 1945 to bring about this legal result. The framers of the Charter envisaged the sorts of tensions we have today and deliberately gave the monopoly on force to the Security Council and states acting in self-defense. It is a matter of the teleology, the overall design, of the Charter.

Both the Security Council authority and the self-defense article, Article 51, are in Chapter VII of the Charter. That chapter envisages the Security Council acting when it perceives a threat to the peace, breach of the peace or act of aggression. The "threat to the peace" mentioned in Article 39 is the lowest threshold for Security Council action. Article 51 assumes that even though the Security Council has authority and responsibility to act in the case of a threat to the peace, it might not perceive that threat until it is too late. In that case, the case in which an armed attack actually occurs despite Security Council oversight or even action, every state retains its inherent right of self-defense until the Security Council acts to discharge its responsibilities. I see no need to appeal to the principle of *rebus sic stantibus* to drop a key provision of the Charter, when the action contemplated can be brought within the terms of the Charter without amendment or deletion. The Charter has always permitted action in self-defense, and the definition of "self-defense" has always been interpreted, except in academic writings, to be far broader than the *Webster-Ashburton* formulation's high threshold envisaging a necessity that is imminent, overwhelming, allowing no moment for deliberation and no other recourse.

Under this approach, does the UN Charter allow for humanitarian intervention? The answer is simple, and I agree with Prof. *Farer:* No. The Charter authorizes the use of force in only two circumstances: When appropriate decisions are made by the Security Council, and in self-defense. That is why Article 51 is always cited. It is not because states are unconscious of their own humanitarian motives from time to time, but because self-defense is the only argument available to them under the Charter. That is why Israel, for example, argued Article 51 in the Entebbe incident — the rescue mission to Uganda; not because the rescue of a state's own nationals from life-threatening danger in a foreign state is part of the *Webster* formulation of self-defense, but because it was the only argument that could fit Israel's use of force into the terms of the UN Charter.

I had a student who wrote an article on this, published in the Fletcher Forum some years ago, arguing that self-defense in the UN Charter should be construed to include what he called "rectification," a conception derived from the municipal law of many countries, possibly a general principle of law recognized by civilized nations, under which every person is authorized to act to avoid irreparable injury to himself or herself by doing for another the things that that other is obliged to do but is failing to do. In the Entebbe case, it was Uganda's obligation under the 1970 Hague Convention to end the incident, and Israel merely did for Uganda what Uganda was otherwise obliged to do when the results of the Ugandan default would have been irreparable injury to legally protected Israeli interests. Uganda's claim that they were discharging their obligations under the Hague Convention of 1970 was not only unpersuasive on its face, but also negatived by the Israeli success and the fate of Ms. *Dora Bloch,* seen helpless in an Entebbe hospital by a third country diplomat at a time after the Uganda government said she had been returned to the airport.

Similarly, I have argued that the British action to recover control of the Falkland / Malvinas Islands from Argentina in 1982 was much more logically a "rectification" action than an action in self-defense; that Argentina's claim to the Islands was not negligible and that Article 2, paragraph 4's prohibition of the use of force was restricted to such use against the territorial integrity or political independence of another state only. I see no reason to delete these words from Article 2, paragraph 4; certainly no practice since 1945 will support a silent deletion. The Argentine default was its violation of Article 2, paragraph 3, of the Charter, requiring international disputes to be settled by peaceful means. (I hear lots of muttering. Those who prefer the British analysis might read my article before making up their minds; it has many footnotes, so it must be scholarly.) It is noteworthy that the British view (and apparently that adopted by many here) would have been indignantly rejected by all the Latin American states and many others whose voices as sovereign equals must be heard and whose votes count equally with European states' in the General Assembly and Security Council. The fact is that Article 2, paragraph 4, was not mentioned in the Security Council Resolution that ordered the Argentines to withdraw from the disputed Islands and that silence was not accidental. Nor was it necessary to categorize the Argentine invasion as an act of aggression. It certainly was a breach of the peace, and that is all the threshold the Security Council needed under Article 39 of the Charter. From this point of view, the British action was a "rectification" action, doing for another, in this case the Security Council and its supporters, what should have been done by that organ and the states it should have called on to restore international peace and security. The failure of the Security Council to do the things envisaged for it in the Charter left the British threatened with irreparable injury by the default of another, the Security Council, thus authorized to act in "rectification" under an expanded reading of Article 51.

This rationale changes the focus of what self-defense means under the UN Charter (and elsewhere); expands the usually publicized concept somewhat, but only very slightly, and supplies a legal rationale that is consistent with actual state practice, predictable state practice, and has built-in limits. It thus avoids the difficulties that I see in Prof. *Reisman*'s and Prof. *Farer*'s proposals that involve giving authority to individual states or small groups of states to decide on the use of force in the interest of others with whom they have no nexus; no integral relationship.

With regard to humanitarian intervention, it seems to me that the answer to the problem is not to promote humanitarian intervention as if it were a good thing, to be decided by the Security Council or the OECD as matters of policy and politics. It seems to me that the European Convention on Human Rights has shown us a less politicized, sounder way to handle humanitarian problems. It is built on the firm base of positive law. It defines in legal terms, not moral terms, the rights to be protected; it creates and defines the authority of institutions through which those rights can be vindicated without the use of force. It works by encouraging states to adhere to the system through political and diplomatic pressures. The "sanction" for opting out of the system, as was done by Greece for a period, is diplomatic and political, just as the cost to a state of opting out of a constitutional arrangement is not usually the threat of force (although in some deplorable cases it might be, as in the United States in 1861 and in Yugoslavia today) but the loss of advantages inherent in continued participation in the arrangement.

It is, in a sense, the reason for the success of the 1975 CSCE Helsinki process that it was not based on treaty commitments. It has been successful because it is an organization through which publicity is given to internal human rights violations (among other matters) by any member, exposed to public scrutiny at the instance of any other member without regard for the normal rules of "standing." The essence of the Basket III arrangement was that the agenda was to permit discussion of whatever connected with the document was inscribed in it by any party, even if it were an "internal" affair of another party. This institutional process conforms to the Westphalian system, but the institution is structured to permit a multilateral approach and the moral sanctions of diplomatic isolation and public opprobrium to supplement the legal remedies that the Westphalian legal order places beyond the reach of an uninvolved but anguished observer: *res inter alios acta*.

What alternatives are there? Surely not to try to repose authority in "democracies" to make binding choices on how others should structure their governments or their legal orders. Democracies are not necessarily peaceful, as I mentioned before. The United States seems to enjoy sending large numbers of otherwise unemployed military forces into small countries in distant places for short but victorious exercises. And it seems to make little difference whether the place to which those troops are sent is another democracy or a people in the chaotic throes of trying to establish a broadly based responsible government to replace an oligarchy or traditional class structure. The decision by a democracy to intervene in a foreign institution really depends on the internal dynamics of the democracy, whose government will do whatever its own political processes push it towards. And its dominant constituency can be ill-informed, fanatical and bored.

Finally, I would argue for consideration of a somewhat different approach. This is not the place to go into detail; we have had two extraordinary papers already laying out new approaches and my function is to comment on them. Indeed, it has been an extraordinarily challenging task to try to find things to say about those papers that had not been at least hinted in them, and my comments so far have been more expansions of what they said into new areas, rather than disagreements with them.

The different approach I would suggest involves a re-examination of the very notion of law. Historically, in the Greek analyses of the notion, *Plato* is the usual starting place but *Aristotle* created the formulations that have survived. *Aristotle* refers to "natural law," but the word he uses for "nature" is "*physis.*" *Physis*-nature has no moral content; it is the root of our word "physics." In the Nicomachean Ethics, *Aristotle* notes that there are people who believe that the moral notion of "justice" is actually a legal notion based on "natural" law. But, he points out in the usual English translations, the "natural law" under which the fire burns alike in Greece and Persia does not apply to concepts of "justice," which "shift and change." Justice, in his view, was determined as a "moral" question, by weighing competing values and compromising them; finding a "mean."

Aristotle wrote a different book about Politics. Here he applied the notion of "natural law" to find the basic Greek political organization, the "*polis*" to be a product of that law. He did not find the *polis* to be good or virtuous, but the product of natural law as the laws of economics are "natural." Shoemakers should make shoes, the soldiers should fight, slaves should be slaves, women should be women; they should all do the things that nature destined shoemakers, soldiers, slaves and women to do. When they join in a distribution of economic and social services to defend themselves, provide security and sustenance for their families and do other things that "nature" requires that human beings do in order to survive and prosper, they "naturally" form a *polis.*

The transition from that to a concept of "natural law" that includes moral imperatives was crystallized about three centuries after *Aristotle*'s death by *Cicero. Cicero* asserted that there is a "true law *(vera lex)*" which is universal and eternal and discovered by introspection. The command of the Senate cannot excuse our violations of that true law although the command of the Senate is, of course, positive law in Rome. Since introspection can reveal that true law to us, it all comes down to a matter of what *Cicero* called "right reason in harmony with nature *(recta ratio naturae congruens).*" He assumes that all reasonable people will ultimately agree on this natural law. But to the degree that that "law" includes moral values and concepts of "justice," there are problems. As we all know, nothing is more disputed among lawyers than value systems, and when we reason together we often come to different conclusions. None of us can be certain that his or her conclusions are correct unless we assume infallibility. That is a common assumption, particularly among those natural lawyers who interpret divine writ as the only legitimate source of "law." But even there, the assumption that God speaks to all in the same words, and that any particular interpreter hears Him correctly, and everybody else hears Him incorrectly, leads to depressing results. The true believer identifies with the Devil all who disagree with his or her interpretations of divine law; to the believer, truth is a function of faith and not of reason or pragmatic assumption. We end up in Armageddon: two armies of the Lord each fighting the other under the conviction that that other is the army of the Devil. We have witnessed that sort of war throughout recorded history, and are witnessing it today in the Middle East and elsewhere.

The result of this in the real world has been to raise the positive law to the center of the stage; to create the Westphalian system by doing away with divine law systems and monopolies on truth. For that matter, in the legal sphere (although not in politics or morality) we have even done away with the notion that that introspection is exportable; that my perceptions as to what the natural law requires must also be yours unless you are not reasoning correctly, and that therefore I have the right, as a matter of law, to force my conclusions on you and, if necessary to support my convictions relating to the "law," to kill you. Despite the rejection of that position in today's dominant legal theories, there seem to be many still who take that position believing it to be consistent with morality and good politics.

It is primarily because the Security Council and whatever substitutes might be proposed, like the OECD, act on the basis of politics and what they might assert to be special moral insight that I find the conclusions of Profs. *Reisman* and *Farer* both convincing and troubling. To use those insights as the basis for the exercise of a legal power to authorize the use of force, meaning that people should be killed and other people's property should be destroyed, is not likely in the long run to help the cause of humanitarianism. That is why I prefer to try to work within the framework of a positivist system; to structure the system in such a way that institutions can be created consistently with the Westphalian order, within which the conflicting insights, moral and political, can be, if not harmonized, at least discussed, and that war becomes the last resort in case of desperate emergency. I would rather that forcible reprisals and kidnappings of suspected "terrorists" be left to states acting alone which are prepared to defend their actions before all the appropriate forums. In the most significant cases, those actions can be defended in legal forums under a rationale that conforms to the positive law of the UN Charter and an interpretation that meshes the provisions of positive law with the realities that statesmen can understand, like a "rectification" interpretation of self-defense and an emphasis on Article 2, paragraph 3, of the Charter rather than a purported reaction to violations of Article 2, paragraph 4, that seem to me to be based more on political posturing and idealism than on legal analysis. I should also like to see institutions like the CSCE meetings created within the Westphalian system to help bring political and moral community pressures to bear against those elites which violate community standards of human rights. I agree with Prof. *Farer*'s notion that there are lots of things that could have been done institutionally with regard to Haiti, for example, without the direct contemplation of the use of force or an undirected embargo which we all knew was going to impact most severely on the peasantry we were trying to help.

With that I will conclude these comments. They are not entirely directed to the papers as presented, but I think we can have a very exciting discussion of all of this this afternoon.

Discussion

Wolfrum:

It is somewhat difficult to structure the discussion, but nevertheless, I shall try to do my best without hoping for much success. All of the three very fascinating and challenging presentations circled around the same issue. One of the questions everybody approached this morning was the question of security, introduced into the discussion by Prof. *Reisman*. The most accurate formulation of the question might be: "Who determines that there is a threat to security?" Mr. *Rubin* has phrased it by asking "Who authorizes whom to do what?" I am convinced that could and should be a topic of this discussion.

The second point I would like to bring to your attention is the second part of the phrase "Who authorizes whom to do what?" What means are open to us under present international law, or, looking more into the future, what means should be provided for in the future? That would be a second set of questions to be discussed.

Let me now come to the third aspect. *Tom Farer* has especially referred — as did Mr. *Reisman* and Mr. *Rubin* — to the question whether enforcement should be undertaken on a universal, on a regional, or on a — how it was termed — delegated level, a term which came up quite frequently. Is it really possible to delegate the enforcement to be undertaken on a regional level rather than on the universal level? What are the advantages, what are the disadvantages of such an approach? What is the inherent danger of having a delegation of power as to enforcement to single states?

Finally, you may add to my list: One should discuss whether — as has been suggested by *Tom Farer* — one should really refer to or fall back upon reprisals. I know that there has already been a challenge or objection to this approach, but nevertheless, I would like to draw your attention to this topic. That makes four topics which I offer you for discussion, but you are totally free to discuss whatever topic you prefer.

Farer:

I owe you a point of clarification with respect to the question of "who should act and who should make judgments." For I think I detect the conflation of two analytically distinct propositions that I was offering, albeit not very clearly.

I spoke about the possibility of enforcing human rights norms — including a right to participate in government — through regional or other sub-global associations of states that enter into treaties purporting to authorize mutual intervention. And I proposed that intervention pursuant to such treaties is at least arguably compatible with the basic assumptions of the Westphalian legal order. Just to give a certain concreteness to my suggestion, let us suppose that the Anglophonic states of the Caribbean — authentic democracies I think you will agree — enter into a treaty relationship with NATO members which have an interest in the Caribbean: The United States, Britain, Canada, France and The Netherlands. In form, the treaty provides mutual guarantees of democratic governance. In effect, the larger states guarantee continuity of constitutional government in the small ones.

With respect to procedures for effectuating the guarantees, the treaty might provide that in case of a *coup d'état* or any other illegal seizure of power, the surviving official with the highest constitutional status could call upon the other state parties to restore the constitutional order. If no senior official survived (or if no surviving official was at liberty to invoke the treaty), then the member states would meet at the request of any one of them and decide according to some weighted vote whether and how to re-establish a democratic government.

Is this scenario in harmony with the Westphalian system? The closest real case is Cyprus. When Cyprus achieved independence, it conceded to the British and Turkish states a right to intervene to defend the constitutional arrangements embodied in the independence agreement including a veto power for the island's Turkish minority over national legislation. Some years thereafter, the head of state, Archbishop *Makarios,* altered the constitution to remove the Turkish veto. When civil conflict ensued, Turkey threatened to exercise its right to intervene. The Cypriote government countered by claiming, in a debate at the United Nations Security Council, that an inherent feature of national sovereignty is the legal authority to deny foreign military forces access to the sovereign's territory. Therefore treaty arrangements purporting to limit that authority were ineffective. This *ius cogens* argument was not tested; the Turks did not invade on that occasion.

If you were to agree with the Cypriote claim — for reasons I will develop below I hope you will not — then my scenario would seem to fall outside the Westphalian dispensation. It probably falls outside when the *coup* is so successful that by the time the treaty is invoked, the insurrectionists have achieved unchallenged control of the target state. The party enjoying such control has generally been treated as the personification of national sovereignty unless foreign military support was critical to its success.

My distaste for the Cypriote argument stems in large measure from my view that many extant and foreseeable internal conflicts will probably require, as a condition of pacific settlement, the presence of external forces able to protect the contending parties and to guarantee the terms of their *modus vivendi*. To conclude that the government can at any time strip from the peace-keeping force the legal basis for its presence is to deny the international community a valuable instrument for the maintenance of minimal order and the defense of human rights. So I would like us to conclude — and here I think it is a question of choice, for you cannot reach a definitive conclusion either by Charter exegesis or logical derivation from the imagined nature of international relations — that temporally limited treaty arrangements of the kind I have outlined are legally binding. If, however, the cession of authority to exclude non-indigenous forces purports to be permanent, then I would probably concede a violation of Westphalian *ius cogens*.

That was what I had in mind when I spoke of armed intervention to enforce human rights norms, including the right to democratic governance. At the very end of my remarks, I opened the question of whether the great human problems of the new age can be addressed adequately if we cling to a formally egalitarian state system. I was suggesting that the sheer number of sovereign entities, coupled with the endemic weakness and irresponsibility of certain regimes, argued in favor of a more hierarchical international system in which some territorial entities now deemed sovereign states would be converted into protectorates or trusteeships. Such a proposal clearly carries us far away from the Westphalian system.

Kühne:

The remarks I have to make concern your first point. It seems to be a philosophical one. But if you take a closer look, it has very practical implications for the future development of international politics as well as of international law. Both speakers made the notion of "threat" a focal point for their analysis of the problem of peace and security in the world today.

I am sceptical whether this is an adequate approach in the post Cold War era. The notion of "threat" may not describe the most important challenges we face with regard to security in the future. It therefore could lead our thinking about what kind of security arrangements we need in the wrong direction. May I remind you that even NATO in its Rome communiqué from July last year shifted its language and chose "risks" instead of "threat" as the basic notion for its future activities. That is significant! In view of a rather breathtaking accumulation of risks endangering our survival, "risk prevention" and "management of risks" seem to be the real problem of the modern world. Of course, in academic circles like this, this distinction seems to be just a matter just of semantics. We could agree that "risks" equal "threats" because both entail dangers with regard to stability and the *status quo*.

Yet outside this room, in real political life, the situation and the dynamics of these two notions are different. There "threat," quite in difference to "risk," carries the whole baggage of traditional military thinking with it. And, perhaps even more important, if you define "risks" as "threats," people will automatically look for an enemy, who is responsible for this threat. Defining something as a threat will in most political cultures, and definitely in ours, lead to a search for the enemy, who has to be fought. Inevitably, a socio-psychological dynamic is unleashed, which almost will lead to war, at least if there are no powerful regional or global institutions to break this dynamic. Former Yugoslavia and the former Soviet Union are good, or for that matter bad examples for such a dynamic. The choice between "risks" and "threats" is, therefore, not just an academic one. It is about choosing between going back to the security culture of the nineteenth century or advancing to a modern, more cooperative one.

The distinction between "risks" and "threats" is also important for the future fate of North-South relations. If the many "risks" which have to be managed in this relationship, in particular the so-called "global challenges" like migration, ecological problems, drug-traffic, terrorism, etc., are defined as "threats," the door for a cooperative solution will be closed and we may end up with another huge bipolar confrontation between the poor countries, mostly in the South, and the rich, industrialized ones.

There is another point which I disagree with somewhat. It concerns the notion of monopolarity. The fear of a monopolar global domination by the U.S. is quite popular these days. I think it is an exaggerated one. The U.S. has the power for monopolar domination only in a very limited sense, i.e. when it comes to the nuclear level or to wars like the one just fought in the Gulf. With regard to the latter, one may even question the U.S. power, as the U.S. was financially quite dependent on other powers to fight this war, like Japan, Saudi Arabia, and the Gulf States, as well as Germany. Anyway, most experts consider the war to be an exception rather than the rule of future military conflicts. So-called soft power, i.e. economic and related power, is becoming more important with regard to the overall distribution of global power (or the "correlation of forces," as Marxists used to say) than military power. There is no monopolar domination by the U.S. in this field.

Watts:

I would just like to start with your first suggestion, namely security, and what is meant by security. It is something on which we have to focus. One of the things that strikes me about that term is that it is one which has got steadily broader over the last forty or fifty years. When the UN Charter was agreed, it had a predominantly military connotation. But now, it is extended very much more widely than just that. It is in that area that, it seems to me, a lot of our present problems arise. Another point I should make about security is that in state practice what we are essentially talking about is the security of individual states. There is, I think, in an academic or an objective sense something called international security, but what motivates states is their own security. They may dress up what they do as in the interest of international security, but, by and large, states are not altruistic. They do things for their own national interests.

Where do the contemporary problems with security lie? It seems to me that they lie essentially in the problem of moving frontiers. I use that term "moving frontiers" in three separate senses. In one sense, purely literally, there are frontiers in the territorial sense; secondly, they occur in a conceptual sense; and thirdly, in a topical sense. Let me take each in turn.

In the literal, territorial sense of moving frontiers, there is a relationship between security and stability. It is not exact, but it is there. One of the problems, it seems to me, with the UN Charter is that it is essentially an instrument for preserving the *status quo*. It is often more concerned with going back to where matters stood immediately before a troublesome situation became active, rather than with resolving the underlying problem. And yet, somehow we have to come to grips with change in the *status quo* and how we manage it. If you look at the Charter and at what has happened since the Charter was adopted, you see an enormous increase in the number of states as members of the international community; there are the consequences of the break-up of states, something of which we are very much aware today; there is still great scope for the concept of self-determination, which started with the colonial problem, but has a long, long way to go, in ways which may be quite difficult for many existing states to absorb. In all those areas, enormous changes are taking place in purely territorial contexts. At a more theoretical level even — and I think somebody mentioned it, it may have been *Tom Farer* — is the question of territorial sovereignty. I really find that it is living in the past to talk too much about territorial sovereignty. *Tom Farer* did not, he talked about authority, in which, I am sure, he is absolutely right. I find it astonishing that we still find in a concept such as sovereignty, which is so politically emotive and jurisprudentially opaque, something which is still thought to be a useful legal tool. Anyway, territorial "moving frontiers," we have to come to grips with.

Turning to concepts, there are a number of relevant concepts in the security area which are also moving. The notion of security — as I have already mentioned — is getting much, much broader than it was when the Charter was adopted. The concept of self-defense has become through force of circumstances considerably adapted, enlarged possibly, from what it originally was. I would also note in particular the concept of "internal affairs." What is appropriately a state's internal affair is now very different from what it was in 1945. Take a current situation, Yugoslavia. It appears to me we have there almost a classic case of difficult problems in the internal affairs of a state, which it should be left to sort out for itself. But that is not how the international community has reacted. What would sixty years ago have been regarded as a classic civil, internal war is now regarded as something with which the international community ought to concern itself. I am not saying that this is in any way wrong. I am just pointing to the change which has taken place, and noting that it is one with which the international community has found it difficult to get to grips.

Another very obvious example is in the field of human rights where fifty years ago people tended to accept that what a state did with its own nationals in its own territory was purely a matter for that state. Gradually that has changed, to quite an astonishing degree. And it is in that context where the concept of humanitarian intervention is relevant. I would have had little difficulty, thirty or forty years ago when I was a student, in saying that that humanitarian intervention should not be allowed. But now I really find it very difficult, given the concern which all states have today with human rights, to deny the possibility of outside states taking some action to stop gross violations of human rights involving the risk of large-scale killing and so on. We know the situation. I find it very difficult to say that states cannot intervene, cannot "interfere," whatever word you want to use, and that states must stand and watch because the Charter is said only to allow the use of force in cases of self-defense or if the Security Council authorized it. That does not seem to me a realistic or acceptable position for states to have to take. And yet, we are stuck with the Charter which says the things that it says. Somehow the change in the relevance and weight of human rights (which are, of course, themselves acknowledged in the Charter) has changed the balance of the Charter's language.

Prof. *Rubin,* I think it was he, suggested that the right way has been shown by the European Convention of Human Rights, establishing an institutional structure available for the resolution of these problems. With all respect, I do not think that solution fully works, because the problem with situations which give rise to humanitarian interventions, just like the problem with situations giving rise to calls for self-defense, is urgency and immediacy, and any institutional structure in the real world today is unlikely able to respond quickly enough. If you are faced with a serious and actual humanitarian problem, to say "well we will go and ask the Security Council to debate about it for several weeks" is just not good enough in the modern world.

If the territorial and conceptual frontiers are moving, so, too, are the topical frontiers, by which I mean the topics with which the international community is concerned. Human rights, again, obviously; the extent of international concern with human rights has expanded enormously. So, too, with security in its broader sense, security issues for all states. The environment is a broad, new area, which many states even regard as raising issues of security in its broad sense. Migration flows of people create very serious problems of order and security within states into which the migrants are moving.

Indeed, all these areas of moving frontiers give rise to problems which can be generally regarded in a wide sense as security problems. Yet the current UN security framework of dealing with these problems is now perhaps no longer appropriate but is out of date. Not surprisingly: the Charter is nearly fifty years old. It was designed for an international community as it existed in the late 1940s. It viewed a world which was to some extent rather static, and it is not designed to cope with some of the fluidities that we see in the modern world in this general security area. Maybe, the organized international community is overreaching itself in trying to deal with quite so many issues without first having established the appropriate institutional structure. The community may be too ambitious.

There is also a need to guard against assuming that the present unity of purpose within the Security Council is going to be a permanent feature of the years ahead — and I consciously talk about the unity of purpose of the Security Council, not just the five Permanent Members. That may also be important, but what has been striking in the last couple of years has been how the Security Council resolutions within a number of areas have been adopted either unanimously or virtually unanimously. Only time will show whether that is going to be a new pattern or whether, as I rather fear, we will find that we have been living through a period which will prove to have been in this respect just an exceptional period in world affairs.

What can be done about tackling these problems is not easy to see. There may still be some scope for using more fully existing Charter provisions. One very clear example of an area of which more use might be made is Article 52, concerning regional arrangements. Although there are difficulties about that concept, there is something there that the United Nations has not made as much use of as perhaps it might. But there is a great danger, it seems to me, in taking the process of using the existing Charter text too far if it means a distorted interpretation of the Charter language. Creative interpretation is all very well, but if we try to stretch a legal text too far, we damage respect for international law as a whole. And that could only be bad. However much it may solve an immediate problem, in the long run it is bad for respect for the Charter and for respect for international law.

But then, if we refrain from going too far down the track of creatively interpreting the Charter to cover everything we want to cover, what are the alternatives? One is to amend the Charter. But I would not be at all optimistic — I doubt if anyone here would be optimistic — about trying to get agreement on formal amendments of the Charter, by which I mean changes to the existing language. I would be a little less pessimistic, I think, about the possibility of an amendment by way of addition to the Charter: one might leave the existing Articles as they stand, but add an extra Article *bis* covering new areas that at the moment are not dealt with. There might also be a possibility in trying to develop something like an updated version of the Friendly Relations Declaration covering a new ground: in effect an interpretative declaration of what is already there. The 50th anniversary of the Charter might have been an appropriate time for that kind of declaration, but it is probably too late to start now. But one might think of a declaration for the year 2001 — the start of the next millennium, for example.

To return to Article 52: The idea of going down the route of delegating the UN's authority to regional bodies, I have to say, leaves me nervous, although I can still see considerable scope in regional arrangements. Delegated authority to solve some security problems is perhaps all very well if one is talking about a security problem arising *within* the regional group to which one is delegating authority. But a lot of problems which are arising are not of that kind. Again, take Yugoslavia. It is not within the proper range of activity of any of the European bodies that have been trying to deal with it, except possibly the CSCE which has not got very actively involved, and Yugoslavia is not part of the European Community, which has been very active in trying to find a solution. That, in my view, is not using a regional group in quite the appropriate sense. I am talking about a positive delegation of authority to a regional group to act, or an implied authority in the absence of some express withholding of authority to a regional grouping to act. I can see that it might be acceptable within the kind of group around this table to think that a delegation of authority to NATO would be all right, as would delegation of authority to the OAS. You only have to look around the rest of the world, however, to find that delegations of authority could in fact easily be simply a licence to a local tyrant to do whatever he wanted to do. The whole of the world is not very well organized in regional groupings. A further danger I see in resort to regional groupings is that it could easily, to the extent that it was successful, result in setting up competing centres of power which would erode the authority of the United Nations. That is not an attractive option as far as I am concerned.

That is the last of my substantive points. There are a lot of problems, and finding solutions is not at all easy. There are some avenues which, it seems to me, it would be helpful to pursue. Some of them need to be used with considerable caution, if one looks at their possible applications worldwide, rather than just in selective parts of the world or in relation to selective problems.

Morrison:

I will make two sets of comments which are somewhat contradictory. The first set of comments is to raise the question about whether we are talking about the scenarios involving the break down of the Westphalian system. That is the emergence of nationalist groups without defined territory, and so on. Much of the structure we have traditionally been talking about, as *Sir Arthur* commented, is defined by the expectations of 1945 in defined state entities, etc. That is something we have to look at and find some other kinds of principles to cope with the new reality. One of the things that led me to rethinking is the suggestion about the pyramidal solution. It may be that the pyramidal solution is not the best solution, but the least worst solution, until some other kind of solution can be found. All the other options do not look very attractive. Therefore, one has to take the least worst solution rather than one that is optimal, simply to preserve some kind of order.

Two further preliminary comments. One of them is that I was amazed this morning that the Third World seems to have sunk into the sea. It was not there in the discussion. What we were talking about, it seemed to me largely, was a series of security concerns of relatively well developed countries. One of the big problems we have is that we have a very large number of very weak non-developed countries, which somehow have to be brought into the equation. Maybe the Westphalian system has already died. A system of sovereign equality, "one country, one vote," is causing us to develop legal fictions and habits of mind to avoid its logical consequences.

A final preliminary comment: I was taught, when I was a law student, that law evolves by legal fiction; it evolves by exception. The comment about Yugoslavia and what *Sir Arthur* made about the Yugoslav situation, if applied to Spain in the 1930s, would have justified immediate recognition of some kind of danger. This indicated to me that we are changing the basic fundamental rules of law about a good many things by creating legal fictions. We have decided that Croatia is an independent country in order to enforce human rights and are recognizing it, not because of the rules of recognition, but because of responses to other kinds of questions.

But with all those preliminary comments, which seem to be asking "is there really law there?" and "is law in a greater state of chaos than we think that it is in?," I came back to thinking about a comment Mr. *Kühne* has made about threats to the peace. I am really concerned about that and the tenor of nearly all presentations of this morning. They seem to be moving away from bright-line rules, which have been the traditional stuff of international law, and on to rather subjective rules in which one opinion is as good as another as to whether there is a risk or threat to peace; and if my opinion is as good as yours, as to whether I am entitled to use force, I guess I might as well go ahead. Maybe that is reality but I am not sure that it is law. I thought we are moving fairly far away from legal standards into policy judgments this morning. I know, *Michael Reisman* was doing that intentionally because he is trying to create policy about where the legal standards should go. But I have said so far that we have got a better grip on what law is or should be, as opposed to what the policy is or should be.

Riedel:

First of all I would just like to come back to what *Sir Arthur* said a minute ago on states that are not altruistic. I think in the general way that you put it one can probably agree, but it depends largely on how you define what is altruism, and more important still, what is egoism of states. Is it egoistic to think of one's future in giving development aid to save the global commons, for instance? That is defined according to one's own egoistic interest. I think one gets into very deep water if one uses that phrase. *Lon Fuller* once said that man is capable of at least limited altruism. Does that not apply to states as well?

Now to the first question that the chairman put to us at the beginning of the session, regarding the security questions. I would like to endorse what Prof. *Reisman* said right at the beginning of his presentation, that it must be an international effort; that it is indispensable to see it from that perspective. If I understood Prof. *Farer* right that his argument was that the problem is policing and not agreeing on norms, I spy a vast divergence of opinions, but maybe, in reality there is not such a big divergence of opinion after all. You then said, Prof. *Farer,* that we are not in a situation of unipolarity but in a multipolar world, and then offered us the picture of a pyramid and a whole horizontal system underpinning it. But you raised that as a question, I think, although I have the feeling that you came down on the horizontal system in your answer, you left it open for us to discuss.

If I may hazard a guess, the pyramidal approach suggests policing, suggests strong institution-making, suggests a triangle to the pivotal point, or an apex, in an essentially unipolar world. I think that is possibly very dangerous. If the alternative was the horizontal approach, then we would find that it would be much more difficult to cope with the actors of the system, because one would have to realize that norm-setting and standard-setting becomes much more the rule of the game than fixing it in a particular world-order model. But then the development of criteria for dispute settlement mechanism again throws us back to some form of institutionalization, even under the conditions of unipolarity.

So, if we take the unipolarity as a political fact and take the normative approach of international law, which is an essentially different claim area, then the dispute settlement mechanisms become very, very important. Is the *Habermas* approach of just having an international law discourse the answer? Or should it not rather be an agreement of the international community, because we cannot afford anything but a horizontal approach, we should agree on standards, on norms of right and wrong in international relations? Developing criterias, as *Sir Arthur* has indicated, for which the Friendly Relations Declaration might be a model or something else for the new millennium, should it be criteria of positive and negative peace, as has been discussed in other symposia here? Should it be criteria like that or is that just academic thinking?

I would be very interested to know on which side of the line you two would come down. Personally, I would feel that the pyramidal approach is probably the easier one to argue and to display but probably not the right answer for the future that lies ahead. In opting for the horizontal approach, that would probably not preclude regional and subregional and deputization ideas that you have outlined. I think it goes really for both. But then I find the horizontal approach much more attractive.

Stein:

I would like to come back to what *Tom Farer* said when he started the discussion. I have to admit that I do have my problems with intervention in order to preserve or restore democracy. If my notes are correct, *Tom* listed among the different occasions for the exercise of the Security Council's options the "ideological concerns," and one of them was the overthrow of democratic regimes. If we allow states to intervene, we can probably allow it only under circumstances in which the community of states, and that is basically the UN, could likewise intervene in the common interest. The UN could intervene if democracy is a security item, as Prof. *Riedel* just indicated, saying that intervention in such a case should be a combined effort. But could the Security Council really intervene in order to preserve or restore democracy? I do not think so. Democracy is not a term that is used in the United Nations Charter. If it were a precondition for joining the United Nations to be a democratic state, we would not have far over 160 UN member states, maybe now, but certainly not ten years ago. So I do not see that the Security Council, let alone states, could intervene in order to restore or preserve democracy without violating Article 2, paragraph 7, of the UN Charter.

Delbrück:

I should like to take up the threat / risk terminology problem and relate it to the basic issue we are confronted with at this first day of the symposium. It seems to me that we are facing different kinds of scenarios to which one may or may not apply these two notions. I do not think that it is an either / or question. I do agree with Mr. *Kühne* that there are special Third World related issues or scenarios which could be more appropriately described by applying the notions of "risk" and "risk management." On the other hand, there are scenarios, including Third World scenarios, for which the term "threat" is the appropriate description. In the first case, where we talk about "risks" and possibly "risk management" — I would think of the world-wide migration process, which could very easily develop into a crisis which needs crisis management, but which would be ill-termed if you would think of it in terms of traditional threat perceptions which we have been dealing with within the United Nations and elsewhere. And yet, these risk scenarios may certainly involve questions of enforcing international law. On the other hand, Iraq's or rather *Saddam Hussein*'s behaviour is something which is very closely related to North-South issues. In terms of the rich and the poor, and of the assertion of power by some states within the Third World, I think that this kind of scenario will most likely be one we shall be facing more often in the future; but still they are very close to traditional threat-type situations which would then have to be dealt with adequately and preferably by an international authority. So, I think, I should warn against making an either / or choice in talking about risks or threats. Both are adequate descriptions for the same or only slightly different scenarios depending on what responses are required.

I have already touched upon the question of the authorities to be dealing with a given risk or threat scenario. I should like to elaborate on this a bit. The questions posed are, who is to determine what is to be done; and what situation is to be determined as dangerous, risky or threatening, and by what authority? I think, this is the other major problem we are dealing with. I respectfully disagree with the opinion voiced this morning, namely that conflict resolution by legal process is the only legitimate and lawful answer to the challenges we are and shall be facing. Although this concept is very sympathetic with me, I think it is not a realistic one. It would be wonderful if we could substitute traditional means of international law enforcement, which usually individual states or groups of states took into their hands, by institutionalized mechanisms of, preferably judicial, conflict resolution. Substituting feud by court proceedings was the great achievement which marked the emergence of the modern state. The success of this new form of conflict resolution rested on the centralization of power in the government. We have not come that far yet. The often cited example of the European Convention on Human Rights enforcement system, indeed, is an impressive model of conflict resolution under the rule of law. But it works well because it functions in the politically and culturally homogeneous European region. *Cum grano salis,* the same may be said of the American Convention on Human Rights system. But beyond that, I think, it is unrealistic to assume that in the near future or even in a medium-range perspective we shall have the chance to achieve effective and swift conflict resolution by orderly process of law, considering the kinds of scenarios we have been talking about; and I think, they are not unrealistic ones.

On the other hand, I am also very sceptical about emphasizing so much the unilateral enforcement approach as the fall-back position, if international authority fails. I think, the focus should be on improving the institutional framework for enforcing international law in view of the scenarios which we could possibly face or are already facing today. Yugoslavia is one more case in point. Due to the background and history of this tragic conflict, the international community cannot afford to stand by idle. But who is to react? The United Nations, the CSCE, NATO, WEU/EC? None of the institutions named, for one reason or another, seems to be ready or capable of effectively intervening. Individual states or a group of states could possibly step in — outside the framework of the above mentioned organizations — but would their authority to act be viewed as legitimate and / or legal?

So, allocating the authority to deal with these issues is the no. 1 problem. Where is the authority which determines what is threatening or not threatening and what has to be done about it? Here again, I should think, it is not the choice between either universal or regional arrangements. It looks like I am always trying to get to the nice middle of the road approach, but the right choice of the authority empowered to react to conflicts such as in Yugoslavia seems to be the crucial element in developing the much needed international law enforcement system. Depending on the nature of a conflict, its geographic location and specific historical and cultural background must be one of the primary determining factors for the allocation of authority to deal with it. Thus, it may be a regional authority or a universal, i.e. the United Nations, which would be the adequate authority to intervene.

The only option I should want to rule out is the traditional unilateral approach. Let me explain this in some more detail. The unilateral fall-back position so strongly emphasized by some this morning will never lead to a real effort to strengthen an institutionalized enforcement system. I do find the paradox — pointed out by *Michel Reisman* — very fascinating, i.e. that we have to rely on the unilateral option in order to make the institutional approach work. In a way, this seems to be a very fascinating and realistic description of what is happening. But it may not necessarily be true that the international mechanism would always work badly, if you would not emphasize or rely on unilateral options. This could also work the other way round. States might be reluctant to agree to bring a conflict before the international institution, because then the option to act unilaterally would be open again, if the international institution would fail. My point of view is that allocating authority for international law enforcement must be either universal or regional; and it should be done regionally where it is feasible and appropriate as, I think, the European institutions are — or should be — in a position to do a fairly sufficient job in the Yugoslavian case. The CSCE, for instance, is an institution which is developing very fast. You have all heard about the recent proposals. On the other hand, there are conflicts, particularly North-South conflicts, which cannot be dealt with regionally very well, because, for example, a given region where the conflict occurs may not be very well organized or institutionalized. Other regional arrangements may not interfere in a Third World region, because, for political reasons, their interference could mean really putting oil into the fire. If European institutions, for instance, would intervene in Africa, I cannot envisage that this could be done without — if only politically — aggravating the situation. In such cases the United Nations have to step in.

To sum up, I think it is within the United Nations Charter law that both authorities, international and regional, can and should act. I am not as sceptical as you, *Sir Arthur*, about the adaptability, the interpretability of the Charter. The terms "breach of the peace" or "threat to the peace" and other relevant terms are open to a normatively justifiable interpretation or re-interpretation. To term a situation like the one in Yugoslavia as a threat to the peace, as the Security Council readily did with sanctions following, is not stretching the Charter text too far. Nor would, I think, describing a situation like in Cambodia under the *Pol Pot* regime as a threat to peace. Potentially, these are situations which could develop into a very serious international conflict. Preventive diplomacy or proactive (to use *Michel Reisman*'s graphic language) measures taken by the Security

Council could easily be subsumed under the notion of avoiding or preventing a threat to peace. The fact that this was not done in the past as, for instance, in the Cambodian case does not mean that the Charter would not have allowed for this interpretation. The failure of the United Nations to react adequately to the massacres of the *Pol Pot* regime was not due to legal considerations. There was simply nobody willing to do it because of the mutual Cold War blockade in the Security Council. Yet, there have been in the past — albeit few — instances, as in the case of the South African Apartheid policies, where the Security Council agreed on a broader reading of the term "threat to the peace", i.e. condemning Apartheid as a threat to international peace. Recently, however, we have — and this has been mentioned — no less than five instances where the Security Council very easily found itself resolved to accept certain internal situations as threats to the peace. Thus, I think the trend in the Security Council is to read the Charter broader and to establish and assert its authority in these areas.

Randelzhofer:

I wished I had the floor prior to the intervention of *Jost Delbrück,* because he said a lot of what I intended to say. So it remains for me only to repeat in less convincing words what he said. I, too, pick up your first question, "Who determines whether there exists a threat the to peace?" But I must confess that I take a very positivistic view in trying to answer it. I will come down from the lofty heights to the floor of the Charter. The Charter in its Article 39, in my view, gives a pretty clear-cut answer in saying, let me cite, "The Security Council determines the existence of ..." That naturally means a predominance of the five Permanent Members. This predominance is only mitigated to some extent by the prerequisite that the five of them must be in accordance (or at least that not one or more are cleary against what they wanted to do), and secondly it is mitigated in that they need four additional votes by other states. The predominance is fostered, too, by the fact that the very notion of a threat to the peace is a very loose one, and it is clear that we have no definition in the Charter of what is a threat to the peace. When we remember what a picture *Michael Reisman* gave us of the manifold varieties of possible threats to the peace, we have to think about the impossibility of really making a definition. In his so-called commentary to the Charter, *Hans Kelsen* fights in favour of the view that the threat to the peace is not really a legal notion, but shall leave complete political freedom to the Security Council in deciding whether a threat to the peace does exist or does not. On the other hand, the four categories *Tom Farer* pointed out to us gave us some guidance, but finally I think it is not possible to give a clear-cut definition. We can point to several types to elucidate what is meant, but a clear-cut definition will not be possible.

I got the impression that at present we are about to blame that legal situation, and to blame it in a somewhat contradictory way. We blame it, on the one hand, on the predominance of the five members in the case that they agree. On the other hand, we blame the ineffectiveness of the same system if they are not of the same opinion. That is contradictory, as I see it. The decisive question is, what are the alternatives for the system? Let me confess that I do not see a better system, and so I totally agree with *Jost Delbrück*. The unilateral approach is not really a better solution; it is only in favour of the powerful states, not mitigated by the necessity of the consent of at least nine states. Regionalism has perhaps the advantage that the states in the same region are more concerned with the problem and, therefore, more eager to find a solution, but on the other hand, you have the problem that it is more difficult to bring about military superiority. If the states in a certain region are only small states, it is very difficult to bring about the necessary military superiority to bring the problem to an end without waging war for years and years. That cannot really be the possible solution.

In my view, it is a little bit astonishing and amazing that we are so critical of the United Nations system of Chapter VII, especially after the experience with the Gulf War. I do not understand that because in my view the Gulf War is the first example not of a clear-cut case foreseen by the Charter, but it is in substance a case of Article 39 in combination with Article 42 of the Charter, and it gives me some hope that it can and might possibly be more effective than it has been in the past.

Please, allow me one concluding remark with a different significance. I learnt — especially by Prof. *Rubin*, who was assisted later on by *Tom Farer* and by Prof. *Morrison* — the notion of the Westphalian system, though the Westphalian system is not totally strange to me. I would have hesitated to use it to describe our actual international legal system. It immediately came to my mind that we could at least add, for example, the Utrecht system in 1713, the Paris system of 1856, the San Stefano system of 1878, the Paris system of 1919, and, last but not least, the San Francisco system of 1945. I am always pleased to hear about historical ideas, but I think we are different from the old Westphalian system. The international legal system has developed a lot and we may not forget those other steps. I only alluded to the most important of them.

Tomuschat:

This is a fascinating debate we have embarked on, but it will be difficult to find answers. Maybe we are talking about too many topics at the same time. We are attempting to resolve all the mysteries of world security, and this is, of course, dependent on an extremely great number of different factors. In trying to find concrete answers to concrete questions, let me just make two points. The first point is: The present system, the San Fransisco system, is totally based on the ban on the use of force, which is one of the core elements of our present system of international law and of the international system as a whole. On the other hand, we may presently be witnessing a deep change in that system because of the many claims of self-determination. Existing boundaries are tied up with nationhood and legitimate nationhood. If nations disintegrate and if new peoples emerge, then existing boundaries are going to lose their sanctity. Nobody will readily accept that those frontier lines which exist presently should remain stable as they are for eternity, unless agreement is reached on some mode of peaceful change. So, I really do see a big threat to international security: the multitude of rising claims for self-determination in all parts of the world. Today there was an article in the Herald Tribune which specified that even in Africa the system inherited from the colonial powers, which has been considered "unfoundable" until recently, is now being challenged, the result being that the block continent has passed into a new mentality, where claims for self-determination could be combined with claims for territorial changes. This is my first point.

My second point is focussed on the Security Council. Two questions arise. First of all, what can the Council do in legal terms, and second, what can it do in factual terms? What are the factors which condition its action? There are so many elements which have to be taken into account that first I would like to focus on the legal element, the criteria which regulate actions by the Security Council. In that respect I agree with *Jost Delbrück* when he pointed out that the formula employed by Article 39 is extremely broad. Article 39 talks about the existence of any threats to peace or breaches of the peace. All this is subject to interpretation of what is peace. I should like to recall once again what he already pointed out, namely that, as far as South Africa is concerned, the Security Council in many instances has ruled that, for instance, a modification of the constitution could amount to a threat to international peace and security. Indeed, the Security Council declared that some of those changes were null and void. Thus we have already embarked on what began many years ago, a new stage in the development of international law. It is not totally excluded to speak of a right to democracy. Given the human rights guarantees as they are laid down in the Universal Declaration and the two Covenants, of which the Universal Declaration (Article 21) and the Political Covenant (Article 25) speak of a right to democratic participation, it is clear that everyone has a right to participate in the conduct of public affairs of his country. So, if there is a massive violation of that right, that again can be characterized as a threat to peace and then justify intervention by the Security Council. This is at least debatable, for there are strong indicia at the present time that a majority of the world community would view massive violation of the right to democratic participation as justifying Security Council action.

But here I would like to distinguish between two situations. First of all, there are situations which can be remedied by just a short action of the Security Council, or, put otherwise, a surgical strike, for instance if you free hostages. Or take the Grenada situation where a whole country was liberated from a group of self-made dictators, which had taken that entire country as hostage. Such a type of intervention is easy, the costs involved are not very high. But on the other hand, if you have to face a situation like in Iraq or in other countries where the society has totally desintegrated, a surgical strike is not enough. You would then have to assume responsibility for a country for a couple of years, maybe for five or ten years, as the Allies did in Germany in 1945. This is an example which should never be forgotten, a sort of test case of new necessities which may emerge in the future and have already emerged.

Take the situation in Cambodia, and then we can have again two situations: One, the country is prepared to accept intervention by the international community — this is presently the Cambodian situation. Outside interference could also go against the will of the country like in Iraq, where, however, the United States did not continue its advance towards Baghdad, probably out of fear that they would indeed have to assume responsibility for that difficult country for a couple of years, which nobody was prepared to do. What we are faced with is the necessity of having some kind of a new trusteeship system. A trusteeship system was thought to be needed just for a transitional period until all colonial countries had achieved independence, but now we have to recognize the fact that such a system may also be needed as a rescue system for shorter periods, when a country has broken down, when the political system does not operate any more, and the society is deeply divided. Let us hope that in that sense the UNTAC action could become a model for future situations which will undoubtedly emerge.

The Cambodian example, however, also shows the high costs involved, the costs in money, the costs in human beings — because you have to send troops there, and troops, that means human lives, that means boys which have to be sent to some country or territory. This is a difficulty which cannot be overcome. Who is interested in rescuing Somalia? The international community certainly does have some interest but is not prepared to pay a high price. Who is interested in rescuing Sudan? Again, there is widespread agreement that it would be nice if Sudan could be rescued, but not at a high cost. This question of costs embodies a structural difficulty, and in this respect I agree that regional organizations should play a bigger role than they have played until now.

O'Connell:

I found Prof. *Tomuschat*'s comments very worrying. I was not going to speak to this point, but I will say a little bit on it first. I do not find a normative value in intervention generally. I think one of the problems with the discussion so far is that I do not actually see any interest by governments in intervening. I think that is actually a positive development in international history and one that, I think, will continue. That means that the security discussion, which we have had so far, must be built on a different basis. I do not see a world full of pyramids, even if that pyramid is a UN interventionary force instead of a U.S. interventionary force or a U.S. dominated world security structure. In the United States we have come through a period of twenty years of economic stagnation, and while we are coming out of a very deep and difficult recession, the predictions, the best predictions, are for another generation of economic stagnation. That means the people in the United States who are reaching middle age, an age of political power in the next ten, twenty years, have a very different life experience than those who currently rule the United States, a very different world view. Not only do they have that economic experience, but they will not have experienced the communism against which the previous generation has oriented U.S. policy for fifty years. They no longer have this reason or continued feeling of why the United States should be a dominant power, or the dominant power in some kind of pyramidal or unipolar system.

What I see instead is a return to a more natural American viewpoint of its role in the world, which is not at the top of the pyramid. We will be much more internally focussed in terms of our economy and other interests. What this means for world security and shaping security into the future is, I think, that the U.S. will prefer a multilateral security system, not a pyramidal one. I think that the current civil wars, which we see — Yugoslavia is a very good example — do not interest the United States. This trend will continue. We do not see even Haiti, so close to us, as a threat to the United States and so we do not use military force there. That will be the view in the future. I actually think that that is best for the people involved, having lived all of my life in an interventionary America that did not necessarily enhance human rights in the countries in which it intervened.

I am sceptical about whether intervention can enhance human rights generally. I think the U.S. instead will see threats to security based on terrorism and arms control, escpecially nuclear proliferation, which *Mike Reisman* referred to this morning. The way to attack those kinds of threats to security will be through a multilateral mechanism such as the IAEA, which we are seeing now getting more attention than it has ever had before and being the kind of institution the U.S. and the Europeans and the Japanese should be interested in promoting.

I also think that the UN is capable of reform at this junction, and certainly even more in the future than at this end of the Cold War period. The European Community and Japan can in the next one or two decades convince the United States to change the current structure of the Security Council, and I think they can do that through a re-discussion of economic distribution or economic payments for the kinds of initiatives that these various countries are interested in undertaking. We could do it now, but I do not quite see the end of the current power structure in the U.S. for another ten years. But that is how I see the future, and I think it is a longer task than *Mike Reisman* sketched out. But I actually think that it would be a more peaceful one and one that promotes human rights more effectively than using force to try to do so. *Jost Delbrück* and I have a debate on this in the upcoming Indiana Law Journal, so I will not say any more about intervention and civil war. I really want to make the point that I think the

U.S.'s view of the future is one of multilateralism and not necessarily of unilateralism that we heard discussed so much this morning.

Ferrari Bravo:

I wish to start from something which should be evident. It is evident that a threat to peace does not always mean that a state is committing a breach of the peace. A threat to peace is a general situation which can also occur inside a single state. I think this to be quite evident and to stem from the logic of the UN Charter: suffice to remember the events in Congo 1960. The second obvious remark relates to Article 4 of the Charter which says that membership of United Nations is open to all peace-loving states.

It is important to underline the word "state" because it seems that today we are watching a very peculiar situation. We have threats to peace in some territories. We do not know how to deal with these threats (I am referring here to the situation in the geographical area of the former Soviet Union and of Yugoslavia). What are we doing to face such situations?

We decide that some new states exist and we admit them to the United Nations as we did a few days ago. So we are paradoxically reversing what *Kelsen* stated some decades ago, that is that the solidity of the internal legal order was a factor of fortifying the weakness of the international legal order. We are thinking exactly in the reverse way. We create an international person to protect a weak national legal order and hope that a network of international legal obligation may lead to build an effective constitution. I believe this is a very important point to be borne in mind when you speak of collective security or of security in general.

Second point: during the present situation very much was said about self-determination of peoples, but still this remains a very critical subject. Mention was made of the situation which justified what has been called a humanitarian intervention in Iraqi Kurdistan, an intervention which certainly was a unique one so far, as no one has thought, not even for one moment, of Turkish Kurdistan which, by the way, is bigger and more populated.

A previous speaker pointed to the migration of people, probably in the framework of the problem of minorities. We may have people migrating and at a certain moment settling in a place as migrant workers, perhaps with some turnover. I refer, with *Sir Arthur Watts'* permission, to the migrant people who settled in the Falkland Islands some decades ago. For these people a war was waged in the name of the principle of self-determination. But what about the new peoples, the very new peoples in Europe? We have had new peoples when the Russian pushed into the Baltic region and settled there. Or we can take — as our discussion takes place here in Germany — the territory which is now somewhat floating after the collapse of the U.S.S.R., namely the territory around the old city of Königsberg, which I do not know whether it is still called Kaliningrad.

There the German population was expelled from the territory after 1945 and replaced by Russians. To which people does the right of self-determination now belong, to the old or the new one? We have similar situations in territories which Italy lost in favour of Yugoslavia.

Besides that, in Yugoslavia the determination of what a people means is really an almost intractable problem. The Badinter Commission merged the self-determination principle and the principle of inviolability of frontiers by using the *uti possidetis* doctrine. This theory was derived from the African experience of decolonization. Therefore, internal frontiers between Yugoslav Republics, some of which were rather artifical like parts of the frontier between Slovenia and Croatia were promoted to the rank of international frontiers. Of course, the problem of what the peoples are in Yugoslavia remained and we now need very cumbersome constitutional arrangements decided upon at an international level, like the one which is foreseen for Bosnia-Herzegovina where probably there will be a Constitution based on cantons which in turn will be established according to ethnic criteria. You see that there are a lot of factors which in the name of the quest for security, and also of international security, leads us to revisit old concepts of international law and particularly what is a state, what is a subject of international law, and so on.

And then we have also in this direction the possible resurrection of old figures which were thought to have completely disappeared. You certainly remember the old handbooks of the 19th century speaking about *état suzerain* and *état vassal*. Think of a state like Turkey. It may become again an *état suzerain* vis-à-vis certain local populations located in the Russian federation. And this may be a factor of peace-keeping. In general, if we look at the situation the Soviet Union was in we may be brought back to the 19th century constitutional history of Germany; I mean the period of the formation of the First Reich in which some semi-independent states co-existed (like Bavaria or Württemberg) with entities which had lost their international standing.

In this moving context we have to place the role we want to assign to the United Nations Organization. I personally share the view of those who are sceptical about giving a role to play to all possible regional organizations. That may be the case when we think of NATO or of some European organizations, but the United Nations may not accept intervention by so many regional entities. I rather see a more likely successful mediation in order to solve a conflict in Africa if it is carried on by a former colonial power like Portugal in the case of Angola; or by my own country in the case of Mozambique. This is one thing I also wanted to say just to focus the role of the regional organizations.

A last remark. Many of you seem to be very much optimistic about the role of the Security Council. Certainly, in the last three years the Security Council has worked well, but I am not so sure that we can keep for much longer the same unity in the Security Council and also the same general composition. Under this last point I do not mean increasing the number of the Permanent Members or changing their identity, no. But regarding the current approportioning, the subdivision by regions, of the non-permanent seats, I am not so sure that we can keep it for much longer. The General Assembly, when it elects non-Permanent Members of the Council, may react badly if the Security Council is viewed by the developing countries as an agent of the developed world.

In the same spirit and in a similar framework, think as an example of the threat which was announced in the press the other day in connection with the current Libyan affair (the Lockerbie disaster). I mean the hypothesis of a group of states that just say good-bye to the United Nations: Would the Security Council remain effective in such a situation? I am sorry, I have raised too many points, but while working as I do, as the Legal Adviser to a country, I cannot refrain from thinking on my own.

Bothe:

In a way it is a funny discussion. "New international order" seems to be such a positive notion, but nobody really seems to enjoy it. This circle seems to be overwhelmed by the multitude of problems, and perhaps the best way to distort these problems is to try to simplify them. The essential content of the discussion is: Who does what in which situation? And doing also means pain, something which is sometimes forgotten. What we are trying to do here is to establish a kind of categorization of situations, and to each of these categories we try to assign competences of various actors to react to those situations. The categories I sensed from the discussion are as a matter of fact five: the good old domestic affairs; second, situations where there is an international concern; third, situations where there is a grave international concern, and you call that a security question; fourth, situations where there is a very grave international concern, and you call that a threat to the peace; and finally, the ultimate pathogenic situation which is the armed attack or the aggression.

If you now assign competences to react to various actors, you have on the one hand the extreme of the domestic affair, where nobody is entitled to intervene, and you have as the other extreme the armed attack, where any state is allowed to unilaterally use force. The interesting situations are, of course, those between these two extremes. There was much debate about the characterization of these various steps. On purpose, I use this graduation: concern, grave concern, very grave concern. It shows that it is very difficult to really discern exact thresholds. It is fair to say that situations are moving, not only *de lege ferenda,* but *de lege lata,* from one category to the other. The good old human rights used to be a domestic affair, now they have moved from international concern to security problems and even perhaps to the level of threat to the peace. You can repeat that with other questions. The notion of "environmental security" has been discussed. Some like it, some do not like it, but it is a serious discussion, or at least it ought to be a serious discussion. "Economic security": you can discuss an economic situation in terms of a threat to security, and that means a grave international concern perspective.

Basically, what we seem to face here is the issue of unilateralism *versus* multilateralism. But there is not a clear-cut distinction. The Gulf operation is a nice example of a mixture of both. Some say it was unilateral, others say it was multilateral, because it was an enforcement action. The truth, in my view, is in the middle. It was a unilateral action with very serious multilateral ingredients. The problem we have with the unilateral approach is that it presupposes that some countries are more equal than others. There are those who can intervene, there are those who cannot act unilaterally because they are too weak. And there are a number of countries in between which may well be the victim and also the actors of some kind of unilateral action. The problem we have with the multilateral approach is the inability of the multilateral organ to come to decisions.

In this connection, I doubt whether the possibility of a unilateral action really serves as a good means of pressure in order to make the multilateral process work. The decision adopted by the Security Council to authorize the action of the "governments cooperating with the government of Kuwait" was not taken because those states who were reluctant to agree, or might have used their veto power, were afraid of the action being taken anyway. Quite to the contrary! They may have had an interest to say, "Well, let them do it and take the blame, we will not agree." Thus, I have some doubts about this argument in favour of maintaining the unilateral option.

A problem we have with both options, with the unilateral and the multilateral, is that of selectivity. It was fashionable in the United States to criticize the United Nations for their selectivity on human rights issues. It has also been fashionable to criticize the United States concerning their selectivity regarding various aggressors or even the same aggressor in two different situations. In any political process, that problem of selectivity is apparently unavoidable, and you will not — at least the world is not ripe for that — replace that political process, which means selectivity, by a judicial process, which by definition means — or at least should mean — non-selectivity or strict equality before the law.

A final word on the "Westphalian system": I understood this term to mean — maybe I am wrong — the international system where we have the territorial states as an exclusive class of actors. It is quite appropriate to take the Westphalian peace treaties as the point where the development towards this modern territorial state was finalized, and where that new political animal was finally well established. The question whether this system should be maintained involves the question of the relevance and of the place which other actors have in our international system. What does this exclusivity of the territorial state in international relations really mean? It means that certain bureaucratic elites, which are the organs of those territorial states, dominate the problem-solving process at the international level. Traditionally, if something goes wrong anywhere that has international implication, the bureaucratic organs intervene and protect the interests which are situated in their own countries against any intrusion from others. That is the idea behind diplomatic protection. But this is no longer the only valid scenario. I take a very simple example: environmental protection. Governmental elites may agree on something which is against the perceived interest of important groups existing in their various countries. The existing system hardly takes into account the multitude of interests and forces existing within the countries, but also transcending borders. These forces have become very mobile, mobile for various social causes. It is quite clear that in this situation the question "Should we add, should we take aboard new actors, other actors which are not government elites?" is a very real one. You will notice that I have a cautiously positive stance towards a better inclusion of those forces in the UN system.

Simma:

Since I am going to treat you to a rather lengthy paper next morning, I will really be brief tonight. I have to confess that I was struck by three features of this morning's papers. First, I was struck by the fact that there was so little emphasis, so little focus, on rules. Especially listening to *Michael,* I felt quite comfortable in my rule-oriented approach. What you were advocating, seemed to me to be a return to — in your language — a pro-rule world.

Reisman:

Pre!

Simma:

Pro! You said pro meaning pre.

I had a little exchange with *Lucius Caflisch* on a rule-oriented *versus* a rule-less world. And it occurred to me that these continental or German sociologists of law have pointed out that the main function of rules is to relieve you of a task, which the New Haven approach is really making its own, namely that of reinventing solutions in each and every new case. I just wonder whether the scenarios, which you sorted out, could possibly be handled in more urgent situations following your complex approach. Why do we not accept that there might be more wisdom, frozen or crystallized, in rules that some people accept? Article 2, paragraph 4, of the Charter is a very good example to me.

Secondly, I was struck by the fact that there was so little focus on the UN Charter. It was hardly mentioned, only mentioned in passing, especially by *Tom.* I would submit that the capacity of the UN Charter, both of its law and of the practice under it, to accommodate and handle new situations, threats, and risks might be greater than some people assume. I do not belong to those for whom the handling of the Iraq crisis by the Security Council amounts to a victory for the UN. I see things much more cynically, I am sorry to say. We might go into this tomorrow. But to take up two issues which *Sir Arthur Watts* referred to: You mentioned human rights, and I have the impression that what you were saying was that the UN system, as it stands today, does not really have the capacity to handle, to accommodate the new challenges in the human rights sphere. From my own very modest experience of the UN human rights system, I have come to the conclusion that what is lacking there is not the framework. What is lacking is the will, the readiness, also of Western powers, to really implement that framework. I am thinking particularly of the United States. This is a German-American Colloquium, so why not be frank, we are among friends. I would submit that the main reason for the UN human rights business going so badly is the absolute lack of interest of the United States to do something about it, except in those cases where the United States instrumentalizes the UN, for instance, for the purpose of Cuba-bashing. *Sir Arthur,* you mentioned another point, namely that of movement of persons as a new threat to the borders of central and Western European states. But could we say that, for instance, UNHCR and its legal framework would be an obstacle in the way of an adequate solution? I agree that UNHCR might be an obstacle to some of the "solutions" which some Western European States have in mind, but I would hesitate to say that this role of UNHCR could be regarded as negative from the point of view of our topic here. I think that we ought to first test the capacity of the Charter before we give up on it (I have to interject at this point that I have a vested interest in the Charter remaining in force for a while).

The third point, and that is the last point that I want to make, is that I was again struck by the fact that there was no focus, no mentioning of Third World issues this morning. We were talking about new challenges to world security, etc. The Third World did not exist. We have heard from different people "Who decides?" The answer which was implied was: us — us meaning U.S., the Security Council, which also means us, and the OECD. We have heard about a pyramid, and this pyramidal example strucks me not only as being a bit phallic, but also as smacking of colonialism. I would go as far as saying that this pyramidal image strikes me as an attempted return to colonialism. *Mary* told me last night that there is a book review in the most recent issue of the American Journal, a review by *Martti Koskenniemi* of *Tom Franck*'s book on legitimacy, and at the end *Martti* comes out by saying "well, where is justice?" Please, allow me at this point to ask, where was justice this morning? I think, the word "justice" was not mentioned by anybody. I think, when talking about how to handle new scenarios and new threats, we should engage in a little more exercising Rawlsian-ism, if you like.

Ginther:

I would like to make a few comments and maybe provoke reactions from the speakers of this morning. I found also something lacking, and this was what I would call the "constitutive process." It was referred to by Prof. *Delbrück* and others that with Article 2, paragraph 4, and the entire Charter as an effort of the state community to organize itself, a constitution was provided and, I think, the core part of it is Chapter VII, meant to install "limited government" in international relations to control the use of force. Of course, in the beginning there was paralysis. It was not applied, especially not since the focus of the international security problem was in Europe (and this was due to the deadlock of the East-West confrontation), a region which could not be subjected to the UN system. But in that situation the Charter proved to be flexible; and self-determination became one of its major objectives.

Today we face again the issue of how to define peace and security. If one compares the Security Council Resolutions in the case of sanctions against Rhodesia in 1965 and 1967 and then in the case against South Africa, one sees what difficulties there were to grasp self-determination in two places very close to each other, Southern Rhodesia and South Africa. In the case of South Africa, the threat to security was seen in the acquisition of arms by South Africa. In the case of the the unilateral declaration of independence of Southern Rhodesia, the threat to the peace was seen in the withholding of self-determination.

What I suggest to discuss today is the question of how the Security Council promoted and successively developed and where it got stuck with the problem of defining threat to the peace, especially looking to Third World interests. We come at the end to the notion of democracy in the Third World today under new international regimes geared towards "good governance." Here we have a change of language, showing that we may have to link the security system in the United Nations with new regimes and new strategies. Within the United Nations, the peace-keeping operation system showed a highly sophisticated structure with respect to accountability, with respect to control of supervisory powers exercised on behalf of international institutions; a sophisticated system which was totally lacking in the case of the Gulf War. Resolution 678 is, I think, appalling. Everything is lacking. The state which should be responsible or the states authorized to act are not named; they are not called to be accountable to any authority. This is a field which one should explore. It was explained to us that it had to do with the bargaining process to come to a concurring vote of the Permanent Members of the Security Council. I still think that the outcome should be criticized; it is something which cannot be taken as such, one has to confront it.

This brings me to a further aspect. The Gulf War had a global security aspect, but it was in fact part of a process of establishing a regional regime, a regional order. What Prof. *Delbrück* suggested, which I fully support, is that one should not think in terms of global or regional security, but the two systems and strategies as being complementary. Maybe the question is, "Which takes precedence in some situations?" The regional order might under certain conditions be the more important one. Europe now faces this situation with Yugoslavia, the United Nations is stepping in just because Europe did not manage, but as soon as it would manage, one would expect the United Nations to step out and to leave it for Europe to develop its security system.

The issue of migration was also mentioned as a security risk, and since sovereignty and territoriality, territorial integrity, was addressed several times, I would like to refer to the idea of deterritorialization of statehood, meaning that the territorial aspect is becoming less and less important, while people are becoming increasingly more important. It is not that states would attack Europe, but people would move into Western Europe. So it is the movement of people and not the change of frontiers which is the cause of deterioration of the security system or the peaceful order. This brings us to the question which *Bruno Simma* just addressed, "What does peace mean in a positive sense?" Some years ago there was a conference on the Charter of the United Nations and its evolution in this house. One major theme was the distinction between peace in a negative and in a positive sense. Is there a basic consensus on peace in a positive sense, i. e., material notions of how to distribute resources and to come to terms with cooperation in letting all the people of Europe develop at a just pace?

As regards the Third World, *Tom Farer* talked of the OAS, the American System, the Declaration of Santiago, and there we face a wave of states moving towards formal democracy, more multiparty democracies, and now agreeing that any toppling of a government or a putsch would provoke a reaction of the state community. But what about other regions like Africa, where you cannot expect a multiparty democracy in the near future, but where the installing of "good governance" is pursued under a broader international regime of international development cooperation? I am thinking of the regime emerging now under the title "Global Coalition for Africa" from a conference two years ago in Maastricht, which most of the African governments attended. There the people were invited to take an active part. I think this is the request Prof. *Bothe* had in mind when he asked whether the states are receding somewhat, the sovereign states, as the actors in the international system. I think there are some indications that even consolidated states now accept that people have a certain active part to play, and this state of affairs should then be linked to the security system as it exists now within the United Nations.

It was suggested that some new parts could be added to the Charter; but the Charter developed to a large extent on soft law basis, soft constitution development. Maybe the promotion of democracy as a newly emerging objective of security policy within the UN system should be given a basis in an amendment to the Charter, but more likely just on the basis of a second edition of the Friendly

Relations Declaration or on the basis of some other declaration of the General Assembly.

Frowein:

I have a very short remark, which, I think, ties to a certain extent into some of what the last speakers have said. We are all for a division of powers in our national systems. We should not forget that the United Nations Charter and the international system as a whole is built on some idea of division of powers, I would submit. It is not by accident that the Security Council is called the Security Council, and that you have in Article 39 a very clear description for triggering the possibilities under Chapter VII. I do not think that we should completely forget about it.

As some members have said from the perspective of Third World countries, the security of frontiers against violent action is really the basic requirement for a peaceful situation. I think, it is really this that we should be concerned about when trying to analyze the possibilities of the Security Council. I do not deny, of course, that we have new issues, hydrocarbons and food for many Third World countries. Should we tie that in with the same system? I have difficulties, I must say. I think that only under very special circumstances the bridge really can be made or crossed. That is something quite different from saying that in Cambodia under *Pol Pot* conditions, there may be a reason for even armed intervention, but I would not call that a threat to the peace in the same sense. I would argue, as in fact some of you did, on a different basis. I am not going to go into that.

Let me end by saying that I find it difficult that the civil war discussion so far has not taken into account a very long development, which started in 1947 when the Security Council discussed the "Dutch Police action," as it was called at the time in Indonesia, and discussed in detail why civil wars, where military force is applied, may easily lead to reactions from other states and may be called a threat to the international peace. There we have a line of case law, and I would consider the Security Council as making its case law, although it is not the International Court of Justice, but it works within legal restraints.

Democracy: I fully accept that where a state has become an aggressor, and the question is how do you restore peace in the area, the question of democracy can arise. But I have great difficulty in saying that even on the basis of the International Covenant, there is some basic requirement of democracy internationally binding for member states, that can lead to a threat to the peace in the sense of Chapter VII.

Schreuer:

Let me start by saying that I found *Michael Reisman*'s effort this morning extremely valuable, although it may not live up to *Bruno Simma*'s normative standards. What he is trying to tell us is that we need scenario-building in a more systematic manner. After all, we are doing that intuitively or consciously, all the time. We all make projections about the future. Most of the time, however, we do it in a rather mono-dimensional way, and most of us and most politicians, I believe, usually only envisage one particular train of events. It is extremely valuable to realize that we do have to systematically envisage different pictures of the future.

Let me treat you to a short anecdote just to illustrate the difficulty of anticipatory thinking in international politics. In the spring of 1989, I attended a conference of international relations experts from both sides of the Atlantic. All these luminaries of international politics and international relations were talking about the future of Europe. Mind you, in the spring of 1989! Not a single one of them anticipated in the slightest manner the momentous events which were going to take place later that very year in Europe. Not a single one of them foresaw the impending collapse of Communism.

Institution-building in the 20th century, in the sense of international institutions, is a history of reactions to past events in a very narrow way. Look at the League of Nations: Basically, the League of Nations was a reaction to the First World War. It tried to prevent a recurrence of the First World War, under very narrow assumptions that really mirrored the events of 1914. Again, if you take a systematic look at the United Nations Charter: What the United Nations Charter is basically trying to do is to prevent the recurrence of 1939. Perhaps the most extreme example for this is the establishment of the International Energy Agency. It just looks very narrowly at the scenario of 1973/74 and tries to prevent or forestall a repetition. One of the reasons why the Security Council was able to react in an effective manner to what was happening in Iraq and Kuwait in August 1990 was simply because the behaviour patterns of *Saddam Hussein* resembled those of *Hitler* so closely. If you look into the newspapers or listen to politicians now, everyone seems to be worried about reincarnations of *Saddam Husseins* all over the world. I am not excluding that possibility but would say that this is not necessarily the most likely thing that is going to happen. This obsession with little *Saddam Husseins* all over the world is just another example of an intuitive and relatively limited mono-dimensional scenario.

Another remark concerning structural changes in the international society to improve the chances for peace: *Tom Farer* made some tentative remarks about the role of democracy and of democratic regimes for the maintenance of peace and security. I think, *Tom,* you left the question open ultimately as to whether the evidence was really conclusive. My reaction would be to say "yes and no." On one side — *Alfred Rubin* pointed that out already — you have this high popularity of little wars in democracies. I am rather uncomfortable about the danger of short-term political considerations, especially with a view to the next election influencing the next decision about the use of force, for instance, by the United States. On the other hand, an uncontrolled concentration of power in the hands of a dictator is certainly potentially destabilizing and could easily be described by the Security Council as a threat to the peace in the sense of Article 39. On this particular point I tend to agree more with Mr. *Delbrück* than with what Mr. *Stein* said.

As to *Tom Farer*'s pyramidal model: I would perhaps rather call it hierarchical or vertical. When we talk about a pyramid, we may well envisage the apex of that pyramid in the shape of a pentagon, and that is hot really what we are looking for. That would rather upset my sense of international geometry. It should be a vertical system, in which international institutions play a decisive role. On the other hand, it is not particularly realistic to expect the big powers to hand over vast areas of foreign relations competences to an international organization. However, we need not be altogether defeatist about the role of international institutions in security-building. In this respect, cooperation is not restricted to the area of high politics. Technical cooperation plays a very important potential role and has an unexhausted potential. Very close technical cooperation in economic and other fields very often makes disruptive behaviour by individual members of the international community much more costly. That in itself may create a strong incentive towards conformity of behaviour and may create spin-off benefits for international security, even if the institutions concerned were not primarily directed towards international security. The history of the EEC is a very good example for that. Nowadays, disputes between EEC members simply do not have a military dimension for that very reason. On the global level, we can still gain very much from that particular experience.

Eitel:

We are here in this symposium discussing law enforcement, and I think all of us are quite happy to see the law enforced. What disturbs most of us, and Mr. *Bothe* referred to it, is the selective use of that law enforcement, which we see around the world. And this is more so, since more and more moral standards are creeping into it. Having one superpower left, we are in the presence of moral standards which tend to be the moral standards of one superpower, which is a sort of a Holy Alliance of one. For us, who are either part of that one or who are hopefully close to it, this may be all right. But for others, it may not.

I had not heard much about the Westphalian system before, but those who know me as a home proud Westphalian will not be amazed to see me come out in defense for any Westphalian system. I may take it that if there is still a Westphalian system, then it is a down to earth approach. Westphalians are not known for their loftiness, and I wonder whether we should not, in that sense, become a little bit more down to earth. The UN Charter and the Security Council system, which has what I would call the veto defect, have the following quality in common with democracy: *Sir Arthur* will know it better than I do, there is a quotation by *Churchill,* I think, that "democracy is a very bad thing, but unfortunately there is nothing better than that" or something to that extent.

Reisman:

"Democracy is the worst system except for all the others."

Eitel:

Exactly! I am afraid that is what we have with the present system in the UN and in world organizations. Therefore, I would like to draw the attention of all of us back to Article 2, paragraph 1, of the Charter, to the sovereign equality; the sovereign equality, I think, belongs to at least all member states of the United Nations. I wonder how then it is reconciled with the fact that the CIA director travels around the globe trying to find helpers for subversive action against the ruler of Iraq, *Saddam Hussein,* who, it is sure, is not liked; but either he ought to have been ousted during the Gulf War or he has to be accepted as being there. I would assume that by dispatching the CIA director to the Middle East recently it was intended to make it known that now the superpower would try to topple that ruler. I think that is something remarkable and so far I have not heard anybody protest or even only wonder about it.

Thus, I think we should, as long as we have not got anything better, stay where we are with the notion that states, even in international organizations, pursue not the happiness of everybody but their own interests.

I make an exception for one field, that is human rights. I think selectiveness there is bad, but it is better than nothing. If we or somebody else take up one case of human rights out of a hundred, then it is better that this case be taken up than that no case at all is taken up. So, in human rights, I think, we should go beyond what we have in the Charter and elsewhere and try to interpret it creatively. But in all the other fields which have been mentioned, political, economic, social, and so forth, we should really stick to the Charter as long as it has not been amended.

Caflisch:

I have come here to hear what others think rather than to speak, so do not expect too much. If I have understood the discussion correctly, the scope of the concept of security has been vastly enlarged, and so have the challenges to it. As a result, we witness the shrinking, for instance, of the well-known concept of domestic jurisdiction. So the basic question asked this morning and, again, this afternoon is: "Who will act?" Will it be a central authority, possibly a regional one, or will it be essentially individual states? The extension of the challenges in question seems to have led to the suggestion of a broader scope for unilateral and decentralized action, witness the resurgence of the so-called humanitarian intervention. This alleged institution was born at a time of total decentralization of the international order. I find it paradoxical that it should be revived at this particular time. It is not only being revived, it is being developed, since the French Government now even refers to a duty to intervene incumbent on individual states. Accordingly, we find ourselves in an astonishing situation. One should have, one would have expected that recent events, in particular the improved functioning of Chapter VII of the UN Charter, would bring about a renaissance of collective security, whatever be its precise definition. I find it amazing that we should sit here discussing the possibilities of individual intervention, and how far such interventions may go, rather than asking ourselves how to improve the system of collective security.

Therefore, I venture to suggest that perhaps some of our remaining energy would be well spent debating the normative future. More specifically, what should the normative future look like in the United Nations framework and, even more specifically, what should the Security Council look like in the future? Should we democratize the Security Council, should we abolish or modify the veto system, should some attributions of the Security Council be delegated to other organs, and if so, to which? Or to regional organizations? Should we leave things as they are? Perhaps we could also examine the question of how to turn the Security Council into more of a "prosponding" agency.

Rubin:

Rather than respond to everything, I will respond selectively. If I do not seem to respond to points you have made, you can assume that I agree with you, or do not think the points worth responding to; I will leave it to you to decide which.

First, some people seem to assume that there is no feasible response to a crisis between inaction on the one hand, or United Nations or great power action on the other. What I have suggested in reaction to both Prof. *Farer*'s and Prof. *Reisman*'s papers was a system of isolating spasms of violence; discouraging outside intervention; encouraging those most immediately affected to find ways consistent with their own best interests as defined by themselves to solve their political problems without killing their ethnic minorities or political dissidents. I did not argue the desirability or inevitability of the *status quo*. It should be made clear to mini-states and others, like the Eastern Caribbean states, that if they are going to have problems arising from actions of lawless foreigners, the "mafia" in New Orleans, they have a solution to hand that does not depend on outside intervention: They can stop being mini-states by doing what the United States did in the 18th century, or what Germany and Italy did in the 19th. They can consider joining together and creating larger political units that can stand by themselves in the strenuous conditions of the modern world, to paraphrase the League Covenant. Their position is not inevitably hopeless or dependent on great power intervention.

Nor do I think that ethnic self-determination is necessarily the bottom line in international society. If people choose ethnicity to determine statehood in disregard of other factors, they must suffer the consequences. Despite *Woodrow Wilson*'s penchant for "national" (i.e., ethnic) self-determination, it is politically, morally, and legally nonsensical to expect a benign outsider to come and help them establish or maintain an ethnically "pure" polity.

In the Westphalian world, absent inherited authority, nobody climbs to the top of his or her local "slippery pole" of political power without a great deal of ruthlessness and experience in local politics, which is one of the most vicious blood sports imaginable. Even in my own country, the United States, people forget that in 1803 the Vice-President shot and killed the former Secretary of the Treasury in a duel over electoral politics. We have never had a benign system, and I do not understand why anybody believes that we should, or can, make the Grenadan or Panamanian system benign. The people who live under those systems must take care of themselves, and if they cannot yet take care of themselves, the only way they will learn is by foreigners not intervening, just as a parent must ultimately leave a child to learn what the real world is like, even though it can hurt very much.

But what about ethnic or other aggression; the plight of the helpless? A rapid reaction institution other than the Security Council would be nice. I am not sure that it would be feasible. There are possibilities for new organizations, I suppose. There are certainly possibilities of defining situations in which different kinds of organizations should act. Article 19 of the 1979 International Law Commission Draft on State Responsibility, for example, defines five different types of state behavior that might be considered internationally "criminal." The draft does not draw conclusions as to what the legal result would be of a state committing such "crimes," but scholars in various learned articles have made serious suggestions.

And why not authorize the Security Council itself to consider massive pollution or a pattern of gross violations of human rights as a "threat to the peace" justifying community counteraction? Why not create new institutions with regional or technical expertise, and give them the authority to react to such pollution or human rights violations in the foreseeable cases in which the Security Council cannot marshal the necessary will? This is the approach proposed by Prof. *Farer*. If such new organizations are not feasible because it is foreseeable that whatever political problems the Security Council has will necessarily arise in any other organization built upon the Westphalian system, then that is a fact with which we must learn to live.

I do not see our discussion as necessarily saying that we must either strengthen the United Nations or create undemocratic or non-useful institutions. I see a whole range of possible choices. We do not live in a dialectical world where the only choices are extremes or an unrealizeable synthesis.

A greatly underrated publicist of the 1930's, *Thomas Baty,* is quoted by *Clive Parry* in his Melland Schill book, saying that "It is universally agreed that, in spite of modern theories ... International Law ... nevertheless has something to do with States." The Westphalian system in fact has never been an exclusively state system. The English East India Company was founded in 1601 and was a very effective international actor in its own name through 1648 and a reorganization in 1701. It was not brought under firm parliamentary control until 1784. It made treaties, maintained an army and was very much a part of the system. The United Dutch East India Company was founded in 1602. There were many other such companies. The Papacy has existed as an influential international actor for much longer and still exists and acts in the international arena. Transnational actors abound; the Westphalian system is not composed exclusively of states and never has been. It is a complex system in which states, asserting themselves to be acting in a secular order even if their constitutions are religiously based, interact with each other and with their own and their neighbors' legal creations, corporations, and many other transnational actors, all competing for authority and profit.

Article 2, paragraph 1, of the United Nations Charter is still binding in positive law and prescribes the "sovereign equality" of all members; and under Article 4 only "states" can be members. Therefore, states are the dominant, in some ways the only, actors within the world of the UN. But the international arena is far larger than the UN. It seems to me that there has been some confusion in our discussion between the Westphalian system and the world of the UN Charter; the two are related, but not identical.

It is common to suppose that something our ancestors did was simple in theory, but has degenerated. I disagree. Nothing is simple in theory to the people who are doing it; nothing is simple in theory today. Our descendants will attribute extraordinary brilliance or stupidity to us, as we attribute extraordinary brilliance or stupidity to our intellectual ancestors. In fact, we, like our ancestors and, one hopes, our descendants, are just people trying to get along in a complex world. Thus, the notion that somehow it is impossible to give authority to regional organizations generally because that would mean empowering the Arab League or some similar non-European-based institution whose values we believe to be not conducive to peace and security and ethnic calm, is false. I know nothing inherently vicious about Arabs or their organizations, and nothing unreasonable about them, although I think I operate with a value system that is inconsistent with the usual Arab systems; but then my personal value system is inconsistent with that of many Americans and Europeans, too. About a fifth of the world's population is Muslim, and I see no way to ignore that fifth, or China, for that matter, and still purport to be acting in accordance with international law or morality. We do not have a Europe-oriented system any longer, and we cannot centralize authority in the UN or any other universal organization through which our values are to be enforced and the values of more than half the world ignored or worse. This is not to say that the Chinese, or Arabs, or Muslims generally have better or higher values than we do, or even that their values are acceptable to us in all cases. But we cannot purport to act for the world and then disregard the value systems we dislike.

Somebody mentioned that nobody had discussed the UN Charter except for some side-mention by Prof. *Farer*. I had thought that I spent much too long discussing Article 51, the teleology of the Charter, and "rectification." I will not spend any further time on that.

I do have a problem with those who have criticized recent Security Council actions on the ground that they are legally not acceptable; not clear enough for a careful legal analysis. No law-making process is clear enough for lawyers once the problems begin to arise. I know no statute passed through the most delicate system that can stand close examination when real cases arise. If I remember correctly, it was *Bismarck* who pointed out that nobody should see how a law or a sausage *(Gesetz oder Wurst)* is made.

With regard to the notion that it is better to help rectify one human rights situation than none, my world is more complex. It all depends on the situation and what the implications of the particular intervention are. It is possible that addressing one human rights abuse might have the side effect of appearing to endorse human rights abuses not addressed; it is possible to do infinite harm in the system by selecting the one for political reasons and ignoring the others, thus implying that the others are not violations or are not significant within the system, or that the one is somehow worse or more significant than the others, or that human suffering of one ethnic or national group is more a violation of "right" than the equivalent or worse suffering of another. This is not to say that no human rights cases should be addressed unless all are addressed. It is to say that the choice of whether you can usefully address a human rights abuse is a far more complex choice than can be resolved by quoting an aphorism.

Finally, it seems to me that we are left with the notion that however we structure the world, some problems will not be effectively resolved. In trying to get the Third World more deeply involved in the system, we discover that many Third World states are not really interested in solving the problems we are interested in solving. We cannot educate them in our ways without permitting them to try to educate us in theirs. If we reject their insights, it is hard to understand why we think that they should be more open to ours.

But because some of our values are so important to us, and we have the military power to act on our convictions, there will remain some necessary scope for unilateral action and we will be convinced, rightly or wrongly in the retrospect of history, that unilateral action in some cases is infinitely preferable to inaction regardless of all that I have said. In any event, some unilateral action by those with the capacity to undertake it is inevitable in the Westphalian system, and we must accept reality as the bottom line of all our discussions, even though we are lawyers.

It does not bother me that we cannot structure a system that will solve, or even alleviate, all problems. I know of no system that is capable of solving or alleviating all, or even many, problems. It seems to me that we are stuck with a world in which we live, and our best course is to try to minimize the problems that exist and grapple with those we can grapple with without doing too much harm. We cannot restructure the world, only refine it a bit around the edges. I would compare international human rights problems, then, to the problems municipal legal orders face when trying to grapple with child abuse; what is feasible is unsatisfactory; what is desirable is not feasible; we do what we can, and suffer with the knowledge that it can never be enough.

Farer:

I yield to no one in enjoying the cut and thrust of debate and in recognizing the temptation to enhance the amusement of debate by exaggerating differences. The differences among us, I would suggest, do not arrange themselves along a transatlantic divide. Rather, as *Bruno* remarked during one of our breaks, the differences among European scholars largely mirror those among legal scholars based in the United States. Some hint of that mirror image can be detected in our own discussions.

All of you are familiar with the American literature and therefore know how sharply we have differed among ourselves, if not over the basic values that normative arrangements and interpretative strategies should serve, then certainly over assumptions about causal relationships, about what kinds of material and intellectual inputs are most likely to generate desired outputs.

I have found all the interventions this afternoon extraordinarily stimulating. It is very rare that I can say that when I have been listening as opposed to speaking. This is one of those remarkable occasions. I was, however, particularly struck by Professor *Randelzhofer*'s point about the need for modesty in claims about the character of the post-Cold War era . . . At least I thought that was your point, and if it was not, of course it should have been.

Randelzhofer:

What do I know what I say?

Farer:

There again is a sign of the modesty I admire. You have properly insisted on the extraordinary difficulty we all face now even in precisely defining problems, much less in prescribing normative solutions. We list the problems; we juggle and repackage familiar normative responses; but we do so without firm convictions about the political, economic, and social context in which problems and inherited normative responses will have to be addressed in the years ahead of us.

It seems to me that the transnational order is riddled with dialectical tensions. Take, for example, the movement of peoples. If there were a right to enter, corresponding to the recognized right to leave a country, the authority of states and the significance of frontiers would be radically diminished. In fact, we now witness a growing effort to assert such a right, an effort proceeding behind a slight veil. The notion of refugee status has been stretched to such a point, and the inefficacy of frontier policing has risen to such dramatic heights that states eager to export people and non-governmental advocates of persons migrating to escape war or poverty often act almost as if there already were a right to enter. Not only do states refuse to invest resources to discourage their citizens from violating the immigration laws of other states; in addition, they sometimes complain bitterly when a neighbor proposes to adopt more effective enforcement measures.

In light of these developments, one cannot be sure that the traditional view about a sovereign's unqualified right to restrict access to national territory will long endure. It may, because the growing porosity of national frontiers has triggered harsh reactions in a number of countries. Consider, for example, the anti-immigrant movements spreading in Germany, France, and elsewhere in Western Europe. Interestingly enough, reaction in the United States to the great surge of immigration, much of it illegal, has been muted by comparison to responses in early periods of mass migration.

Seeing the volatility of reaction to a capacity and will to emigrate that may soon assume proportions with few historical precedents, we cannot make confident predictions about normative developments even if we are as relentless in accumulating data as *Michael* and his colleagues of the New Haven School enjoin us to be.

How can the values we jointly hold be expressed in useful norms? How can we improve on the inherited normative responses to the main transnational problems of contemporary world society? One of the reasons we tend to overstate our differences as we struggle to respond to those questions is, in fact, our profound uncertainty, sometimes admitted, about how to go about making the world a place more in harmony with our ideals.

When my genuinely old and close friend *Bruno* asked — a little rhetorically, I am afraid — where was the Third World? where was justice? in the papers presented this morning, I was moved. I looked around, checking out various places on the table to see if justice had inadvertently been discarded. And then I looked at my mandate to see whether I had overlooked one of its commandments.

I was asked to discuss law enforcement under Chapter VII. In doing so, I did address the issues inciting *Bruno*. I did so, however, without naming them. Perhaps my differences with *Bruno* — which I think are altogether more apparent than real — relate to the role of the United States, the unipower question mark in contemporary statecraft. When he solicits our concern for the Third World — while perhaps worrying about a spirit of triumphalism in the West and particularly in Washington — I myself wonder whether he is conflating the interests of Third World peoples and the often brutal, corrupt, and repressive regimes that purport to speak for them. Running through part of our discussion, including *Bruno*'s interventions, there is a certain inconsistency. On the one hand, a state-centered distaste for metaphors which suggest the reality and even the possible desirability of a hierarchy of states; on the other, a tremendously warm concern for the conditions of real human beings in the Third World.

In solicitude for the quiddity of life for real people, not abstractions or reifications, in the Third World (or, for that matter, in the slums of the First and what was once the Second), I yield to no one here. After all, I spent almost ten years of my life looking into the prisons of Third World countries and into countries that had been converted into prisons for all but a small elite and its camp followers. Through a complex stream of causation, economic, political, and military resources have become disproportionately located in the West and Japan. A central issue of our time is how those resources should be employed in relation to the Third World.

I have urged readiness to deploy those resources on behalf of human rights. Although I eschewed the 1970s idiom of North-South relations — in particular its invocation of a "New International Economic Order" — my own purpose is unchanged, the purpose namely of improving the condition of life for people living outside as well as within the West. But I am convinced, as I am sure are many of you, that peoples can steadily improve their conditions only if political elites must compete for their votes, that is to say, only if people exercise some effective control over internally-generated resources and assistance coming from the outside. In short, democracy is a critical element in any scheme for reducing extant levels of misery. If this was once a distinctively Western notion, it is no longer. All of us are struck by the swelling demand in Africa and elsewhere for democratic rule. It is far greater than I anticipated from the perspective of a decade ago. And while we do not know the full dimensions of that demand, they are indisputably impressive.

Let me conclude with a brief reference to the danger of metaphors. Of course we cannot speak other than metaphorically. Eliminate metaphors and we would probably not get much beyond grunts and clicks. But accepting the inevitability of metaphor, let us concede that some metaphors are more dangerous than others, that some metaphors cloud the mind. In our discussions to date the metaphors have been vividly evocative. In debating the proper allocation of authoritative power in the new international order, we have heard talk of pyramids and pentagons. For the pyramid image, I am the original culprit. It is not the image that best reflects my incipient view of what sort of institutional arrangements will best serve the interests of the international community of peoples.

Overlapping circles of authority: That is an image that comes closer to summarizing what I was groping to express. But it too is not entirely satisfactory. Because a substantial number of recognized governments are parasitic internally and / or lethally irresponsible internationally, I do favor a somewhat more vertical authority structure. That is what led me originally to the pyramid metaphor. Some confused it with reversion to something not very different from 19th century colonialism.

Certainly that is not what I had in mind. The 19th century system was state-centered and racist and intentionally exploitative. The question I am putting is whether we would be better off working to develop regional and global directorates, clusters of elites who among them command decisive resources. The directorates would be multi-racial and that fact in itself would distinguish them radically from the 19th century system. I agree that an effort to institutionalize a global directorate that is exclusively North Atlantic and white is both wrong and futile. The directorates would include all elites that enjoy a fair measure of internal legitimacy and practice a statecraft that is moderate or responsible in two senses: First, in rejecting force as a conventional instrument of statecraft, and secondly, in not seeking the maximum of unilateral advantage out of every interaction with other elites.

Where does the U.S. fit in to my inchoate paradigm? Today the U.S. foreign policy community is marked by indecision. It sees virtue and national advantage in the spread of democratic liberties. One segment of the community is prepared to act consistently and, if necessary, imperiously for the defense and promotion of such liberties. Another segment regards democracy promotion as a fringe concern, a pleasant windfall where it coincides with the protection of security and economic interests traditionally conceived. And a third segment takes a narrow view of what is required to defend even traditional security interests and, with respect to democracy, feels that it is sufficient to exemplify its virtues by the success of our domestic life.

I myself see the U.S. as the necessary balance wheel of any healthy international system. Perhaps in order to perform that function efficiently, it must be prepared *in extremis* to act without authorization from the UN or a regional organization to enforce central tenets of international law. But generally, both in order to maintain international and domestic support for U.S. leadership in the realm of multilateral law enforcement, the U.S. needs to be deeply implicated in authentically collective decision-structures for clarifying, applying, and enforcing the law.

Effecting its implication is no easy task. I have been a not infrequent critic of the powerful tendency in U.S. policy to operate unilaterally behind a multilateral fig leaf and even to strip away the fig leaf whenever it proves constraining. You will recall that the United States virtually ceased bringing what is perceived to be hemispheric security issues to the OAS when it ceased to control the weighted majority required for collective action.

But the tendency toward unilateralism is not entirely the fault of the U.S. When multilateralism is no more than a code name for inaction in the face of illegal and destructive behavior by rogue regimes, a great power, much less a superpower, will tend to act alone. A condition of real multilateralism is efficacy. To that end, I think that the mandate of the Security Council requires a broadening interpretation, and its membership also must be broadened. Conversely, proposals for a radically more egalitarian distribution of authority within the United Nations should be rejected. We need more Permanent Members — obviously Germany and Japan, perhaps India and Brazil — together with fixed or revolving representatives of each consequentially self-conscious block like the Islamic states. But in addition we need more and more effective limited-membership treaty organizations organized to deal with problems that peculiarly effect them.

Finally, I would like to respond with great brevity to the point raised by Professor *Riedel* about policing *versus* norm creation and the sometimes understated importance of the latter. I very much share your conviction that norm-making is a central activity of international relations. What I meant to say, in connection with the scenario of abuse of the commons by private persons, was simply that normative elaboration would be relatively easy, that the necessary consensus of governing elites could be marshalled with considerably less effort than that required in this case to enforce norms in the immense space of the commons and against a vast array of potential violators in the ordinary course of business. Moreover, while I doubted that it would be difficult to win agreement on the substantive norms, I anticipated difficulties in achieving agreement on procedural norms.

But speaking more generally about the process of norm creation and elaboration, I am less sanguine. For I see that process as one form of discourse among peoples, and at the present time discourse is still pretty uneven. There is far too little effective communication among all relevant elites. The UN is not a sufficient venue or mediator of sustained and informal dialogue. For the most part it brings together only a very narrow corps of diplomatic specialists. No extant institution organizes regular and structured yet informal dialogue among senior officials and intellectuals from all consequential countries. For example, the evident alienation, the mutual incomprehension of Western and many Islamic elites is as depressing as it is dysfunctional. One task of Western intellectuals is to find ways of increasing the level of authentic communication between peoples.

Reisman:

This has been a very useful discussion for me, though I cannot say that I have agreed with all the views expressed.

I would like to go back to the basic issues and certain misperceptions that may have emerged in the discussion in the afternoon. The name of the conference is "The Future of International Law Enforcement, New Scenarios — New Law." The subject for the morning was "New Scenarios of Threats to International Peace and Security, Legal Bases for Adequate Responses." In line with the general title of the conference and the specific subject of the morning, *Rüdiger* posed some very good questions that sharpen the issues: What is a threat; who determines it; what is to be done, what means should be provided for doing that "what" in the future; and who should do it? The discussion sometimes moved away from these issues. I propose to bring the focus back to the assignment.

Professor *Frowein* talked about security specialization. In every community which perceives that it may be exposed to danger, either internally or externally, security specialists are developed: police, the military, and so on. Insofar as a community, whether national or international, feels that it must address its security, it will focus, in doing that, on security. The fact that, at the same time, it does not talk about long-range justice or terrible violations of human rights does not mean that it is ignoring them. It has identified security as a *sine qua non,* something necessary for the continuity of the existence of the community and, of course, for the community's achievement of any of its longer-range goals. The fact that there is a focus on security seems to me quite justified. The fact that it does not, in this context, address justice is justified as well. There are moments in the lives of nations and in the lives of groups when songs about justice played on guitars, poems, and philosophy just do not do the trick. That is what security is about.

What should the focus of threats to the international community be, as we look towards the end of this century and the beginning of the next? Planners have to try to anticipate which are the critical struts on which our system is based and what will happen if some of those struts are attacked. That is a security threat to the international system. When we say we are excluding a lot of other things, they do not necessarily go off the international agenda. But they are not sent to the Committee or the Council that is primarily concerned with security.

Professor *Frowein* asked whether it is appropriate to extend this notion to include something like the supply of energy. The point is well taken. Professor *Schreuer,* too, said that the question is not what may have been meant by security in 1945. If that were decisive, there would be no reason for us to convene here. We could simply consult the legislative history of the Charter. The relevant question is both projective and empirical: What are the threats likely to cause serious harm, disruption or destruction to our system? I put forward in the first among the six scenarios a construct of a cessation of the supply of energy. Our civilization is energy dependent. When energy is cut off to great cities in my own country, public order breaks down. I cannot imagine Europe's survival if there were a substantial reduction of the supplies on which it is dependent.

The point is that we must consciously look ahead to what sorts of threats are likely to cut the tendons of our system and make it inoperable. They are security threats. This means that certain terrible things will not be characterized as a security threat. The example cited was the carnage in the southern part of Somalia, where 250,000 human beings' lives are at stake. Certainly, something should be done about it. But I do not think we can stretch the notion of security to cover something like that.

Dr. *Kühne*'s notion of using the word "risk" rather than "threat" seems to me inspired. I intend to use it, for the word "threat" definitely implies a "threatener" and thus leads to a polarization. Insofar as one is searching for integrative strategies, this minimizes the likelihood of their development. But I presume that the organizers of the conference selected the word "threat" precisely because it is the term of art that is used in Article 39 of the Charter. It also leads to the next issue that *Rüdiger* raised which is: Who decides?

As *Albrecht Randelzhofer* explained, if we are talking about threat in the United Nations context, a group of fifteen states, anyone of five of whom can stop the show by the exercise of a legal veto, decides. This means that, insofar as we are talking about the definition of "threat" in this particular context, we mean threat as perceived largely by these five. Of course, no organization is impervious to democratic forces. Clearly, other members of the United Nations on whom some of these states are dependent or with whom they have a constituency relationship will be able to influence the outcome. The General Assembly claims under the "Uniting for Peace Resolution" a secondary right to determine and act on threats if the Security Council is blocked. But the Assembly does not dispose of the military assets that the Security Council's members do. The process of definition of threat, however, may be somewhat more open than would appear. If we elect to use the term "risk," it will simply throw us back to the effective power process of the moment.

Who should define threats or risks? The world would be a better place if half of this dilemma were resolved by a centralization and monopolization of force. That would not mean that there need not be unilateral uses of force by certain actors. The intolerably high expectation of violence, which is characteristic of the international arena, would be reduced. But the political process in which the United Nations is embedded is not prepared to assign that kind of power to the United Nations, however it is structured. Insofar as the power process does assign power, it is given to a mini-organ within the United Nations, which replicates the fundamental distribution of power in the international political system. The "who" question is thus a continuing problem. The "who" is not yet the United

Nations. Yet we do not want to authorize unilateral force, but when we talk about security, we are talking about something that demands a reaction, often a rapid response by someone. If it cannot be the Security Council or the United Nations as a whole, who will the someone be? It is unreal to assume that those whose interests are threatened will not act if there is no international agency to protect those interests. It is, however, appropriate to ask them first to try to exhaust international arrangements, even to try to create them if time allows.

As to the relationship between international or multilateral action and unilateral action, Professor *Ginther* said that there is a formal structure which is inclusive of the United Nations and there is an informal process, the elementary or primitive, if you like, world power process or what my colleagues in New Haven call the effective power process. How are they to be related? I have suggested that, given recent history, the availability of the option of unilateral action on the part of states that might still prefer, for a variety of reasons, to do things multilaterally puts pressure on the multilateral institutions and probably increases the likelihood that they will respond and obviate the need for unilateral action. In this respect, I think that, as we design a variety of scenarios for dealing with risks in the future, it is probably better to continue to allow some role for unilateral action in the hope that even its possibility will press the multilateral institutions to do something. But it is an arguable point. Some believe that the recent Iraq-Kuwait War might have gone better had the United States not been in the wings and threatening to go it alone. That is an interpretation I do not find persuasive but I appreciate its force for others.

Finally, the issue of regional and even individual delegations for coercive action on behalf of the international community: The passionate discussion may have obscured some of the critical issues. It seems to me that where an international organization cannot operate but a regional organization is available, it is better that the regional organization operates. If a regional organization cannot operate, it seems to me that where there is a genuine security threat, a unilateral reaction is better than no reaction at all. To say that does not mean that one plumps in favor of all regional organizations in all cases. There are circumstances in which NATO would be quite appropriate and there are circumstances in which NATO would be inappropriate, in much the same way that there are circumstances in which certain states that routinely wish to contribute to peace-keeping forces are acceptable, and other cases in which the Secretary General does not invite those states to participate. One has to make judgments about these things.

Nor should one assume that in all circumstances in which regional action would be authorized, it would be European or North-American organizations or states that would be engaged. The carnage in Lebanon in the late 1970s was suspended for a period of time when Syria, at the invitation of the Arab League and with no objection from the United Nations, went in and re-established a minimum order. It turned out to be messy. It was done incorrectly. Perhaps the conditions were wrong. Certainly Syria stayed too long. But for the first year after the intervention, there was a general satisfaction that the appropriate option had been taken. There are circumstances in which the Arab League or a particular state operating under the Arab League may be appropriate, and circumstances in which a European organization would be utterly inappropriate or even provocative.

A final point. *Bruno Simma* asked where the rules were and whether or not I was suggesting that there are no rules. I think rules are important, for they carry important information about how to make decisions in complex situations. But rules do not make the decisions, as, I think, *Tom* and *Al* pointed out. In order for us to design new rules for new threats in new contexts, we need more than rules. We need to look at those contexts. We have to identify the fundamental policies and we then have to shape rules that will serve the common interest in projected futures. When it comes to making decisions, it is never simply a question of applying rules. The range of lawful considerations includes the question of what the rules were seeking to achieve, the social implications for different patterns of application, and the aggregate consequences for security and for other social values.

Legal Consequences for International Law Enforcement in Case of Security Council Inaction

Jochen A. Frowein*

Introduction

The subject of my report contains some inherent difficulties shown by the title. International law enforcement is a rather wide notion. The Security Council is entrusted with the primary responsibility for the maintenance of international peace and security. It is in this area that the members of the United Nations agree, according to Article 24, that in carrying out its duties under this responsibility the Security Council acts on their behalf.

Action or inaction by the Security Council will, therefore, be relevant for law enforcement concerning one of the most important rules of public international law today, namely the prohibition of the use of force. Chapter VII of the United Nations Charter gives the Security Council power to take action where there exists a threat to the peace, a breach of the peace, or an act of aggression.

The issues raised by that subject will be addressed in four separate chapters:

1. action and inaction by the Security Council;
2. collective action without Security Council authorization;
3. regional action;
4. reactions to violations of obligations *erga omnes*, which will be mainly addressed by Professor *Simma*.

I. Action and Inaction by the Security Council

Under Chapter VII the Security Council may take action in accordance with Articles 41 and 42. Article 42 deals with action including the use of armed force. What is action in that sense? This may be of crucial importance for the dividing line between Articles 42 and 51, if there is one.

* Prof. Dr. *Jochen A. Frowein*, Director of the Max-Planck-Institute for Public International Law; Professor at the University of Heidelberg; Vice-President of the European Commission of Human Rights.

Security Council action under Article 42 was frequently interpreted as limited to direct action with forces made available to the Council under Article 43. However, long before the Gulf War it had been pointed out that this is not the only possible scenario.[1]

Under the wording of Article 42, 2nd sentence, actions may include demonstrations, blockades, and other operations by air, sea, or landforces "of members" of the United Nations. No reference is made to Article 43. The wording of Article 48, which may also relate to military measures, is even more telling. According to the latter article, the measures can be taken by all the members of the United Nations or by some of them, as the Security Council may determine. This shows that the Council may authorize specific states to take action.

In this respect, the view is correct that Article 42 does not require troops to have been placed at the disposal of the Security Council according to Article 43. The International Court of Justice certainly had this in mind when it rejected the argument that the Security Council could not take action in a situation threatening the peace, without agreements having been concluded according to Article 43.[2]

It follows that the Security Council can give the armed forces of member states an authorization with respect to a particular mission when the prerequisites of Articles 39 and 42 are met and member states make such armed forces available to the Security Council. The fact that the Security Council cannot oblige member states to place armed forces at its disposal without agreements according to Article 43 is, of course, a clear consequence from the relationship of Articles 43 and 42.[3]

It can be shown by several incidents before the Gulf War that neither the Permanent Members of the Security Council nor states which belonged to it while the discussions took place ruled out the application of Article 42 only on account of the absence of agreements concluded pursuant to Article 43. In 1956, the Soviet Union proposed, with reference to Article 42, that the Security Council should authorize the Soviet Union and the United States to employ armed force in support of Egypt after the outbreak of the Suez Conflict.

---

[1] *Hans Kelsen*, The Law of the United Nations — A Critical Analysis of Its Fundamental Problems, 2nd ed., New York 1951, 756; *Derek William Bowett*, United Nations Forces, London 1964, 160-169; *Leland M. Goodrich / Edvard Hambro / Anne P. Simons*, Charter of the United Nations, 3rd ed., New York 1969, 316; *Jochen A. Frowein*, [Commentary on] Art. 42, in: *Bruno Simma* (ed.), Charta der Vereinten Nationen, Kommentar, Munich 1991, 589 (para. 16).

[2] *Certain Expenses of the United Nations (Article 17, paragraph 2, of the Charter)* (Advisory Opinion), ICJ Reports 1962, 151-308 (167).

[3] *Frowein* (note 1).

The Soviet proposal read as follows:

> ... in accordance with Article 42 of the United Nations Charter ... all States Members of the United Nations, especially the United States of America and the USSR, as permanent members of the Security Council having powerful air and naval forces at their disposal, should give military and other assistance to the Egyptian Republic, which has been the victim of aggression, by sending naval and air forces, military units, volunteers, military instructors and other forms of assistance, if the United Kingdom, France and Israel fail to carry out this resolution within the stated time limits.[4]

While reference was made during the discussion to the fact that an action according to Article 42 against a Permanent Member of the Security Council would not be conceivable, it was not argued that such an authorization would be unlawful.[5]

In the famous Resolution of 9 April 1966, the Security Council authorized the United Kingdom to prevent, by the use of force if necessary, the arrival of vessels reasonably believed to be carrying oil destined for Rhodesia and empowered the United Kingdom to arrest and detain the tanker known as the Joanna V.[6] Again, this decision contains an authorization for the United Kingdom to apply armed force. It is of interest whether this should be distinguished from the earlier examples because at the time Greece as the flag state of the Joanna V had probably agreed to the measures.[7]

Where an authorization is made under Article 42, the justification for the enforcement action in relation to the state against which armed force is used lies in the decision to take measures under Article 42.[8] This is confirmed by the distinction made in Article 39 between, on the one hand, recommendations and, on the other hand, decisions to take measures under Articles 41 and 42. This should also furnish the answer to the question sometimes put whether non-binding recommendations under Article 39 can justify enforcement measures under Articles 41 and 42.[9] Enforcement measures must have a binding character against the state subject to the measures. This cannot be achieved through recommendations.[10]

---

4 UN Doc. S/3736.

5 Repertoire of the Practice of the Security Council, Supplement 1956-1958, 172.

6 SC Res. 221, 9 April 1966.

7 However, the authorization was wide enough to cover the use of armed force in general as to vessels of that category. See *Frowein* (note 1), 590 (paras. 18, 19).

8 The measures under Art. 42 are enforcement measures. *Cf. Certain Expenses of the United Nations* (note 2), 164-65.

9 *Michael Schaefer,* Die Funktionsfähigkeit des Sicherheitsmechanismus der Vereinten Nationen, Beiträge zum ausländischen öffentlichen Recht und Völkerrecht 77, Berlin / Heidelberg / New York 1981, 35; *Eric Stein,* Collective Enforcement of International Obligations, in: Zeitschrift für ausländisches öffentliches Recht und Völkerrecht (ZaöRV) 47 (1987), 56-66 (60).

Under Article 42 the Security Council can take action with forces made available to it under Article 43 or authorize specific member states, which are prepared to do so, to use armed force with a clearly circumscribed goal. The precondition is that the Council has determined a threat to the peace or breach of the peace in the sense of Article 39.[11] Authorization in this sense is action by the Security Council.

Inaction by the Security Council may become important after the Council has authorized states to use force. This issue arose in the context of the Gulf War. It is clear that a justification under the United Nations Charter to use armed force under a Security Council resolution exists only as long as states applying force keep within the limits of the authorizing resolution. Where the text of the resolution is vague, this may create space for uncertainty.[12] Since a new resolution by the Security Council terminating the use of force may be vetoed, considerable dangers exist with regard to open-ended resolutions. Had the United States taken the view that for "restoring international peace and security in the area" Baghdad had to be occupied, it could have vetoed any resolution trying to stop it from doing so.

It is here that a real dilemma can arise. One must hope that the Security Council and its members will act responsibly when drafting and implementing resolutions.

II. Collective Action without Security Council Authorization

Collective action is also authorized by the Charter as collective self-defense under Article 51. It presupposes the existence of an armed attack. It was a great innovation that the United Nations Charter recognized for the first time that the protection of a state's right to existence may always be implemented through collective measures.[13] This implies that an armed attack as the requirement for

---

[10] It is of great importance that the distinction between recommendations as non-binding resolutions and measures of the Security Council with binding force be maintained. When the International Court of Justice accepted that decisions outside Chapter VII may be binding under Art. 25, it certainly did not imply that recommendations may be binding; *Legal Consequences for States of the Continued Presence of South Africa in Namibia (South West Africa) notwithstanding Security Council Resolution 276 (1970)* (Advisory Opinion), ICJ Reports 1971, 16-333 (53).

[11] This determination should clearly refer to Chapter VII as it seems to become the rule now.

[12] Resolution 678 of 29 November 1990 reads in the relevant passage: "Authorizes Member States — to use all necessary means to uphold and implement resolution 660 (1990) and all subsequent relevant resolutions and to restore international peace and security in the area."

[13] *Cf. Jost Delbrück*, Collective Self-Defence, in: *Rudolf Bernhardt* (ed.), Encyclopedia of Public International Law (EPIL), Instalment 3 (1982), 114-117.

the applicability of measures of self-defense is being seen by the Charter as an attack on the most fundamental common value of the system.

In the *Nicaragua* case the International Court of Justice has made it clear that the right of collective self-defense may not be used to apply force where the state being attacked does not consider the situation as being one of armed attack.[14] This is an important clarification making it impossible that collective mechanisms will be used disregarding the interests of the state whose rights are at issue. The Court even went so far as to require that the state which regards itself as the victim of an armed attack should make a formal request permitting the exercise of collective self-defense.[15]

More important and more difficult to accept is the Court's reasoning in the *Nicaragua* case which concerns possible reactions by third states to forcible interventions. According to the Court, the lawfulness of the use of force by a state in response to a wrongful act of which it has not itself been the victim is not permitted when this wrongful act is not an armed attack. The Court underlines that under international law in force today, whether customary international law or that of the United Nations Charter, states do not have a right of collective armed response to acts which do not constitute an armed attack.[16]

The Court has thereby limited the possible reactions of third states to the use of force which remains below the threshold of armed attack very considerably indeed. It is not clear whether this limitation will be in fact observed by member states in difficult situations. A state against which forcible intervention takes place may certainly react by the use of force in a similar way. A weak state against which force is being used under those circumstances may be left without a meaningful possibility to defend itself.[17] Prof. *Reisman* has correctly drawn our attention to a possible consequence: more covert action. The majority of the Court probably believed that since you cannot control covert action anyhow, you should at least not legalize it. I have real doubts here. Of course, one should realize that active support from the territory of the victim state by a third state always remains possible. The third state is only precluded from acting directly against the state using force outside the territory of the victim state.[18] It must be remembered in this context that the Court expressly recognizes that the sending of armed bands under the conditions circumscribed by Article 3 (g) of the

---

14 *Case Concerning Military and Paramilitary Activities in and against Nicaragua (Nicaragua* v. *United States)*, ICJ Reports 1986, 14-546 (104).

15 *Loc.cit.*, 105.

16 *Loc.cit.*, 110.

17 See *Jochen A. Frowein*, Collective Enforcement of International Obligations, in: ZaöRV 47 (1987), 67-79 (71-73).

18 Judge *Jennings*, in his dissent, strongly questioned the underlying rationale according to which "forcible response to force" is forbidden, at least collectively; *Nicaragua* case (note 14), 543 *et seq.*

definition of aggression annexed to General Assembly Resolution 3314 (XXIX) can constitute an armed attack.[19] The Court denies, however, that mere support to rebels is already an armed attack while it accepts that it may be a use of force.[20] The distinction may become very artificial.

However, there is a more difficult consequence concerning collective action without Security Council authorization following from the *Nicaragua* judgment. The ICJ has held that the United States, by introducing a trade embargo against Nicaragua, has violated the Treaty on Friendship, Commerce, and Navigation with that country of 1956. The Court stated that no state is bound to continue particular trade relations longer than it sees fit to do so, in the absence of a treaty commitment or other specific legal obligation. But where there exists such a commitment, of the kind implied in a Treaty of Friendship and Commerce, an abrupt act of termination of commercial intercourse such as the general trade embargo of 1 May 1985 will normally constitute a violation of the obligation not to defeat the object and purpose of the treaty. The Court did not accept that the action by the United States would be justified under Article XXI as necessary to protect the essential security interests of the United States.[21]

The Court did not address the issue, not raised by the United States in its submissions on the question of jurisdiction, of whether the trade embargo could be justified as a reprisal against Nicaragua. This is quite astonishing. The ICJ takes as established that Nicaragua had used force in violation of international law against some of its neighbours.[22] If one accepts the proposition that the United States could not use Article 51 against Nicaragua because the use of force by Nicaragua remained below the level of armed attack, the question should have been answered what sort of reactions against the violation of the prohibition of use of force could be taken by any third state.[23]

Today the probhibition to use force is generally seen as a rule of public international law belonging to the category of *ius cogens* and creating obligations *erga omnes*. Reactions against "transborder military incursions into the territory of Honduras and Costa Rica" which are attributed to Nicaragua should give rise to the possibility of collective sanctions of an economic nature.[24] It may be in

---

19 *Loc.cit.*, 103.

20 *Loc.cit.*, 104.

21 *Loc.cit.*, 137, 138.

22 *Loc.cit.*, 87.

23 *Jochen A. Frowein*, Das Staatengemeinschaftsinteresse — Probleme bei Formulierung und Durchsetzung, in: Staat und Völkerrechtsordnung. Festschrift für *Karl Doehring*, Berlin / Heidelberg / New York 1989, 219-228 (227 *et seq.*).

24 *Jochen A. Frowein*, Die Verpflichtungen erga omnes im Völkerrecht und ihre Durchsetzung, in: Völkerrecht als Rechtsordnung — Internationale Gerichtsbarkeit — Menschenrechte. Festschrift für *Hermann Mosler*, Berlin / Heidelberg / New York 1983, 241-262.

this context that the non-appearance of the United States before the Court on the merits had its most questionable result.

Where an armed attack occurs, Article 51 permitting the use of force as collective self-defense must be seen as the legal basis for all other collective measures against the attacker.[25] Where the use of force is justified as response, third parties may also use other remedies. This was confirmed by state practice when Argentina invaded the Falkland Islands as well as when the Soviet Union threatened Poland with the use of force.[26] Although the use of force in the case of Nicaragua, according to the Court, did not amount to an armed attack, the violation of the prohibition to use force under the United Nations Charter should be recognized as giving rise to the possibility of applying peaceful reprisals.[27]

Some problems exist as to the limitations of Article 51. While there is general agreement that Article 51 is limited by the second part of the first sentence referring to the Security Council, the Gulf Conflict has shown that this limitation is less clear than one had believed. According to the Charter, the right to individual or collective self-defense exists "until" the Security Council has taken measures necessary to maintain international peace and security. The second sentence underlines that the measures taken by member states shall not in any way affect the authority and responsibility of the Security Council to take at any time such action as it deems necessary in order to maintain or restore international peace and security.

One would have thought that that excludes a combination of Article 51 and Security Council action under Articles 39-42. However, the political compromise behind Security Council action in the Gulf seems to indicate that especially the United States wanted to keep Article 51 intact as basis for its military involvement. According to the Charter system, this is difficult to accept. Either military action is taken by or authorized through the Security Council which triggers off the limitation in Article 51, or this is not the case. One should not overlook Article 2, paragraph 5, of the Charter in this context. All members shall give the United Nations every assistance in any action it takes in accordance with the present Charter and shall refrain from giving assistance to any state against which the United Nations is taking preventive or enforcement action. This obligation is conditioned by the existence of preventive or enforcement action which means action by the Council under Chapter VII.[28] Properly speaking, it would not seem correct to include Article 51 as a possible basis besides enforcement action.

---

25 *Alfred Verdross / Bruno Simma*, Universelles Völkerrecht, 3rd ed., Berlin 1984, 907.

26 *Rainer Hofmann*, Zur Unterscheidung Verbrechen und Delikt im Bereich der Staatenverantwortlichkeit, in: ZaöRV 45 (1985), 195-231 (223 *et seq.*).

27 *Frowein* (note 24), 253.

28 *Jochen A. Frowein*, [Commentary on] Art. 2 Ziff. 5, in: *Simma* (ed.) (note 1), 91 (para. 2).

It is rather clear that the United States wanted to create an additional legal argument for possible unilateral continuation of hostilities when it relied on Article 51. I would submit that authorization by the Security Council for enforcement action takes away the right under Article 51. Only where the Council expressly limits its action to a recommendation, as it did in the case of Korea, Article 51 remains intact.[29] Here, the limitation under Article 51, 1st sentence, is not applicable.

One must admit that the different possibilities of action opened for the Security Council may easily create doubtful situations, and it is true that there is a certain artificiality in making the distinction just proposed. Where the Security Council only recommends, it does not take any action in the sense of Article 51. It strengthens the position of those acting in collective self-defense for the victim.

Should that be otherwise where the Council goes one step further and authorizes armed action by the states willing to cooperate with the victim and the Security Council? I am of the opinion that it makes a difference. Where the Council lends its authority to authorize armed action, it must use Articles 42 and 48 if we analyse the matter from a juridical point of view. As soon as these articles come into operation, the limitation in Article 51 applies. From then on self-defense is no longer applicable.[30]

It is not unlikely that the precedent of the Gulf War will be used to show that states may rely on the title of Article 51 even after authorization by the Security Council which can only be based on Articles 42 and 48. This will have the consequence that the limitation in Article 51, for all practical purposes, has disappeared.

We may also consider here to what extent recommendations by the General Assembly can become of importance as a basis for collective sanctions. The Uniting for Peace Resolution has certainly been accepted in its procedural parts as forming part of proper law in the United Nations. Many emergency sessions by the General Assembly have been convened on the basis of this resolution.[31]

The substantive aspect of Resolution 377 (V) to recommend action including use of force has never been clearly settled. The General Assembly may of course recommend measures for a peaceful adjustment of any situation according to

---

[29] On 27 June 1950 the Security Council adopted Resolution 83 (1950) which reads: "... Recommends that the Members of the United Nations furnish such assistance to the Republic of Korea as may be necessary to repel the armed attack and to restore international peace and security in the area."

[30] For the contrary view *Eugene Victor Rostow*, Agora: The gulf crisis in international and foreign relations law, continued. Until What? Enforcement Action or Collective Self-Defence?, in: American Journal of International Law (AJIL) 85 (1991), 506-516 (510 *et seq.*).

[31] *Eric Stein / Richard C. Morrissey*, Uniting for Peace Resolution, in: *Bernhardt* (ed.), EPIL, Instalment 5 (1983), 379-382.

Article 14 of the Charter. It would seem to be generally agreed today that the Uniting for Peace Resolution cannot create a legal title for enforcement action, otherwise in violation of public international law.

This does not mean, however, that a resolution by the General Assembly could not have a certain justifying effect where the recommendation is within the competence of the United Nations. The justification would probably lie in the recommendation because the view expressed by the competent United Nations organ must be deemed to have expressed a correct appreciation of the legal situation.[32]

This is not a completely independent substantive justification but rather an important procedural presumption created by the recommendation. Boycott measures as implemented against South Africa[33] on the basis of General Assembly recommendations would seem to find their justification at least partly in the consensus reached by the states in the General Assembly.

III. Regional Action

With the Security Council having become unblocked, the relationship of its competence to regional arrangements or agencies under Article 53 may become quite important again. The use of peace-keeping forces under the umbrella of European organizations was discussed concerning Yugoslavia. Of course, there were no European institutions competent to set up peace-keeping forces.[34]

Enforcement action taken under regional arrangements or by regional agencies must be authorized by the Security Council according to Article 53. Inaction by the Council can never amount to authorization. However, the question may be asked whether a general authorization would be in line with the Charter. Assuming that a European system with a machinery for peace-keeping would be set up, could the Security Council authorize that system to take what would be considered enforcement action under the Charter? The question may be less theoretical than it appears at first sight. A general authorization would make it impossible to veto a specific decision by the regional agency to use force. But it would not be in line with the prerogative of the Security Council to give a general authorization.[35] This prerogative, however, is limited to enforcement action.[36]

---

32 *Jochen A. Frowein*, Collective Enforcement of International Obligations, in: ZaöRV 47 (1987), 67-79 (70).

33 *Cf.* International Legal Materials 24 (1985), 1464 *et seq.*

34 The CSCE has formally declared that it is a regional security system, Declaration of Helsinki 10 July 1992, para. 25.

35 *Cf. Georg Ress*, [Commentary on] Art. 53, in: *Simma* (ed.) (note 1), 681 (para. 10).

36 *Certain Expenses of the United Nations* (note 2), 164-65.

Measures taken against a state which are clearly justified by its consent may be called enforcement measures in a wider sense, because arms are being used, but can certainly not be violations of public international law. Where the state has given its consent, even measures implying the use of force are lawful. Where United Nations peace-keeping forces use their weapons in line with the specific agreements, no question under Article 2, paragraph 4, can arise.

In several cases the Security Council has accepted that peace-keeping forces may be set up by regional agencies without a formal authorization by the Council. The matter was discussed for OAS forces in the Dominican Republic 1965. When the OAU sent a peace-keeping force to the Chad in 1981, the Security Council took notice of that without authorizing the decision. This is in line with the wording of Article 53 which limits the need of authorization to enforcement action in the proper sense, i.e. action against the will of the state against which action is taken.[37]

Assume for a moment that within the European Security System states would agree in advance to peace-keeping by specific international intervention forces.[38] Could one overcome Article 53 by arguing that no enforcement measure takes place? The argument is certainly a difficult one because Article 53 wants to concentrate a monopoly for the use of military force in enforcement proceedings with the Security Council.

However, I would not exclude that a formula could be found by which a specific intervention force could be seen as not acting against any state in enforcement action. Intervening to suppress military action in a civil war context could furnish a good example for enforcement action not directed against a state in this context. There is in practice general agreement that the recognized government may consent to foreign intervention to suppress a civil war. Although sometimes criticized by legal doctrine, this rule is frequently the basis for action.[39] France has concluded treaties with many African countries providing for French assistance where a government is threatened by internal upheaval, and French armed forces have been used in several instances on that basis.[40]

---

[37] *Ulrich Beyerlin*, Regionalabkommen, in: *Rüdiger Wolfrum* (ed.), Handbuch Vereinte Nationen, 2nd ed., Munich 1991, 673-679 (678); *Joachim Wolf*, Regional Arrangements and the UN Charter, in: *Bernhardt* (ed.), EPIL, Instalment 6 (1983), 289-295 (292-294).

[38] In its declaration of 19 June 1992 the Western Europe Union declared its readiness to use military units for peace-keeping and for peace-making, i.e. intervention to restore the peace.

[39] *Cf. Nicaragua* case (note 14), 126 (para. 246): "Indeed, it is difficult to see what could remain of the principle of non-intervention in international law if intervention which is already allowable at the request of the government of a State, were also to be allowed at the request of the opposition." See also *Michael B. Akehurst*, Civil War, in: *Bernhardt* (ed.), EPIL, Instalment 3 (1982), 88-93 (90 *et seq.).*

[40] For a discussion of this practice see *Robert Jennings / Arthur Watts*, Oppenheim's International Law, 9th ed., Harlow 1992, 435 *et seq.* with references.

The line between enforcement action and peace-keeping may be even more difficult to draw in some areas. It is not excluded that in a regional context with strong institutional structures even military intervention against a state will lose the notion of enforcement action. According to the *Certain Expenses* Advisory Opinion, enforcement action is action not justified by the actual will of the state concerned.[41] The question arises, however, to what extent a state may enter into obligations which will justify intervention by peace-keeping forces even where the actual will of the state at the time of intervention may be different.

The debate concerning the withdrawal of UNEF from the Sinai in 1967 may be of some importance in that context. After the withdrawal a discussion arose to what extent Egypt had entered into formal obligations *vis-à-vis* the United Nations not to withdraw its consent for the stationing of the peace-keeping force without a specific procedure.[42] It was assumed, at least in some statements, that this would have excluded a change of quality of the action if the peace-keeping forces had remained on Egyptian territory even without the actual consent of the Egyptian Government. Where this consent was withdrawn against a clear procedural rule agreed beforehand, the withdrawal should be considered legally irrelevant.

It should not be excluded that the notion of enforcement action in Article 53 can be limited to those cases where the state has not entered into clear commitments for regional peace-keeping beforehand. The regional peace-keeping arrangement would, of course, be known by the Security Council. The Council could debate the structure and legal implications if need arose.

Another question in that context concerns non-military sanctions. It is frequently advanced that enforcement action in the sense of Article 53 concerns also non-military sanctions in the sense of Article 41 of the Charter.[43] This would mean that economic measures including embargos or boycotts could not be applied by regional organizations without the authorization of the Security Council. However, this view seems to be too restrictive. During the discussions in the Security Council on the complaints by the Dominican Republic in 1960 and Cuba in 1962, the majority of the member states assumed that both the imposition of economic sanctions on a state as well as its exclusion from a regional organization were not enforcement actions in the sense of Article 53.[44]

This must be the correct approach. One has to bear in mind that no general prohibition of economic sanctions or other reprisals exists in public international law including the United Nations Charter. This is the crucial difference between

---

[41] See note 36.

[42] UN Doc. A/6730 Add. 3; *Schaefer* (note 9), 240.

[43] *Cf. Beyerlin* (note 37), 678; *Wolf* (note 37), 292.

[44] *Wolf* (note 37), 292.

the application of economic sanctions on the one hand, and the use of armed force on the other. While the use of armed force has to be justified under the United Nations Charter to overcome Article 2, paragraph 4, no such need arises with economic sanctions. Therefore, regional agencies may apply economic sanctions wherever they have a legal title to do so within their regional system.

Where authorization is needed under Article 53, it must be prior authorization.[45] However, this does not necessarily mean that the authorization must be expressed in a formal resolution. If the matter is before the Council and the Council does not take any action contrary to authorization, one may argue that it has tacitly authorized the regional agency to act. Such a tacit authorization could be seen to be in line with the specific obligation of Article 52, paragraph 2, for members of the United Nations entering into regional arrangements to make every effort to achieve pacific settlements of local disputes through regional arrangements before referring them to the Security Council. However, this priority is limited to pacific settlement of disputes and can be of no importance where enforcement action is envisaged.

Nevertheless, since the development of a dispute may be such that pacific settlement and intervention is difficult to distinguish, one should not completely exclude such a possibility of tacit approval of regional action by the Security Council. Experience with recent situations as in Yugoslavia has shown the reluctance of the Security Council to intervene where a regional organization is dealing with the matter.

It has sometimes been argued that enforcement measures by regional organizations may also be directed against states which are not members of that given regional arrangement or agency. According to that view, authorization by the Security Council could also cover enforcement action against third states.[46] This seems to be rather difficult to accept, given the clear need for a title *vis-à-vis* the third state in the regional system. Action against a third state could only be taken with the authorization of the Security Council under Articles 42, 48 of the Charter, the regional organization being used as "some" of the members of the United Nations in the sense of Article 48.

Here again one must, of course, draw the important distinction between enforcement action including the use of military force and reprisals taken by a regional agency. Wherever public international law permits the use of reprisals, any regional agency or organization which under its statutes is able to coordinate the measures of its members may use reprisals against states violating public international law.

---

[45] The United States have sometimes argued that authorization could be given after the action. *Cf. Wolf* (note 37), 293.

[46] *Cf. Wolf* (note 37), 294.

A very good example for action of this sort was the resolution taken on 22 April 1980 by the Foreign Ministers of the European Community within the European Political Cooperation to apply sanctions against Iran because of the hostage-taking of American diplomats.[47] On 18 May 1980 a formal decision was adopted according to which all contracts concluded after 4 November 1979, when the hostages were taken, should be suspended. The EEC ministers referred to the threat for peace and security in the world created by the action and to the draft resolution submitted to the Security Council which was blocked by the Soviet veto. EEC member states, although not directly affected by the taking of the hostages, were of the opinion that they could apply sanctions which would amount to the neglect of otherwise applicable rules of international law against Iran to collectively respond to the breach of law. The economic sanctions applied by the EEC after the invasion of the Falklands / Malvinas by Argentina 1982 are of a similar nature.[48]

In case of inaction by the Security Council regional agencies may in fact play an increasing role for international law enforcement in the area of peace and security.

IV. Community Interest and Reactions to Violations erga omnes

Without encroaching too much on the topic to be dealt with by the following speaker, let me stress the need for clarifying the relationship between *erga omnes* obligations and possible reactions without a formal Security Council authorization. The American Restatement puts it very bluntly: "The principles governing unilateral countermeasures apply as well when a state responds to a violation of an obligation to all states (erga omnes)."[49]

According to the International Court of Justice, obligations *erga omnes* derive, for example, in contemporary international law from the outlawing of acts of aggression and of genocide as also from the principles and rules concerning the basic rights of the human person, including protection from slavery and racial discrimination.[50]

Under those circumstances peaceful reprisals by any state can be justified without Security Council action.[51] It is less clear, however, where the violation

---

47 EC-Bulletin 1980, No. 4, 26 *et seq.*; *Frowein* (note 32), 74 *et seq.*

48 EEC-Regulation of 16 April 1982, Official Journal of the EC, L 102, 1, 3.

49 Restatement of the Law Third, The Foreign Relations Law of the United States, Vol. 2 (1987), 381 (para. 905).

50 *Case Concerning Barcelona Traction, Light and Power Company Limited, Second Phase*, ICJ Reports 1970, 3-358 (32).

51 *Frowein* (note 24), 241; *Verdross / Simma* (note 25), 909; *Jonathan I. Charney*, Third State Remedies in International Law, in: Michigan Journal of International Law

of human rights conventions is at issue. The Court stated in the *Nicaragua* case that where human rights are protected by international conventions, that protection takes the form of such arrangements for monitoring or ensuring the respect for human rights as are provided for in the conventions themselves.[52] Only where persistent and gross violations are concerned, collective enforcement measures without Security Council authorization can be envisaged. It is probably in this area where development of public international law in the future will become of greatest importance.

---

10 (1989), 57-101; *Antonio Cassese,* International Law in a Divided World, Oxford 1986, 244 *et seq.*

[52] ICJ Reports 1986, 134.

Does the UN Charter Provide an Adequate Legal Basis for Individual or Collective Responses to Violations of Obligations erga omnes?

Bruno Simma*

In earlier times, cartographers used to fill blank spots on their maps with the words *hic sunt leones:* here is where the lions roam. The treatment of obligations *erga omnes* in international legal literature reminds me of this description for two different reasons. First, although the notion of obligations *erga omnes* appears to be here to stay, we are still far from having a clear picture of its precise ramifications and implications for an international law traditionally viewed from a strictly individualist — or bilateralist — perspective. But *hic sunt leones* would also be fitting with regard to the use, or non-use, of the concept of obligations *erga omnes* and of the faculties which it entails in actual state practice: like chunks of meat thrown to the lions, such legal constructs are either devoured or neglected by states, depending on their political "appetite" or lack thereof at a given time. Just compare the readiness of the United States in resorting to the pipeline embargo against the Soviet Union in 1982 as a reaction against the declaration of martial law in Poland, or the energy displayed in countering the Iraqi invasion of Kuwait, with the absolute lack of interest in doing anything that could have forced Indonesia to have second thoughts about its annexation of East Timor.[1]

Thus, any observer entering the terrain of obligations *erga omnes* should be aware that one will be moving on largely uncharted and dangerous grounds, where the animals whose actions we will observe rarely display the tameness — or the willingness to perform — which some academic guidebooks so readily foresee. Viewed realistically, the world of obligations *erga omnes* is still the world of the "ought" rather than of the "is"; the concept marks the direction in

* Professor Dr. *Bruno Simma,* Director of the Department of International Law, University of Munich; Professor at the University of Michigan, Ann Arbor.

1 The noteworthy exception here is Portugal which filed a claim against Australia in the International Court of Justice on 22 February 1991, seeking a declaration from the Court that by entering into the Timor Gap Treaty with Indonesia — a treaty arranging for the exploration and exploitation of off-shore resources — Australia has not only violated Portugal's rights as the competent authority in East Timor but also the rights of the people of East Timor: *Case Concerning East Timor (Portugal* v. *Australia)* (Order of 3 May), ICJ Reports 1991, 9-10.

which international law will have to move rather than a clear course already steered today.

The organizers of this Conference have asked me to consider whether the Charter of the United Nations can be said to provide an adequate basis for individual or collective responses to violations of *erga omnes* norms. At first glance, this reference to the UN Charter seems to introduce an element of certainty and orderliness into the matter. The lions secured behind more or less solid bars of Charter law, so to speak. However, upon closer examination, we see that in the lions' favorite spot, these bars are frighteningly far apart. I am talking about the Security Council, of course. And I recall Secretary-General *Perez de Cuellar* telling "Der Spiegel" a few months before his retirement: "Supermächte sind mir verhaßt", that he hated superpowers.[2] Dangerous ground again. Moreover, what we have heard yesterday and this morning has not brightened the picture.

I am going to proceed as follows:

In the first part of my paper, I will try to map obligations *erga omnes* within the coordinates of international law. A few rough sketches must suffice in this regard. In particular, I will not have the time to delve into the doctrinal interrelations between obligations *erga omnes,* the concept of *ius cogens,* "international crimes" of states as foreseen in the ILC's draft on state responsibility, crimes against the peace and security of mankind according to the Commission's recent draft code and, finally, possible limits of the *pacta tertiis* rule (understood in its broadest sense).

In the second part of my report, I will investigate how the UN Charter accommodates the securing of performance of obligations *erga omnes.* Does it provide enough room in that respect? And, even more importantly, does it contain the necessary safeguards against power politics under a communitarian — or humanitarian — guise?

Let me begin with a few remarks on the underpinnings and the regime, if any, of obligations *erga omnes.*

I assume that everyone present here will be familiar with the *obiter dictum* of the International Court in its 1970 judgment in the *Barcelona Traction* case. Let me recall: At the outset of a highly technical discussion of diplomatic protection of shareholders, the Court emphasized that an essential distinction should be drawn between the obligations of a state towards the international community as a whole and those arising *vis-à-vis* another state in the field of such diplomatic protection. By their very nature, the Court said, the former obligations are the concern of all states. In view of the importance of the rights involved, all states can be held to have a legal interest in their protection; they are obligations *erga omnes.* And the Court went on to say:

---

[2] *Javier Pérez de Cuellar,* "Supermächte sind mir verhaßt", in: Der Spiegel, No. 27/ 1991, 126-128.

> ... Such obligations derive, for example, in contemporary international law, from the outlawing of acts of aggression, and of genocide, as also from the principles and rules concerning the basic rights of the human person, including protection from slavery and racial discrimination. Some of the corresponding rights of protection have entered into the body of general international law ..., others are conferred by international instruments of a universal or quasi-universal character.[3]

It would be interesting to speculate on the reasons why the Court spelled out its view on community interest in the observance of rules of international law that had absolutely nothing to do with the substance of the case before it. Had the new majority on the Court been waiting for an opportunity to make up for the 1966 *South West Africa* judgment — a pronouncement so disgraceful to the progressive observer?[4] Whatever the Court's motivation might have been, however, the notion of obligations *erga omnes* gained quick acceptance and has met with only sporadic criticism in doctrine.[5] In light of the controversies that accom-

---

[3] *Case Concerning Barcelona Traction, Light and Power Company Limited, Second Phase*, ICJ Reports 1970, 3-358 (32). For a (critical) comment see *Hugh Thirlway*, The Law and Procedure of the International Court of Justice 1960-1989, in: The British Year Book of International Law 60 (1990), 92-102.

[4] For two prominent voices in this regard see *Richard Falk*, The South West Africa Cases, in: International Organization 21 (1967), 1-23; *Rosalyn Higgins*, The International Court and South West Africa — The Implications of the Judgement, in: International Affairs 42 (1966), 573-599.

[5] From among the pertinent literature, *cf.* the following voices (with a special emphasis on the enforcement aspect): *Antonio Cassese*, Remarks on the Present Legal Regulation of Crimes of States, in: International Law at the Time of its Codification. Essays in Honour of *Roberto Ago*, Vol. III, Milan 1987, 49-64; *Jonathan Charney*, Third State Remedies in International Law, in: Michigan Journal of International Law 10 (1989/90), 57-101; *Christine Chinkin*, Third Parties in International Law, Oxford (in print); *Benedetto Conforti*, In tema di responsibilità degli Stati per crimini internazionali, in: Essays in Honour of *Ago (supra)*, Vol. III, Milan 1987, 99-111; *Charles Dominicé*, Observations sur les droits de l'Etat victime d'un fait internationalement illicite, in: Droit international, Vol. 2, Paris 1982, 1-73; *Pierre-Marie Dupuy*, Observations sur la pratique récente des "sanctions" de l'illicite, in: Révue générale de droit international public 87 (1983), 505-508; *Jochen Abr. Frowein*, Die Verpflichtungen *erga omnes* im Völkerrecht und ihre Durchsetzung, in: *Rudolf Bernhardt et al.* (eds.), Völkerrecht als Rechtsordnung — Internationale Gerichtsbarkeit — Menschenrechte. Festschrift für *Hermann Mosler*, Berlin 1983, 241-262; *idem*, Collective Enforcement of International Obligations, in: Zeitschrift für ausländisches öffentliches Recht und Völkerrecht (ZaöRV) 47 (1987), 67-79; *idem*, Das Staatengemeinschaftsinteresse — Probleme bei Formulierung und Durchsetzung, in: *Kay Hailbronner et al.* (eds.), Staat und Völkerrechtsordnung. Festschrift für *Karl Doehring*, Berlin 1989, 219-228; *idem*, Die Staatengemeinschaft als Rechtsbegriff im Völkerrecht, in: Liechtensteinische Juristen-Zeitung 12 (1991), 3-7; *Giorgio Gaja*, *Jus cogens* beyond the Vienna Convention, in: Recueil des Cours 172 (1981-III), 271-316; *Rainer Hofmann*, Zur Unterscheidung Verbrechen und Delikt im Bereich der Staatenverantwortlichkeit, in: ZaöRV 45 (1985), 195-231; *A. J. J. de Hoogh*, The Relationship between *Jus Cogens*, Obligations *Erga omnes* and International Crimes: Peremptory Norms in Perspective, in: Austrian Journal of Public and International Law 42 (1991), 183-214; *Günther Jaenicke*, International Public Order, in: *Rudolf Bernhardt* (ed.) Encyclopedia of Public International Law (EPIL), Instalment 7 (1984), 314-318; *Menno T. Kamminga*, Inter-State Accountability for Violations of Human Rights, Leiden 1990, 156-164 and *passim; Manfred Lachs*, Quelques réflexions sur la communauté

panied the entry of *ius cogens* into the codified law of treaties, such a warm welcome is surprising. To some degree, the explanation may lie in the undeniable lack of critical interest in theoretical issues which marks our discipline, or in the merciful dark in which the lofty words of *Barcelona Traction* left all the nasty details. However, I think the main reason goes deeper and is more positive than that. It is to be seen in the growing recognition — be it explicit or implied — of the need to re-think some of the basic tenets of international law in order to enable it to meet the new challenges for which the old bilateralist paradigm is so terribly ill-equipped. Such re-thinking is well under way; the *Barcelona Traction* dictum was only one step, albeit a decisive one, among others in the ongoing process of developing international law into a more socially conscious legal order.

The recent book by *Philip Allott,* "Eunomia," traces this process in a particularly vivid and illuminating way.[6] We do not have to go as far as *Allott* and denounce traditional, Westphalian, *Vattel*ian, international law as the "phantom-law of an interstatal unsociety."[7] But can we really deny that *Allott* captures the essence of the morally uncommitted nature of precisely the international law that *Prosper Weil*[8] and others feel nostalgic about, by pointing out that this traditional law left it to governments "to will and act internationally in ways that they would be morally restrained from willing and acting internally, murdering human beings by the million in wars, tolerating oppression and starvation and disease and poverty, human cruelty and suffering, human misery and human indignity, of kinds, and on a scale, that they could not tolerate within their internal societies"?[9]

internationale, in: Le droit international au service de la paix, de la justice et du développement. Mélanges *Michel Virally,* Paris 1991, 349-357; *Paolo Picone,* Obblighi reciproci ed obblighi *erga omnes* degli Stati nel campo della protezione internazionale dell'ambiente marino dall'inquinamento, in: *Vincenzo Starace* (ed.), Diritto internazionale e protezione dell'ambiente marino, Milan 1983, 15-135; *Oscar Schachter,* International Law in Theory and Practice, Dordrecht / Boston / London 1991, in particular 208-218, 342-345; *Linos-Alexandre Sicilianos,* Les réactions décentralisees à l'illicite: des contremesures à la légitime defense, Paris 1990, in particular 135-177; *Bruno Simma,* Bilateralism and Community Interest in the Law of State Responsibility, in: *Yoram Dinstein* (ed.), International Law at a Time of Perplexity. Essays in Honour of *Shabtai Rosenne,* Dordrecht / Boston / London 1989, 821-844; *idem,* International Crimes: Injury and Countermeasures. Comments on Part 2 of the ILC Work on State Responsibility, in: *Weiler / Cassese / Spinedi (infra),* 283-315; *Giuseppe Sperduti,* Les obligations solidaires en droit international, in: *Jerzy Makarczyk* (ed.), Essays in International Law in Honour of Judge *Manfred Lachs,* The Hague / Boston / Lancaster 1984, 271-275; *Vincenzo Starace,* La responsabilité resultant de la violation des obligations à l'égard de la communauté internationale, in: Recueil des Cours 153 (1976-V), 263-317; *Hubert Thierry,* Cours général de droit international public, in: Recueil des Cours 222 (1990-III), 61-70, 104-107; *Joseph H.H. Weiler / Antonio Cassese / Marina Spinedi* (eds.) International Crimes of States, Berlin / New York 1989.

6 *Philip Allott,* Eunomia. New Order for a New World, Oxford / New York 1990.

7 *Op. cit.,* 243-253.

8 *Prosper Weil,* Towards Relative Normativity in International Law? in: American Journal of International Law (AJIL) 77 (1983), 413-442.

This law has been, again in *Allott*'s words, the "minimal law necessary to enable state-societies to act as closed systems internally and to act as territory-owners in relation to each other,"[10] nothing more.

International law was thus left entirely in the hands of sovereign states, predicated on their bilateral legal relations, on the intrinsically bilateral character of legal accountability, and on a delict-property-contract ethos.[11] Such bilateralism has stood in the way of a development of international law in the directions that are demanded by the development — and for the survival — of international society. Bilateralist international law has fallen far behind the state of consciousness of international society — which is increasingly transcending national boundaries and growing impatient with the value-poverty of the traditional law. Within the modern state, the development of the role of government has enabled organized society to intervene as a third party in any bilateral legal relation, not merely in creating and enforcing legal relations but as an active participant in such relations through the exercise of public power. In other words, domestic constitutions granted public authority the power to control property-holding in the social interest. International law is in urgent need of such a re-conception as a system of *public* law based on social responsibility and accountability of its subjects.[12] In fact, it has been taking steps in this direction for some decades. The rapidly increasing international concern with human rights, the environment, the spread of nuclear weapons, and economic interdependence, to name just the most obvious examples, amply illustrate that there is a world-wide social consciousness at work today that "publicizes" international relations far beyond the rituals of governmental interaction. Forces as diverse as Amnesty, Greenpeace, and satellite TV are building up a feeling of world-wide solidarity which cares little about legal finesses and the sovereignty-sensitivities of governments.[13] Such social consciousness and solidarity cannot but spill over into the world of international law, with theories such as those on *ius cogens* and on obligations *erga omnes* serving as the jurisprudential *Leitmotiv* of this process.

Now, if these theories are just a sign of the overdue "socializing," "warming," and "greening" of international law, why are they considered a mixed blessing by *Prosper Weil* and others? The reason is, I think, that these concepts also reveal a fundamental tension in contemporary international law — the tension between the need to make international law express and support what are assumed

---

9 *Allott* (note 6), 248.

10 *Op. cit.*, 324.

11 *Op. cit.*, 335.

12 *Op. cit.*, 336-337.

13 *Cf.* from the address delivered by UN Secretary-General *Pérez de Cuellar* on 22 April 1991 at the University of Bordeaux: "We are clearly witnessing what is probably an irresistible shift in public attitudes towards the belief that the defence of the oppressed in the name of morality should prevail over frontiers and legal documents." UN Press Release, SG / SM/4560 (24 April 1991).

to be universally held moral beliefs, and the need to make it firmly reflect the political context. As a consequence, the observer is constantly torn between a feeling of satisfaction that international law is finally being imbued with some of the social consciousness long developed in domestic law, and the fear that the still primitive, still essentially bilateralist structure of contemporary international law will turn out to be too weak to come to terms with the implications of the concepts of *ius cogens* and obligations *erga omnes.* There is indeed legitimate reason for concern that such new conceptions are being grafted upon international law without support through, and any serious attempts at, adequate institution-building. What is going to happen if the concept of legal obligations in the common or public interest, which is being implemented in domestic systems through the intervention of public authority endowed with a monopoly of physical force, is left to the play of individual auto-determination of duties and self-enforcement of rights? Will chaos and violence come to reign among states, as *Prosper Weil* foresees,[14] or will a more socially conscious substance of the law make states more prepared to equip the international "community" with an adequate institutional framework?

If taken seriously, acceptance of obligations *erga omnes,* as conceived by the International Court, asks for a lot. Such obligations presuppose not only universal agreement on certain values to be protected by and enshrined in international law (which, in a certain sense, is the case with all norms of universal international law, also with those that are then left to bilateral application). The concept of obligations *erga omnes* requires, in addition, universal agreement to the effect that the enforcement of the rules embodying these values is not to be left — or at least not totally — to the discretion or power of individual states, and, further, that the principle *volenti non fit iniuria* ought not to apply to infringements of such rules. But does a consensus on the values and norms that are to enjoy such superiority or on the means by which the international community may take action actually exist? How are we to perceive the achievement of such universal agreement? As to the *substance* of the obligations *erga omnes* claimed by the ICJ and others, of course everyone will accept the broad principles — the prohibition of the use of force, respect for human rights, the duty not to stand in the way of self-determination, and the like. But most cases out there in the real world will be "hard cases" where principles conflict or where we have to find our way through a normative penumbra. For instance, is a state employing military force abroad to protect its own nationals, the human rights of nationals of the target state, or democracy pure and simple, violating an obligation *erga omnes? Michael Reisman* or *Tony D'Amato* would never agree with me on such issues.[15] Is the execution of minors or mentally retarded criminals to be seen as

---

[14] *Weil* (note 8), 433.

[15] For my own views *cf. Alfred Verdross / Bruno Simma,* Universelles Völkerrecht, 3rd ed., Berlin 1984, paras. 261, 473, 494, 1208 and 1338. During the discussion of,

contrary to an obligation *erga omnes* to respect the fundamental human right to life?[16] Or would non-recognition of Croatia and Slovenia have to be considered in violation of these peoples' right to self-determination? In this context, it is to be hoped that the *East Timor* case currently pending before the ICJ[17] will develop beyond the jurisdiction stage and thus give the Court the opportunity to provide some guidance on these and related problems.

Moving to procedural aspects of our inquiry, the rule remains that the questions I have just asked will be subject to auto-determination, and this simple fact ought to restrain our admission of individual countermeasures against alleged breaches of obligations *erga omnes*. Such a right should, in principle, rest with the *"omnes,"* that is, with the international community of states as a whole. Agreed, but where precisely do we find this "community"? Does it consist of all states *ut singuli?* Or does the *Weltgeist* prefer the more exclusive company of the Great Powers? Or is a certain qualified, representative majority of states deemed to have the power to proclaim obligations *erga omnes?*

At the 1968 session of the Vienna Conference on the Law of Treaties, after the Drafting Committee had agreed on the text of what was to become the Treaty Convention's Article 53 on *ius cogens,* its chairman explained the meaning of the condition that a peremptory rule would have to be accepted and recognized as such by "the international community of States as a whole" in the sense "that there was no question of requiring a rule to be accepted and recognized as peremptory by all states. It would be enough if a very large majority did so; that would mean that, if one State in isolation refused to accept the peremptory character of a rule, or if that State was supported by a small number of States, the acceptance and recognition of the peremptory character of the rule by the international community as a whole would not be affected."[18]

If we read this together with what is probably the majority view on the effect of — or rather lack of effect of — persistent objection to an emerging rule of *ius cogens,* namely that such objection cannot exempt an "outsider" from the

---

inter alia, the present paper, *Michael Reisman* considered humanitarian intervention by military means to be the "primary technique for enforcing some *erga omnes* norms concerned with human rights" and came out strongly in defense of the U.S. intervention in Panama. The most hilarious attempt to whitewash this blatant violation of international law is probably that by *Anthony D'Amato:* The Invasion of Panama was a Lawful Response to Tyranny, in: AJIL 84 (1990), 516-524; see also *id.*, in: AJIL 85 (1991), 331. *Contra Tom J. Farer,* Panama: Beyond the Charter Paradigm, in: AJIL 84 (1990), 503-515.

16 See, for instance, the decision of the Inter-American Commission on Human Rights of 27 March 1987 in the case of *Terry Roach* and *Jay Pinkerton:* Resolution No. 3/87, Case No. 9647 (United States), Inter-Am. C.H.R., OEA/ser.L/ V/II.69, doc. A, para. 56.

17 See *supra* note 1.

18 United Nations Conference on the Law of Treaties, First session, Official Records, UN Doc. A / CONF. 39/11 (1969), 472 (para. 12).

binding force of a peremptory rule,[19] we have probably arrived at the formula which most observers would employ to answer the question of the quality as well as the quantity of agreement necessary to spell out an obligation *erga omnes.* But can it really be argued, that, *de iure lato,* a majority of states, albeit a very large one, may posit precisely the most fundamental obligations? I submit that the very formula "international community (of states) as a whole" characterizes the *interim* position which international law currently takes with regard to community interest in the law — a stage in which, to some, highly desirable manifestations of such community interest find themselves caught in the Procrustean bed of bilateralism.

The UN Charter has not changed this situation — it, too, epitomizes an international society and its law in a time of transition from a "private law" system of feudal landowners, as *Philip Allott* would say,[20] into a community under a truly public law, reflecting the tensions and contradictions of such a period. Just contrast the sovereign equality of UN member states consecrated in Article 2, paragraph 1, with the system of collective security established in Chapter VII and the claims at the basis of Article 2, paragraph 6; the apparent impossibility of organizing collective enforcement measures within Chapter VII in the centralized, that is, "public law" mode designed in Articles 42 and 43; or the jealous safeguarding of domestic jurisdiction by Article 2, paragraph 7, *vis-à-vis* the clauses of Articles 55 and 56, obliging states to open themselves up, so to speak, in the very fields which Article 2, paragraph 7, was designed to keep closed.

Before I finally turn to the law of the Charter, let me make a number of slightly more technical observations regarding obligations *erga omnes.* Again, I will have to be extremely brief and leave many questions to our discussion period.

First, I suggest that we maintain a distinction between obligations *erga omnes* in the *Barcelona Traction* sense and rules of general international or multilateral treaty law whose structure of application, if I may use this expression, is such that they cannot be split up into a number of parallel bilateral relationships.[21]

---

19 *Ian Brownlie,* Principles of Public International Law, 4th ed., Oxford 1990, 11 note 56, 514; *Louis Henkin,* International Law: Politics, Values and Functions (General Course on Public International Law), Recueil des Cours 216 (1989-IV), 50; *Maarten Bos,* A Methodology of International Law, Amsterdam / New York / Oxford 1984, 246; for an extensive discussion of this question *cf.* with further references, *Ted L. Stein,* The Approach of the Different Drummer: The Principle of the Persistent Objector in International Law, in: Harvard International Law Journal 26 (1985), 457-482 (in particular 474 *et seq.).*

20 *Allot* (note 6), 246 and *passim.*

21 On the different ways in which rights and obligations run in multilateral treaties *cf. Verdross / Simma* (note 15), paras. 539, 733, 754, 794/5 and 813; *Gerhard Hafner,* Bemerkungen zur Funktion und Bestimmung der Betroffenheit im Völkerrecht anhand des Binnenstaates, in: German Yearbook of International Law 31 (1988), 187-229;

Certain uses of the high seas, for instance, cannot be agreed upon by pairs of states without encroaching upon the rights and interests of others. But this does not necessarily mean that obligations of such integral structure will also constitute genuine obligations *erga omnes*. I submit that the factor distinguishing the latter can only be seen in a particular value judgment according to which the international community as a whole considers observance of certain obligations as imperative. From this perspective, the core provisions of the great human rights or humanitarian conventions also referred to by the *Barcelona Traction* dictum might be taken as examples where integral treaty and truly *erga omnes* obligations coincide.

My second observation concerns the law-making process from which obligations *erga omnes* emerge. A satisfactory treatment of this issue calls for a paper of its own — and *Philip Alston* and I have indeed dealt with its human rights aspects at greater length elsewhere.[22] Let me just say the following: If obligations *erga omnes* denote international legal obligations which do not arise from particular legal relationships established between pairs or groups of states, then such obligations do not — at least not necessarily — come about through a process whereby each and every state binds itself *vis-à-vis* each and every other state through the vehicles of treaty or customary law-making. Rather, what happens in the case of genuine obligations *erga omnes* is that, at a certain stage of the law-making process, an international community (admittedly not yet defined in any satisfactory and precise manner) regards all states as legally bound, irrespective of any individual manifestations of consent.

To give just one example: Would it help a state accused of genocide to argue that it had never consented to the respective prohibition contained in the 1948 Convention and in unwritten international law? Thus, obligations *erga omnes* — or the emancipation of such an obligation from a treaty provision which initially proclaimed it *inter partes* (as in the case of Article 2, paragraph 4, of the Charter as acknowledged in the *Nicaragua* judgment)[23] — come about more or less spontaneously. This does not necessarily mean instantly (just compare the emergence of the prohibition of slavery with that of genocide in this respect). Obligations of this nature are carried in by the tide of an overwhelming *opinio iuris*, a sense that a certain statal behaviour simply has to be outlawed in the profundest way international law has to offer, that it cannot any longer be left

---

Kamen Sachariev, State Responsibility for Multilateral Treaty Violations: Identifying the "Injured State" and its Legal Status, Netherlands International Law Review 35 (1988), 273-289 (all with extensive further references).

22 *Bruno Simma / Philip Alston*, The Sources of Human Rights Law: Custom, *Jus Cogens*, and General Principles, in: Australian Yearbook of International Law 12 (1992), 82-108.

23 *Case concerning Military and Paramilitary Actions in and against Nicaragua (Nicaragua* v. *United States of America)*, ICJ Reports 1986, 14-546 (98-102).

to moral condemnation alone. I think that the outlawing of genocide soon after 1945 or the emergence of a universal legal prohibition of torture as well as of some other fundamental norms in the field of human rights illustrate this process — a process which can hardly be reconciled with the accepted modes of formation of customary law[24] and, indeed, with the axioms of legal positivism.

At the basis of my third remark lies the notion of injury. I consider it essential — particularly in view of my paper topic — to distinguish between two different types of obligations *erga omnes* from that viewpoint. First there are those whose violation directly and materially "injures" another or certain other states in the more or less traditional, tangible mode, like the prohibition of aggression or of large-scale intentional damage to the environment (as in the case of the burning of the Kuwaiti oil fields by Iraq). In such cases we are in presence of state victims; self-help as well as collective countermeasures are feasible, at least in principle; the same is valid with regard to state responsibility in the established sense.

But there are also those obligations *erga omnes* in the field of human rights or the environment that do not protect states but rather human beings or groups directly, and as such protect these beings even against their own state, or those rules that deal with the preservation of the world's commons, so to speak, like the high seas or the ozone layer. In the case of such rules, traditional international law reflexes geared towards individualized action and material, injury have a hard time both latching on and displaying any real "bite." If individual states nevertheless decide to go through the traditional motions here, the danger of abuse is great, as is the lack of any regularity, objectivity, and even-handedness.[25] In most instances of violation of obligations of this type, states prefer not to respond — or to adequately respond — at all. In these cases, the only remedy is to be found in the elaboration and application of specific, "custom-tailored" regimes which take into account and overcome the lack of an inter-statally bilateralizable delict-injury-reparation mode. The various implementation procedures to be found in human rights treaties or the respective regime emerging within the CSCE may serve as examples.

---

[24] Even authors who argue strongly in favor of the feasibility of human rights prescriptions having been transformed into customary law have had to admit that the traditional prerequisites of international custom must be handled in somewhat of a cavalier fashion in order to arrive at this result. *Cf. Henkin* (note 19), particularly 223-224; *Schachter* (note 5), 335-342 (note the differences *vis-à-vis* the original text, in: Recueil des Cours 178 (1982-V), 338-338).

[25] *Cf. Gaetano Arangio-Ruiz,* Third Report on State Responsibility, UN Doc. A/CN.4/440 (10 June 1991), 2 (para. 4): "... one must register cases of partial collectivization of measures on the part of rather occasionally concerted groups of States against a current wrongdoer mostly outside of the tendentially universal institutional framework: practices which, while keeping in a sense within the classic bilateral 'injured State — author State' pattern, do not seem to offer ... the indispensable guarantees of regularity and objectivity."

Perhaps one could say — and this brings me to my fourth observation — that, with the exception of the prohibition of aggression, obligations *erga omnes* tend to be coupled with "soft responsibility," to use an expression coined by Professor *Kiss;*[26] that is, such obligations are either equipped with the conventional *leges speciales* which I have just referred to and which only very rarely provide for genuine restitution or enforcement; or responsibility for their violation turns out to be soft in the sense that the general legal consequences of illegal behaviour, although available in law, are hardly ever invoked in fact. What we see then, is almost paradoxical: Obligations accepted as peremptory, of general concern, of the most fundamental importance, are pretty much left out in the cold when it comes to countering their violation: infringements of the "hardest" obligations appear to be followed by particularly soft responses.

Please do not get a wrong impression here: I repeat that I consider obligations *erga omnes* as deriving from rules of international law in the full sense, that is, from rules embedded, in principle, in the general law on responsibility and on countermeasures against international wrongs. But the problem is, first, that this general regime fits obligations *erga omnes* rather badly from the beginning and, second, that its practical application leaves a lot to be desired, above all any regularity and objectivity.

I cannot offer much of a consolation, except that I see this state of affairs as a consequence precisely of what I have called the "public law" character of the obligations *erga omnes* referred to: There already is (some) agreement on the substance of these prescriptions in the public, not only in the bilateral, interest; but agreement has not yet been reached on how to provide this "public law" with an adequate infrastructure, with the necessary institutional support to ensure truly collective enforcement. What we have, therefore, is an incremental "public" international law (in my sense!) desperately seeking the public authority enabling it to counter violations on a regular basis and in an objective manner and thus saving the law from the whims of bilateralism (I don't know if any of our American participants have come to Kiel by car but just imagine the German *Straßenverkehrsordnung* left to German drivers for enforcement . . .).

Leaving aside European Community Law which by now appears to have definitively elevated itself above the dangerous grounds of our discipline, I have come across (only) one area where the possibility of a truly "public" international law is currently being explored and advanced in a sort of juridical laboratory. I am referring to the European Convention on Human Rights which, through the jurisprudence of its organs and the laudable indulgence of its states parties, is outgrowing its conventional, interstatal framework and developing into what the Convention organs themselves have for a long time been labeling as an "objective

---

26 See, e.g., *Alexander Kiss / Dinah Shelton,* International Environmental Law, New York / London 1991, 362.

public order," and what the European Commission a year ago in the *Chrysostomos* case did not hesitate to call a "constitutional instrument," facilitating the "collective enforcement" of human rights.[27] Here we not only have the public law substance but also something like a public law infrastructure: Convention organs which, for instance, through their control of reservations and declarations of acceptance and their dynamic method of treaty interpretation, have established themselves as "masters" of their treaty to a degree unparalleled in the history of international law, and have approximated their activity to that of a constitutional court. From these Strasbourg heights it is a long way back down to the United Nations scene.

Let me now turn to these UN aspects by taking up again the question of the enforcement of obligations *erga omnes*. It is this enforcement stage which constitutes the moment of truth for the entire concept of obligations *erga omnes*. Here, the first step of any argument must certainly be the observation that, since *erga omnes* norms are binding *vis-à-vis* the community of states as a whole, and since all states are regarded to have a legal interest in the protection of the rights involved, these *"omnes"* must also be considered as in some way entitled to bring about performance of such obligations by employing the range of means provided or allowed by international law. Where we proceed from there will depend, first, on how we are prepared to interpret "all states" for purposes of such a *droit de regard* and, second, in what measure we want to put the instruments I have just referred to into the hands of that variant of the *"omnes"* which we prefer.

As regards the first point, we have the following choices: We could decide to remain within the traditional paradigm and understand *"omnes"* in the sense of literally all states individually, *ut singuli*, or we could transcend such multiple bilateralism and denote a somehow organized community of states, be it the United Nations or some other more perfect configuration to come about in the future. But we could also combine these abstract possibilities to the effect that states *ut singuli* as well as the organized community of states will have their respective role to play in the enforcement of obligations *erga omnes*. If we put it in still more concrete terms and establish the necessary priorities, we arrive at the answer which, I submit, corresponds best with the current transitional state of the law as well as with the *lex ferenda:* According to this view, performance of obligations *erga omnes* may be enforced by the mechanisms provided for this purpose in the Charter of the United Nations, or, if United Nations procedures are lacking, or insufficient, or prove to be unworkable, by states collectively or individually through means which are in conformity with — or justified by — both the Charter and general international law.[28]

---

27 Decision in the Case of Chrysostomos and others, 4 March 1991, reprinted in: ZaöRV 51 (1991), 156-176. See also the case note by *Jörg Polakiewicz, loc. cit.*, 145-155.

If we accept this formula we can proceed to make it operational by inquiring, in case of each obligation for which *erga omnes* status is being claimed, to what extent states have empowered the UN to take enforcement in its hand, and, conversely, if the organization does not or cannot respond to violations of *erga omnes* rules, what faculties remain for states, acting individually or collectively, outside of Charter procedures. In this regard let us consider, for example, from the list of obligations *erga omnes* provided in *Barcelona Traction* (a) the prohibition of aggression and (b) fundamental human rights.

As to *use of force,* it is relevant to my topic from two different perspectives. First, the use of military force, whether direct or indirect, reaching the level of acts of aggression constitutes a breach of an obligation *erga omnes* enshrined both in the Charter and in general international law.[29] The law of the Charter counters acts of aggression with the most comprehensive and potentially most effective set of reactions available in case of violations of *erga omnes* obligations.[30] As to the limits of such reactions, I fully adhere to the continental mainstream[31] — and *Henkin / Schachter*[32] — view, according to which the prohibition stipulated in Article 2, paragraph 4, of the Charter outlaws any exercise of military force except individual or collective self-defense against an armed attack (meaning an "armed attack" in the genuine sense of the term, nothing different and nothing less) and, of course, military enforcement measures according to Chapter VII. To take up the question I have been asked to answer: Yes, the Charter does provide an adequate basis for responses to acts of aggression by foreseeing collective responses on the basis of Chapter VII as well as unilateral action in self-defense *stricto sensu;* any other use of force is — and should remain — illegal. Let me just note in passing that a lasting revitalization of UN enforcement measures under Chapter VII — of whatever variety — would inevitably deprive what could be called the *Bowett* / New Haven reading of Article 2, paragraph 4,[33] of persuasive power as well as legitimacy.

---

28 The statement in the text seems to me to be in essential conformity also with the debate that has taken place so far in the course of the International Law Commission's work on State responsibility. *Cf. Marina Spinedi,* International Crimes of State: The Legislative History, in: *Weiler / Cassese / Spinedi* (eds.) (note 5), 7-138; *Arangio-Ruiz,* Third Report (note 25), Add. 1 (14 June 1991), 2-7; *idem,* Fourth Report on State Responsibility, Addendum, UN Doc. A / CN. 4/444/Add. 2 (1 June 1992), 20-37.

29 *Nicaragua* case (note 23), 98-102. For a recent survey on the literature see *Albrecht Randelzhofer,* [Commentary on] Art. 2 Ziff. 4, in: *Bruno Simma* (ed.), Charta der Vereinten Nationen. Kommentar, Munich 1991, 67-90.

30 *Cf.* the commentaries on Chapter VII of the UN Charter by *Jochen A. Frowein* and *Brun-Otto Bryde,* in: *Simma* (ed.), *op. cit.,* 559-617.

31 As exemplified in the commentaries by *Albrecht Randelzhofer* on Articles 2 (4) and 51 of the Charter, in: *Simma* (ed.), *op. cit.,* 67-90, 617-635.

32 *Henkin* (note 19), 142-162; *Schachter* (note 5), 106-134, 389-417.

33 To name just the early expositions of this view: *D. W. Bowett,* Self-Defence in International Law, Manchester 1958; *Myres S. McDougal / Florentino P. Feliciano,* Law and Minimum World Public Order. The Legal Regulation of International Coercion, New Haven / London 1961.

Allow me just one brief glance at the reality of collective enforcement of the obligation *erga omnes* not to use force in contravention to the Charter: An intensive debate, here and in other fora, has focused on the question of whether the collective military action against Iraq on the basis of Security Council Resolution 678 (1990) constituted an implementation of Chapter VII Articles 42 and 48 or was rather to be seen as an instance of collective self-defense, with an unusually explicit and far-reaching blessing by the Security Council, so to speak.[34] Neither of these alternatives fits neatly: The Article 42/48 view does considerable violence to the wording and systematics of these provisions, while the Article 51 position would render the "remainder" of Chapter VII virtually meaningless. In my opinion, a correct analysis of Chapter VII (including Article 51) leads to the result that it does not provide for a dichotomy of reactions by military means but in reality comprises a trichotomy, namely, (1) action according to Article 42 under the operative command and control of the Security Council, (2) action by UN member states authorized by the Council through a recommendation according to Article 39, and (3) measures of individual or collective self-defense against an armed attack under the sort of control of the Council envisaged by Article 51.[35] This view is derived from the wording of Article 39, according to which the Security Council first makes a determination, followed by either recommendations or decisions as to enforcement measures to be taken.

I regard already the first step of Council action, namely the determination of the existence of one of the three elements enumerated in Article 39, as a "decision" in the sense of Article 25 of the Charter. As a consequence, this determination is not only binding on all UN members but — and this is the decisive point — it also legally justifies the (non-military as well as military) measures taken by member states against the aggressor, regardless of whether these measures are carried out on the basis of a mere Council recommendation or pursuant to a decision.[36] The Articles 42 *et seq.* provide the framework only for action under the genuine control of the Security Council, while measures recommended by the Council are subject to the regime and limitations spelled out in the respective Council resolution itself. Applied to the Gulf scenario, what I am suggesting is that we should not try to fit the Allied action into the strait-jacket of either Article 42 or 51 but rather view it as a distinct category of collective enforcement under the Charter, with a legal framework of its own that could be summarized in the formula: authorization = determination + recommendation.[37] From this

---

[34] See, for instance, the contributions on the legal aspects of the Gulf War by *Oscar Schachter, Eugene W. Rostow* and *Burns H. Weston,* in: AJIL 85 (1991), 452-473, 506-535. See further the discussions of the present Symposium.

[35] I follow here the analysis made by *Stefan Brunner,* Militärische Maßnahmen nach Kapitel VII UN-Charta, in: Neue Zeitschrift für Wehrrecht 34 (1992), 1-15.

[36] *Cf. Alfred von Verdross,* Idées directrices de l'Organisation des Nations Unies, in: Recueil des Cours 83 (1953-II), 1-77 (54-55).

[37] *Brunner* (note 35), 11.

perspective, the military action against Iraq was based on a decision by the Security Council which authorized (and legally justified) the use of force beyond the limits of Article 51 and consequently could also legitimate the "humanitarian intervention" in favor of the Kurds (Res. 688 (1991)). Such authorization by the Security Council is not limited to cases of "armed attacks." I will return to this aspect in a second, but let me first say that I am personally convinced that future collective measures under the aegis of the Security Council will be of the mode that I have tried to identify as a third, distinct way of implementing Chapter VII. The full-fledged Article 42/43 approach presupposes a degree of solidarity specifically on the part of the major powers which may have existed among the war-time coalition that drew up the Charter.

At present, and again from the perspective of the interests of the United States and the other major industrial powers, very little — or nothing — speaks in favor of surrendering the operative command of military measures to a supranational body.[38] Thus, it is to be expected (or feared) that future Security Council enforcement practice will display features of what *Charles Krauthammer* has called "pseudo-multilateralism": "[A] dominant great power acts essentially alone, but, embarrassed at the idea and still worshiping at the shrine of collective security, recruits a ship here, a brigade there, and blessings all around to give its unilateral actions a multilateral sheen."[39] Whether we like it or not, this again mirrors the transitional stage in which the international community finds itself — on the way to its "public" law but not quite there yet: We are in favor of policing the world but we prefer doing it as *beliehene Unternehmer* — by a sort of international citizen's arrest, if you will.

I see a certain probability that in the future such policing might increasingly be effected through regional organizations or groupings, but as long as the UN Charter is recognized as the higher law of the international community, any regional enforcement action employing military force or, as in the case of economic sanctions, affecting the rights of third parties will require an (express) authorization by the Security Council.[40]

With this, I turn to another relationship between the use of force and obligations *erga omnes*. Put as a question, under which circumstances may violations of

---

38 This evaluation has recently been corroborated by the mainly (and in case of the United States, totally) negative response to the proposals made by Secretary General *Boutros Ghali* on 17 June 1992: "An agenda for peace, preventive diplomacy, peacemaking and peace-keeping." (UN Doc. A/47/277, 13). *Cf.* Frankfurter Allgemeine Zeitung of 11 July 1992, 8.

39 *Charles Krauthammer*, The Unipolar Moment, in: Foreign Affairs 70 (1991), No. 1, 23-33 (25).

40 *Cf.* Article 53 paragraph 1, of the UN Charter. In principle, such authorization could also be granted in a general way, covering future regional enforcement action undertaken by specific regional organizations under circumstances and within both substantive and procedural limits set out by the Council.

obligations *erga omnes* other than acts of aggression be countered with military means? Let us consider, for example, violations of human rights such as genocide, racial discrimination and other grave infringements of "the principles and rules concerning the basic rights of the human person," as the International Court expressed it.[41] I am restricting my analysis to clear cases of grave breaches of such principles and rules, first, because I think that the moral judgment legally expressed in the very notion of obligations *erga omnes* to respect human rights only extends to universally recognized rights and only to reliably attested, gross and persistent violations, to use the classic formula introduced by ECOSOC Resolution 1503;[42] and second, because only in cases of this magnitude will humanitarian interventions involving the use of military force be considered.

As I understand the law of the Charter, any such military response to violations of human rights taking place in another country is legal only if it is either requested or authorized by the Security Council on the basis of a determination according to Article 39 of the Charter (the distinction between "requested" and "authorized" use of force referring back to the understanding of possible variants of Chapter VII enforcement action developed earlier).[43] On the other hand, manifestations of "military humanitarianism" (to quote the title of one of the background papers to this Conference)[44] on the part of individual states or groups of states without the blessing of the Council must be considered illegal in the light of Articles 2, paragraph 4, and 53. The last thing we need to achieve respect for human rights are self-appointed "kind-hearted gunmen" — to use a phrase coined by Professor *Brownlie* about 25 years ago to counter an earlier instance of "military humanitarianism," overcoming some American colleagues.[45] If you agree with the direction in which I traced the origin and *raison d'être* of obligations *erga omnes* in international law earlier on, you will have to concur that any encouragement or liberal justification of unilateral use of force by states to enforce these duties would run counter to the very essence of such a concept. Nowadays, there is a wide array of peaceful means available to states eager to

---

41 *Barcelona Traction* case (note 3), 32.

42 This resolution provided a carefully and deliberately constrained procedure by which the UN Commission on Human Rights could pursue situations which appear to reveal "a consistent pattern of gross and reliably attested violations of human rights": *Philip Alston*, The Commission on Human Rights, in: *idem* (ed.), The United Nations and Human Rights: A Critical Appraisal, Oxford 1992, 126-210 (144 *et seq.).*

43 For the most recent analysis to the same effect see *Kelly-Kate S. Pease / David P. Forsythe*, Human Rights, Humanitarian Intervention and World Politics. Paper prepared for the Atlanta Conference of the International Studies Association, April 1-4, 1992 (manuscript). See also *Randelzhofer*, in: *Simma* (ed.) (note 29), 84-85; *Ulrich Beyerlin*, Humanitarian Intervention, in: EPIL, Instalment 3 (1982), 211-215 (all with extensive further references).

44 *Thomas G. Weiss / Kurt M. Campbell*, Military humanitarianism, in: Survival 33 (1991), 451-465.

45 *Ian Brownlie*, Thoughts on Kind-Hearted Gunmen, in: *Richard B. Lillich* (ed.), Humanitarian Intervention and the United Nations, Charlottesville 1973, 139-148.

induce, or enforce, the observance of human rights in other countries, carrots as well as sticks. Such measures just have to be applied in a regular and even-handed fashion.

As I have already stated, violations of human rights obligations do constitute internationally wrongful acts in the classic sense and thus justify, under certain conditions and within certain limitations, peaceful countermeasures on the part of other states.[46] You will recall that a few years ago, in the course of its work on state responsibility, the International Law Commission adopted a definition of "injured states."[47] In so doing, it took the view that the breach of a treaty for the protection of human rights legally injured every other state party to such a treaty, thus entitling any other party to invoke the legal consequences of the breach. If the breach amounted to an "international crime" in the sense of the ILC's famous Article 19, all states, that is, literally all states, were to be considered "injured states." The Commission did add that such a liberal disbursement of "injury" did not prejudice the extent of the legal consequences that these other states could invoke.[48] In this regard a strong opinion in the literature would permit "third-party" responses through measures of retorsion and non-military reprisals if this were the only effective means available to counter gross and persistent violations of fundamental human rights.[49] Although this view gives rise to considerable procedural problems, in particular, concerning the relationship between such countermeasures and the implementation mechanisms provided in human rights treaties or elsewhere, I think it is a correct statement of the law. However, in actual state practice, readiness to go beyond measures of retorsion in order to enforce human rights appears extremely restrained; in most cases, reactions to violations of human rights have not even been discussed — in public — in terms of specifically legal countermeasures. From a policy perspective, I see this as a positive development. Aside from particularly abhorrent and urgent cases, the "sanction of non-participation," as *Wolfgang Friedmann* called it,[50] will be more fruitful than raw coercion.

---

46 See also *Bruno Simma*, Consent: Strains in the Treaty System, in: *R. St. J. Macdonald / D. M. Johnston* (eds.), The Structure and Process of International Law, The Hague / Boston / Lancaster 1983, 485-511 (500-502); *Louis Henkin*, The Age of Rights, New York 1990, 58-61; *Kamminga* (note 5), *passim* (with extensive further references); *Oliver Cortem / Pierre Klein*, Droit d'ingérence ou obligation de réaction non-armée? in: Revue belge de droit international 23 (1991), 368-440.

47 *Cf.* Report of the Commission to the General Assembly on the work of its thirty-seventh session, Yearbook of the International Law Commission 1985, Vol. II, Part Two, 27 (para. 28). For a commentary see *Simma*, International Crimes, in: *Weiler / Cassese / Spinedi* (eds.) (note 5), 296-300; *Bernhardt Graefrath*, Das Verantwortlichkeitsverhältnis im Völkerrecht und die Definition des "verletzten Staates", in: Probleme des Völkerrechts, (East)Berlin 1987, 107-138.

48 Report 1985, 59.

49 *Cf.* the references in note 46.

50 *Wolfgang Friedmann*, The Changing Structure of International Law, London 1964, 88-95.

Human rights considerations should be made an integral, routine, part of bilateral as well as multilateral diplomacy and economic cooperation — and there are many indications that this is precisely what is happening at present. International development assistance has become far more human rights-conscious than was the case a decade ago, labour rights issues are intruding further and further into the international trade regime,[51] and the very legitimacy of governments is being regularly assessed on the basis of their compliance with international human rights norms.[52] In short, "good government," including, in particular, respect for human rights, is increasingly becoming an essential condition for a good rating in all kinds of intergovernmental business. In view of such growing sophistication of the ways and means of promoting human rights internationally, "military humanitarianism" ought to be seen as a dangerous anachronism as well as a contradiction in itself, prone to permanent abuse. The *Weiss / Campbell* paper that I have already mentioned provides a macabre illustration of the latter by calling the U.S. invasion in Panama a "unilateral relief effort."[53]

As I emphasized at the outset, for a decision to use military force on humanitarian grounds to be legally defensible, it must be taken or authorized by the UN Security Council. It is only in this sense that a *droit d'ingérence* by force of arms exists. The same is valid for military enforcement of all other obligations *erga omnes*. The threshold to be passed in all such cases is a determination by the Council to the effect that infringements of such obligations amount to, lead to, contribute to, or are accompanied by, a "threat to the peace" in the sense of Article 39. I am using such unelegant language in light of the fact that the Security Council has, at least until now, been anything but enthusiastic about expanding this formula to embrace more than just threats to negative peace. Contrary to many observers, I do not perceive Security Council Resolution 688 (1991) as a decisive step forward in that respect.[54] But the potential for such an extension is there, and a certain development is undeniably taking shape. It shows that the Security Council has been broadening its initial understanding of "threats to the peace" as frontier-crossing activities, so to speak, to include internal situations with serious transborder implications, as in the case of Rhodesia and, in the most recent instance, also of Resolution 688.

---

[51] *Cf. Philip Alston*, Labor Rights Provisions in U.S. Trade Law: "Aggressive Unilateralism"? Paper presented at the Symposium on Human Rights and Labor Rights in the Global Economy (Yale Law School, March 1992), (in print).

[52] For a particulary noteworthy expression of this trend see the "Declaration on the Guidelines on the Recognition of the new States in Eastern Europe and in the Soviet Union", issued on 16 December 1991 by the EC Foreign Ministers meeting in Brussels, in: International and Comparative Law Quarterly 41 (1992), 477.

[53] *Weiss / Campbell* (note 44), 451.

[54] For an excellent discussion see *Peter Malanczuk*, The Kurdish Crisis and Allied Intervention in the Aftermath of the Second Gulf War, in: European Journal of International Law 2 (1991), No. 2, 114-132.

Legally, nothing stands in the way of further steps by which the Council could steer a course towards adopting a still more dynamic concept of peace — and threats thereto — by linking it to the very values that the notions of *ius cogens* and obligations *erga omnes* consecrate in a legal form. Thus, it cannot be excluded that in addition to the prohibition of aggression, further obligations *erga omnes* will in the future be enforced under the umbrella of Chapter VII. But the Council's role with regard to obligations *erga omnes* does not have to be seen as restricted to that of a trustee of community interest only in the field of enforcement. Particularly in cases relating to international peace and security, Council action might also initiate, intensify, or finally establish a consensus through which an international legal precept or prohibition acquires the particular weight and solemnity giving rise to an obligation *erga omnes*.

Perhaps the treaty prohibition on the proliferation of nuclear weapons is on the way to such a qualitative leap under the impact of the dissolution of the Soviet Union and the accompanying security risks. Thus, a few weeks ago, Foreign Minister *Genscher* envisaged for the Security Council the role of a "patron" of the Non-Proliferation Treaty which ought to threaten violators with complete isolation as well as the most stringent of sanctions.[55] To enumerate just a few more precedents from the past: The barring *erga omnes* of the legality of South African presence in Namibia,[56] the call for non-recognition of territorial entities established in violation of Charter principles as in the case of Southern Rhodesia or North Cyprus,[57] the proclaiming of provisions of a national constitution as null and void,[58] or the current treatment of the issue of alleged Libyan terrorists[59] may be named as instances where the Security Council has played a central role in the formation and concretization of obligations *erga omnes*, as their "patron," so to speak.

I am well aware, of course, that within the UN system the Council does not possess a monopoly for countering breaches of such obligations. The law and practice of the UN provide a range of other measures which could be employed

---

55 In his speech at the plenary meeting of the Geneva Conference on Disarmament, 20 February 1992, Translation of advance text 3-4.

56 SC Res. 276 (1970). Its legal effects *erga omnes* were confirmed by the ICJ: *Legal Consequences for States of the Continued Presence of South Africa in Namibia (South West Africa) notwithstanding Security Council Resolution 276 (1970)*, ICJ Reports 1971, 16-345 (56).

57 On the situation in Cyprus see SC Res. 541 of 18 November 1983 and 550 of 11 May 1984. Starting with SC Res. 216 of 12 November 1965 a whole series of resolutions on the duty of non-recognition of the situation in Southern Rhodesia was initiated. *Cf.* in detail *Vera Gowlland-Debbas*, Collective Responses to Illegal Acts in International Law. United Nations Action in the Question of Southern Rhodesia, Dordrecht / Boston / London 1990, in particular 273-325.

58 SC Res. 554 of 17 August 1984.

59 For a critical account see *Mark Weller*, The Lockerbie Case: A Premature End to the "New World Order"?, in: African Journal of International and Comparative Law 4 (1992), 302-324.

in that context, like the suspension of membership rights, expulsion from the Organization, involvement of the International Court of Justice or the "mobilization of shame" through a whole variety of human rights procedures.[60] In some of these instances, participation of the Security Council is necessary, some other responses are feasible without its involvement. But there is no denying the fact that any "enforcement", in the true sense of the word, of community obligations in accordance with the Charter presupposes a positive decision of the Council, including the unanimity of its Permanent Members.

This statement is certainly more defeatist than exciting. Things look different, however, if we consider it in the reverse. Let me put it a bit provocatively: What checks and balances exist to prevent the Security Council from decreeing anything it wishes as a political or even legal obligation *erga omnes* and attaching the most heavy sanctions to it, provided the "Big Five" have arrived at unanimity and have pressured a few non-Permanent Members into agreement? Two participants in this Conference have provided what could be taken as an answer to this question. In his entry on "Great Powers" for the Heidelberg Encyclopedia, *Albrecht Randelzhofer* speaks of a collective hegemony of the five Great Powers envisaged by the Charter and then goes on to say: "Once the unanimity of the five Great Powers is given, the UN Charter gives them the legal basis for a far-reaching reign and provides for only scarce limitations to secure the sovereign independence of the other States."[61] One might add that the severe regimentation to which Iraq has been subjected under Resolution 687 (1991) furnishes a graphic illustration of the sort of "reign" that the Security Council considers compatible with the fundamental premise embodied in Article 2, paragraph 1, of the Charter.

Michael Reisman attempts to comfort us a bit. In a review of the respective instalment of the Encyclopedia, he criticizes *Randelzhofer* for not taking into consideration what he calls "authoritative evaluative criteria for the use of power." Whatever the effect of the Charter, he adds, "one would have thought that under its normative terms, Articles 1 and 2 would apply to Security Council action no less than to the actions of individual states."[62] A pertinent remark, no doubt, but *quis custodiet custodes?* In light of the dominant reading of Articles 24 and 25 of the Charter,[63] there is very little in law, but particularly in fact, that a target state can do to bring its view to bear. At this point, so-called "realist" observers will interject that, ultimately, might has always been right in world politics and thus the omnipotence of the Security Council ought to be seen as a confirmation

---

60 *Cf.* e.g. the deliberations of the Panel on "Compliance and Enforcement in the United Nations System" at the 85th annual meeting of the American Society of International Law (1991), in: Proceedings, 428 - 447.

61 *Albrecht Randelzhofer*, Great Powers, in: EPIL, Instalment 9 (1986), 142 - 146 (144).

62 *W. Michael Reisman*, in: AJIL 85 (1991), 205 - 207 (207).

63 *Cf. Jost Delbrück*, Commentary on Articles 24 and 25, in: *Simma* (ed.) (note 29), 364 - 383.

rather than a rejection of this truth. We must not rest content with such an oversimplification, however. If the UN Charter is to remain universally accepted as the constitutional instrument of the international community, a Security Council flexing its muscles in newly-won freedom from Cold War stagnation will sooner or later have to overcome what could be termed as its "legitimacy gap."

There is a certain parallel visible here with the notorious "democracy deficit" of the European Community. To put it provocatively again: The more the Security Council lives up to its full political as well as legal potential, the more disquieting its present status and composition becomes. Could we possibly imagine the community of states agreeing on a sort of international *contrat social* and drafting a constitutional treaty to provide it with an institutional framework, not in the traumatic circumstances of 1945 but under present political and economic conditions, and in so doing give the body that is to exercise the incipient "public authority" of this community the unbridled powers as well as the composition of the present-day Security Council? What I am hinting at is not just the desirability of making the Council more representative through granting additional permanent seats — albeit without veto privileges — to certain states. I would also include amendments of the Charter introducing greater coordination between the Security Council and the General Assembly, but also the International Court, for instance, before recourse may be had to enforcement action.[64]

Let me further remind you of the proposal made by former Secretary-General *Perez de Cuellar* to call on a tribunal consisting of "eminent" or "wise" persons to give an opinion on the legitimacy of humanitarian interventions envisaged by the Security Council.[65] None of these ideas should be tabooed or disqualified as "unrealistic" from the outset. Maybe a major and concerted effort, comparable to that undertaken by hundreds of American lawyers upon the initiative of *Manley Hudson* during World War II, could be made to present the UN at its 50th anniversary in 1995 with a comprehensive blueprint for reform, including the field of maintenance of peace and security.

Let me conclude: I think that the question I was asked, whether the UN Charter provides an adequate basis for responses to violations of obligations running *erga omnes* can be answered with a cautious "Yes, in principle." Obligations of this kind witness the attempt in general international law to ultimately overcome the paradigm of individualist, uncommitted sovereignty in favor of some inter-state solidarity. But such solidarity is still far from being "in the blood" of international law; it may exist among friends in some instances, but certainly it is the exception rather than the rule. As a consequence, a world organization

---

64 In the same sense *Brunner* (note 35), 3 (note 10); *Benedetto Conforti*, Non-Coercive Sanctions in the United Nations Charter: Some Lessons from the Gulf War, in: European Journal of International Law 2 (1991), No. 2, 110-113 (112/3).

65 Frankfurter Allgemeine Zeitung of 4 December 1991, No. 281, 2.

built on international solidarity, that is, depending on it for its functioning, would be too far ahead of political reality. The UN Charter, as it stands, encourages and channels rather than presupposes such solidarity. In so doing, it epitomizes a hopefully transitional stage of international society. A thorough reform of the Security Council would contribute significantly towards providing this society with the more mature law and organization that it so urgently needs.

Comment

Christoph Schreuer*

The task of a Commentator, as I understand it, is to highten the entertainment value of an event like this by providing controversy. If this is indeed what is expected of me, my contribution may be a disappointment. The simple reason is that I agree with most of what has been said this morning. Therefore, what I have to offer is more by way of a summary, a shift of emphasis here and there and perhaps an occasional supplementary remark.

Let me start with the topic of obligations *erga omnes* and then turn to more procedural aspects, especially the role of the Security Council. There appears to be consensus that obligations *erga omnes* (like *ius cogens)* signify international law of a higher order. This is not because the entire community of states is necessarily directly affected but because there is a consensus about value judgments. In other words, there is a moral and public order commitment to certain standards. Basic human rights and the prohibition of aggression are offered most frequently as examples. This phenomenon of law of a higher order is familiar from constitutional law. It is qualitatively more important to the community than ordinary law. However, a constitution must also have structural and procedural rules to deal with the creation, ascertainment and enforcement of these substantive standards. The higher constitutional law of the international community is in constant tension with the still largely bilateralist and consensualist structures of international law.

Bruno Simma has referred us to the spontaneous creation of this type of superior law; to a lack of formal consent; to its emancipation from specific treaty provisions or demonstrable state practice. In other words, it cannot be reconciled with the traditional categories of international law. Perhaps this is a good example for the realization that the authoritative decision-making process that we call international law has outgrown the strait jacket of Article 38 of the ICJ Statute. A more traditional explanation would be to see obligations *erga omnes* as guiding principles of international law which can be traced back to a number of positive obligations and which have been internalized by the international community as being part of the overall architecture of international law. Principles of this kind have always existed. Under classical international law they included consent and

---

* Prof. Dr. *Christoph Schreuer*, Department of International Law, University of Salzburg.

pacta sunt servanda. The decisive difference is that these classical meta-principles were value-neutral, whereas modern international law has created a set of value-oriented higher principles.

The chief characteristic of obligations *erga omnes* is that they evoke a higher degree of solidarity. All states are called upon to react individually and through collective measures. In both reports there was a lot of emphasis on strengthening organized community responses and on denouncing unilateral action of a military nature. Both are important and I shall return to them in a minute. But I do believe there is also room for strengthening decentralized responses to violations of obligations *erga omnes*. While community responses are indispensable, I think reliance on responses by indivudal states cannot be neglected at this transitional stage of the development of international law, as *Bruno Simma* has called it. The International Law Commission has developed useful criteria in a related context.[1] They include the non-recognition of situations brought about in violation of such obligations; the refusal to support a violating state and mutual support of states in their efforts to counteract breaches of these obligations. Another strategy which has been suggested recently by Professor *Caron*[2] would involve the lifting of state immunity in all cases before domestic courts involving claims arising from such violations. This potentially effective strategy could be brought about either by a Security Council decision or by concerted individual action of states.

Decentralized responses also include third party responses to human rights violations. I would certainly subscribe to the view that the supervision mechanisms of human rights treaties are not exclusive. They do not represent a self-contained régime in the sense the International Court of Justice has given to this concept in the *Tehran Hostages* case, where it said that any abuses of diplomatic privileges can only be prosecuted within the framework of the law of diplomatic relations, that is declaration of a person as *persona non grata*.[3] In human rights cases, individual action by states not directly affected remains permissible if it is proportionate, non-violent and is not abused for external motives. *Bruno Simma* has advocated such a policy as an integral part of interstate diplomacy such as marginalizing abusive regimes. Needless to say, that such a policy will only work if it is not undermined by double standards. This is not a quantitative statement. I agree that a reaction to some human rights violations is better than none even if this is necessarily selective. Rather, this is a question of credibility.

---

[1] *Cf.* Article 14 of the fifth report by Special Rapporteur *W. Riphagen* on state responsibility, in: Yearbook of the International Law Commission 1984, Vol. II, Part Two, 101.

[2] *David D. Caron,* Iraq and the Force of Law: Why Give a Shield of Immunity, in: American Journal of International Law 85 (1991), 89-92.

[3] *Case Concerning United States Diplomatic and Consular Staff in Tehran (United States of America* v. *Iran),* ICJ Reports 1980, 3-65 (41).

The demise of superpower rivalry is an excellent chance to do away with the distinction between good human rights violators (our allies), and bad human rights violators (their allies).

Let me shift more specifically to Charter law. I think we can make two broad policy statements for our purposes:

— First, less coercive measures should have precedence over more coercive ones whenever possible.

— Second, the stronger the coercive reactions, the stronger the case for community action. In other words, unilateral reaction loses its appropriateness, and legitimacy in community authorization becomes increasingly more important as we move along the spectrum towards more coercive reactions, especially those involving the use of force.

The preference for less coercive action has found its clearest expression in the relationship of Articles 41 and 42 of the Charter instructing the Security Council to use military means only if non-military strategies are inadequate. The preference for organized community action in highly coercive situations is encapsuled in Article 51 allowing even self-defence only within the limits set by Security Council action. This reading of the Charter is not only warranted by its text and underlying spirit but also by subsequent practice. If there is one lesson to be learned from the history of Article 2, paragraph 4, it is that loopholes have to be closed and that the ingenuity of powerful states in inventing self-serving justifications for the use of force has to be contained. It is certainly possible to present extreme scenarios in which the unilateral use of force may seem desirable. But the sad fact is that in the vast majority of cases where force was used unilaterally, the alleged exceptions to Article 2, paragraph 4, were *ex post facto* justifications often of an evidently insincere kind. The International Court of Justice seems to have followed a general policy of disapproving claims justifying the unilateral use of force for allegedly good causes. This is apparent from the *Corfu Channel* case in connection with British mine-sweeping operations,[4] from the *Tehran Hostages* case in connection with American efforts to liberate the hostages[5] and, of course, most spectacularly in the *Nicaragua* case.[6]

In addition to the overwhelming danger of abuse, there appears to me to be another reason for this very strong presumption against the legality of unilateral use of force. It is the close interrelation of two of the most widely accepted obligations *erga omnes,* namely prohibition of the use of force and protection of basic human rights. Quite independently of its permissibility under international

---

4 *The Corfu Channel Case,* ICJ Reports 1949, 4-169 (35).

5 *Tehran Hostages* case (note 3), 44.

6 *Case Concerning Military and Paramilitary Activities in and Against Nicaragua (Nicaragua* v. *United States of America),* ICJ Reports 1986, 14-546 (45-142).

law, the use of force, war and warlike situations almost inevitably involve massive and multiple violations of human rights. Loss of personal liberty and forced labour are among the lesser evils. Inhuman and degrading treatment of military personnel as well as of civilians and systematic and institutionalized killings are the most egregious examples but by no means exhaust the range. The fact that war has always been like that and that some human rights instruments actually contain exceptions relating to war does not make this any more acceptable.

It follows that military humanitarianism is a contradiction in itself. It carries the danger of discrediting and debasing the very goals it declares. This is also the reason why a quantitative choice in the sense of "let's violate a few human rights for a little while in order to forestall more violations for a longer period" is unconvincing. Recent history with its worldwide trend towards democracy and an increased respect for human rights, especially in Latin America and in Eastern Europe, shows that these achievements have been brought about by internal forces of reform supported by external non-military pressure. The years 1989/1990 in Europe are a triumph of non-interventionism.

Let me turn more specifically to Security Council action. I have already referred to the clear preference for community action inherent in Charter law, when it comes to highly coercive action. Articles 42 and 51 are expressive of this choice but also signify the two types of action. Here is one point where I cannot entirely follow Mr. *Frowein* and am much more inclined towards *Bruno Simma*'s interpretation. I think that the "authorization procedure" as used in resolution 678, is a compromise between desirable community action provided for by Articles 42 and 43 and the individualistic response permitted by Article 51. In terms of legitimacy and community support, this is a vast improvement over an unfettered unilateralist approach. But it is also a far cry from action *undertaken by the Security Council*. It is a retreat into semi-decentralized action brought about by the necessities of military and political practicability. Under this halfway approach, the Security Council remains factually and legally dependent on the continued co-operativeness and good behaviour of member states. There is no guarantee that the members authorized to take action will in fact do so. If they do, the Security Council has little control over the exercise of the authority delegated to them. Most important, the Security Council may need to muster a fresh majority to stop activities going beyond its intentions. The danger of abuse to which I have referred a moment ago, arises again in slightly different form. The fact that these problems have not or only very marginally arisen in Iraq and Kuwait does not mean that they cannot arise in the future.

On the other hand, I do not see why the Security Council or for that matter the General Assembly should not also play a role in the exercise of self-defence. It may very well reach the conclusion that it cannot or does not wish to act. Under these circumstances, it can confirm, clarify and also contain decentralized action under Article 51 in a particular situation. Such a flexible and less formalistic approach would be entirely in line with the existing practice under the Charter. After all, the Security Council supported by the General Assembly and the Secretary General have created an entirely new type of action not provided for by the Charter, namely peace-keeping operations sometimes facetiously referred to as "Chapter VI and a half." I can see no reason why practice within Chapter VII must be tied to the strict categories of individual articles as long as it remains faithful to the object and purpose of the Charter.

Next, a word on regional action. I think that control by a supervisory body, the Security Council, has much to commend itself and that the pertinent provision, Article 53, should not be treated lightly. Authorization by the Security Council, as provided there, is also a problem of the degree of control and supervision and will have to be very seriously examined when the situation arises. Consent by the target state alone is no alternative. Envisage the possibility of an abuse or excess by a regional organization. It is inherent in the prohibition of aggression, which is generally accepted as *ius cogens*, that consent will not do. What, if a regional organization gets hijacked by one or a group of extremist states and starts to victimize a member? Participation in the regional organization cannot simply be taken as consent to any decision or action by that system no matter how abusive it may be. Also, I would not discard Article 53 by way of labelling what is going on as peace-keeping rather than enforcement. The distinction may appear clear in theory but the borders may one day become fluid. Peace-keeping, too, can be abused to victimize an unpopular state in the region. Therefore, supervision is essential.

In this context, I would be extremely wary of tacit authorization. Inaction by the Security Council, especially if it is brought about by a veto, would give an inacceptable *carte blanche* to a regional organization. However, I agree that the situation is totally different with respect to non-forcible sanctions by regional organizations. Measures which can be taken as legitimate reprisals by individual members, may be co-ordinated by regional organizations without Security Council authority.

Regional action against non-members may appear unacceptable at first sight simply because the regional arrangement cannot exercise any authority beyond its membership. On the other hand, I can see no reason why a regional organization should not be ordered or authorized by the Security Council to take action under 42 against a non-member state. Why should the Security Council be debarred from turning to a particular regional grouping, if it is free to authorize an indeterminate group like "Member States co-operating with the Government of Kuwait"? Of course, in a situation like this the authority of enforcement action would be derived from the Security Council and from Chapter VII and not from the regional organization itself. For instance, it is entirely conceivable that the Security Council may give instruction or authorization to a future military arm of the EEC to deal with disturbances at the periphery of Europe.

Recently, the Security Council has displayed an unprecedented activism. This is not only demonstrated by its actions against Iraq, especially resolutions 678, 687, and 688, but also in action taken in relation to what used to be Yugoslavia, to Somalia, and most recently, Libya. It is probably no exaggeration to say that in the last two years, the Security Council has been more active than in the nearly 45 years of its previous history. It has also become more intrusive, a fact that has evoked bitter complaints on the part of Iraq. It has taken an extensive interpretation of its mandate and has stretched the meaning of "threat to the peace" in Article 39. In some situations, it has come close to playing the role of a general enforcement agency for international law, for instance in connection with Iraq's financial obligations. I do not think that all this is a cause for disquiet. Even if the Security Council goes beyond the confines of Article 39, it can play a beneficial role in strengthening the international legal system. In Charter terms, this can be justified by reference to the accepted flexible techniques of interpretation, especially object and purpose.

However, I do agree with *Bruno Simma* that a more active Security Council will also require a clearer legal framework for its activities. Checks and balances, as he put it, will be necessary. While community action, especially by the Security Council, is clearly superior to unilaterlism, the purely formal aspect of community authorization or action is not enough to provide legitimacy. An authorization may be abused and even genuine community action may go astray. Some observers have already criticized actions against Iraq and the regime imposed upon it as excessive. Putting limits on Security Council action may not sound very popular at a time when it has at last started to play its proper role. On the other hand, to the extent that it does exercize public authority, the need for legal controls will become inevitable. Police action, as Mr. *Delbrück* called it earlier, also needs supervision. There are clear parallels with European Community law. At the inception of the European Community, restrictions and restraints on Community activity were unpopular and were considerd unnecessary. In the course of time, it was clearly recognized, both by the Community Court and by the other Community organs, that the rule of law, especially adherence to human rights, must be imposed also on international bodies. I think similar considerations must apply to Security Council activity. We cannot rely on the benign nature of collective authority just because we are used to the fact that in the past abuses have resulted from unilateral action.

Let me submit a tentative list of items to be considered in drafting such a legal framework:

— There must be more precise standards for the conditions legitimately triggering Security Council intervention. Article 39 is probably too narrow. The concept of obligations *erga omnes* may be a useful starting point. But to include contract debts clearly would go too far.

— Procedures must be improved. *Bruno Simma* has mentioned the possibility of involving independent experts, "eminent" or "wise" persons as he called them, and a supervisory role of the International Court of Justice. In many cases, such supervision will only take place after the fact. But that is inherent in the concept of judicial supervision of executive action and should be accepted.

— As to methods, the principle of the least coercive method likely to yield the necessary effect should be maintained. It is not undisputed whether this principle was respected in action against Iraq. This would include precedence of non-military over military methods but also a strict observance of proportionality.

— If military action turns out to be indispensable, the highest standards of humanitarian law must be observed. This would clearly include the strict compliance with all relevant treaties irrespective of whether the states providing military units have ratified them.

— Legal protection must be granted to the target community. In order to avoid victimization in a regional or global context, the target state must enjoy legal resort against the measures that are taken. The human rights of the affected population must not only be preserved to the maximum extent possbile but judicial redress and a possibility for compensation must be granted.

Such a legal framework would not only be a barrier to centralist excesses, but should also improve the confidence of the lesser nations of this world and their willingness to co-operate in what is happening in the Security Council.

Discussion

Delbrück:

Just let me recall a few items to bring us back to the context. With regard to the report by Mr. *Frowein,* I should like to mention two major aspects, although these are not really covering his whole report, and therefore, I may do some injustice to Mr. *Frowein* in mentioning only these two. First of all, I like to refer to the question of the various forms of Security Council action we can observe. Particularly, I like to mention the question of delegation by the Security Council of actions held to be necessary and general *pro futuro* authorization as distinct from authorization as part of the action taken *in concreto.* I believe that these were the most interesting forms of Security Council action in the spectrum of such actions which Mr. *Frowein* displayed and from which he then drew several inferences. Then the second set of problems: the scope and limits of the competences of enforcement agents other than the Security Council which formed another intriguing part of Mr. *Frowein*'s report.

Turning to Mr. *Simma,* I should bring to your attention again the section of his report which dealt with the role and function of UN organs in the enforcement of *erga omnes* norms with the subsection, which we should not address too extensively, whether or not there are norms *erga omnes* at all and how they could be doctrinally worked into the fabric of the existing body of international law. I think it would be helpful for our discussion if we would work on the assumption that there is something like *erga omnes* norms around, especially since time is limited, and that we should primarily talk about their enforcement.

As a third set of problems, I should recall that of the scope and limits of non-institutional collective and / or individual enforcement of *erga omnes* norms and finally, especially relying here on Professor *Schreuer*'s comment, the relationship between institutional and non-institutional enforcement action. I refer here to — what I would like to call — the *Schreuer* formula: The more severe enforcement action is necessary, the higher the need for collective and / or institutional action. As a subsection of this latter problem, attention may be paid in the forthcoming discussion to the criteria governing legitimate and legal collective institutional enforcement action. This is just to recollect some of the major highlights which I think the excellent reports have put before us.

O'Connell:

I just have a few comments on each of the speakers. I want to start with *Bruno.* I am a great fan of *Philip Allott* and I am glad that you described his view of our international system as being in transition, because I think that is clearly true. Unfortunately, the other thing you described, since we are in a transitional state, is that there are tensions now in actually knowing whether we are yet in this community that *Philip* pictures or still in the old *Prosper Weil* world or somewhere in between, and from what you said it was hard to answer what is actually the question that *Jost* and I talked about as a possible paper topic. We were debating last year whether or not a third party has an obligation to aid in the enforcement of an *erga omnes* norm. In other words, if a single enforcer has decided to set out on the path of enforcing an *erga omnes* norm, and does so without using force, but clearly has the right to do so because there has been a violation of that *erga omnes* norm, I think *Jost* would take the view that other states are obligated to join in that enforcement effort. I would take the view that under current international law, since the initial enforcer does not have an obligation to enforce, other enforcers would have no individual obligation to join states in a unilateral decision to enforce. Out of the transitional phase that you described it is hard for us to know whether we should go with what looks like more communitarian values of requiring all states to aid in *erga omnes* enforcement action to get a true communitarian view, or whether we should continue with what seems to be closer to the bilateral system you described of state practice, which would allow the individual state to take its own decision whether to join enforcement. I think those are the two possibilities out of that transitional phase that we might be in now. I am not sure which of those you would say is the right one at the current time, maybe there is not a right one now.

The second point (and I guess I have had to change my views on UN intervention to enforce human rights norms): *Oscar Schachter* has taken the view, consistently with you, *Bruno,* that if the Security Council finds a threat to the peace in a situation of serious human rights violation, then the United Nations can intervene to end that human rights violation. I am not sure how far *Oscar* would go in saying that there has to be a real threat to international peace. Compare a situation like the Kurds, where the Kurds lived in several states and the human rights abuse in one state may lead to uprisings in the neighboring states and therefore to a threat to international peace, with Cambodia (where of course there was intervention too, so that is not such a good example, but perhaps a hypothetical example) where the human rights abuse does stay internal and there is no going outside the lines: I am not sure how far *Oscar* would go with that. My view is that state practice does not currently permit that kind of intervention. I think the two latest examples of Kurds and Croatians would undersquare that. If you look at the decisions made in the last year quite carefully, you see that a majority of members of the Security Council were not interested in using force in order to protect human rights. They had an interest in trying to prevent ongoing armed conflict, but they did not authorize the use of force to protect human rights *per se*. I do not think we have moved that far, but I think that I would have to go along now with what I think is a consensus in the group. I took up the opposite position yesterday, but under the *Schreuer / Simma* restraint for the UN to use force in serious human rights situations, I think we just reached a consensus. I do not have good enough arguments to continue to not support that, although I think that the current rule would not support it as interpreted in a traditional way.

Finally, I am surprised that nobody has talked about, at least with regard to *Bruno*'s comments, actually putting into effect Article 43 as a means of accomplishing your organized community response. *Michael* said yesterday that we need to backup our request for security or request for change with real intent to use force. It seems to me that if we have the Article 45 standing force in place and we have a Security Council committed to use force and it is convenient to use it because a force is there, that would give us some of the commitment to use force that *Michael* talked about yesterday.

The points are much briefer for Professor *Frowein:* I was surprised when you said that intervention in civil war would not be against the state. It has always been my view that if we stop recognizing the state during ongoing armed conflict, we may no longer find a government in effective control, but the international community tends not to derecognize the state and require new recognition. In most cases there is one part of a state that even continues after a civil war and without need for new recognition of its smaller status. I think your paradigm was built on the view that we do not intervene against a state, we intervene in civil war. Well, I will wait for you to clarify; that is what I heard and had a note on.

You also made a comment (maybe I heard this one wrongly as well) that there are no limits on economic sanctions when used as countermeasures. And then your next comment went on to say that in fact you can use economic sanctions to enforce *erga omnes* norms. I think those are somewhat inconsistent. My view is that there are limits on the use of economic sanctions and that you have got to use them under the countermeasures rules, so that if you are responding to an *erga omnes* violation, you can use economic sanctions. But when you use economic sanctions, you are inevitably terminating trade treaties, terminating your GATT requirements, freezing assets, doing a host of things that require a violation of international law, usually by terminating treaties. And in order to do that, you have got to be in the countermeasures category. We should be using economic sanctions, but I think the way the United States has used them without a sense of really responding to a real prior violation of international law has left the use of decentralized responses without control. But as you were arguing in favor of real control, you would probably end up by criticizing some of the U.S. uses of economic sanctions in recent years.

Tomuschat:

First of all I should like to thank the speakers of this morning for excellent and most stimulating presentations. I learned a great deal and so I have very little to say because I agree with the speakers on most points, though I do perceive some slight divergencies, which, however, are minimal and not very important.

Let me address just two issues. First of all, the issue of regional security arrangements: According to Article 53, any regional arrangement requires authorization by the Security Council for enforcement action. *Jochen Frowein* dealt with that issue. If in Europe we attempted to establish a European system of security, creating also a "European Council of Security," could we not then vest that European Security Council with exactly the same kind of powers as conferred upon the universal Security Council, and would such a European Security Council then in all instances require authorization by the world Security Council — which means that China would have a say in European matters? Just as states were able to submit to the authority of the Security Council, could they not also submit to the authority of a European Security Council with the effect that no further consent would be required for an enforcement action? I do think that it would be incompatible with peremptory rules of public international law to submit to unilateral decisions of just one state, as happened in the case of Cyprus. To submit to unilateral determinations by foreign states to intervene at whatever time they deem fit to do so is inconsistent with the sovereign equality of states. But I do not see the same obstacle in establishing a system according to which an organization with sufficient checks and guarantees and balances is vested with powers which resemble closely or which are almost identical to those of the Security Council. I fully acknowledge the existence of Article 103 of the Charter which sets forth that the provisions of the United Nations shall prevail in cases of conflict. But my question is: Why should we not be able to establish, for instance, by strengthening the CSCE mechanism, a system of security which would apply only to Europe, conferring on that new type of security council exactly the same powers as held by the present Security Council? That would be my question to *Jochen Frowein*.

Now I should like to address an issue raised by *Bruno Simma*. He rightly pointed out that obligations *erga omnes* are obligations which are value-orientated, as was clearly stated by the Court in the *Barcelona Traction* case. On the other hand, he also showed that we find ourselves in a transitional stage where the question is, what authorities are going to enforce those obligations of a new type, more precisely, those obligations involving new enforcement opportunities? However, where are the enforcers, who are the enforcers? Who really takes an interest in such enforcement action? And again the question is, if you opt for centralization of sanctions, should everything depend on the Security Council? Should any determination require the consent of China? I would draw a distinction between two types of situations. On the one hand — leaving apart for the moment the hypothesis of a European Security Council — states can resort to the use of force. Then, indeed, approval by the Security Council is needed. It is an achievement of the international community that no state may unilaterally resort to the use of force. But there are other instances, in particular, reprisals. Take the case of a violation of obligations *erga omnes*. Why should in all such instances authorization by the Security Council be required? That might lead to a situation where no countermeasures may be taken against the wrongdoer.

Interruption:

Military or non-military?

Tomuschat:

Non-military! I thought I understood you in the sense that sanctions of a non-forcible nature should also be authorized by the Security Council. This is how I took my notes, but if this is a misunderstanding, I am very glad, because it is necessary to have at least a fall-back position, a reserve potential for enforcement. *Jochen Frowein* rightly pointed out those cases — the *Tehran* case and countries which provide a safe haven to air pirates — where states should, for instance, be able to suspend any agreement on air traffic in force in order to compell the state which acts in such an irresponsible manner to behave correctly again. These are my two observations and I do apologize to *Bruno Simma* if I misunderstood him.

Simma:

I must apologize, because my deliberate ambiguities apparently went too far. Let me just remind you that — Professor *Frowein*, you will agree — I started writing about reprisals to enforce human rights, which made Professor *Frowein* write that maybe *Simma* went too far. I am very glad that *Christian Tomuschat* is now misunderstanding me in the sense that I am excluding all this. But I am still in favor. So I hope it is now clear what I mean.

Charney:

I also appreciate very much the excellent presentations that were given today and yesterday. Today's presentations contain, I believe, a fundamental assumption that I disagree with. I think both Professors *Frowein* and *Simma* and some of the other discussants made the assumption that there are or can be specific defined rules of international law that are classified as *erga omnes*, and that you can identify such rules. Professor *Frowein* used the term "legal title" in one context with respect to that, and Professor *Simma* talked about a process for establishing *erga omnes* norms. But both of their presentations also establish the difficulty of discerning or cataloguing those norms. Professor *Frowein* spoke about the prohibition of hostage-taking as being an *erga omnes* norm. But I do not believe that anybody has ever written about those norms as being *erga omnes*. They were, to now move to Professor *Simma*'s view, "spontaneously" declared or established as *erga omnes* norms. Just by the fact that you can "spontaneously" find and declare something to be *erga omnes,* it is very difficult to say that there is an established constitutional process for finding and clarifying what an *erga omnes* norm is. If you look at the *obiter dicta* in the *Barcelona Traction* case, and that is all it was, it also does not help very much to define what an *erga omnes* norm is. If you look at state practice and *opinio iuris,* I think you will have a very difficult time establishing a process by which a particular norm becomes *erga omnes.*

Nevertheless, I think historically, even before *Barcelona Traction,* third states have enforced rules of international law. The question then becomes, "What do you look at?" Perhaps it is advisible to systematize international law to find out what the commonalities of these rules are in order to help us identify the norms. I am more comfortable, at least at this stage, to say that there are no classes of norms that are *erga omnes.* In fact, it is a much more contextual facts-specific situation. One really should not cabin international law in order to define a particular rule as *erga omnes* or not. Surely, in international law *erga omnes* attempts to vindicate basic public international law principles, particularly in situations where there is no effective vehicle by bilateral means for enforcing a rule of international law. Thus, I would say that in the case of aggression against a state, where the state is fully capable of enforcing the rule of international law against the aggressor, there is no *erga omnes* norm allowing any other state to involve itself in that bilateral dispute. On the other hand, in a rather benign situation such as where there is significant pollution of the high seas and no injury to any specific state, there would be an *erga omnes* situation in which a third state or third states, depending on how you construct it, would be able to enforce the rule of international law. I would look at the nature of the violation, the bilateral remedies that are available, and the type of remedies that are under consideration. Is it the use of force where perhaps multilateral considerations are important? Or is it peaceful countermeasures where we perhaps might be more liberal in allowing third states to involve themselves in what might be assumed to be a bilateral situation?

I think one needs also to look to the question of the exhaustion of multilateral forums, I think Professor *Simma* spoke about that. Surely, it is appropriate to consider whether there is an available forum and what kind of remedies would be available. I was pleased to hear that Professor *Simma* is not suggesting that the UN Security Council — I may have misunderstood his presentation — would not, at least at present time (and I would not expect in the future), be the centre for coordinating third state enforcement of international law. The Security Council today has very limited subject matter jurisdiction. I would be very textual in that matter and ask whether or not the particular subject matter was one within the jurisdiction of the Security Council. I would not expect, even though there is talk about reformation of the Security Council and optimism, that it will be very effective in the future. I am not all that optimistic. I would not propose that the Security Council become the forum for coordinating third state enforcement nor do I expect the General Assembly to always or generally be a forum for doing that. It does not have any authority to actually take measures. One would have to look at specific regional and subject matter oriented organizations to see whether those forums should be exhausted before a third state could become involved in such enforcement practices. I would not foreclose the possibility that a third state, without actually going to an international forum, would have the right under international law in a specific case to enforce a rule that many would classify as an *erga omnes* norm.

Farer:

In light of *Christian Tomuschat*'s reference to what I call sub-global organizations, I would like to explore a little further the question of how to incorporate them into a preferred system of law enforcement. Specifically, we need to consider the extent to which and the circumstances in which such organizations should have authority to legitimate armed intervention. Sub-global organizations assume several forms. One is the regional organization anticipated by Chapter VIII of the Charter. Three are now recognized as such: The Organization of American States, the Organization of African Unity, and the Arab League. Why does the mantle not fall on other treaty-based associations of states? Because they have no stated or claimed peace-keeping function? No, since if that were a requirement, the OAU would not comply.

In fact, I have never encountered anything like an authoritative definition. The word "regional" suggests geographic propinquity of some sort, nothing more. One might ask whether insistence on this single type of intimacy should result in enhanced authority for an association of states. What about ideological or economic intimacy? Is some fundamental international community policy served by the distinction? Assuming, as I in fact would not, that Chapter VIII must be read literally and that the Security Council cannot use treaty organizations as agents for enforcement measures unless they satisfy the geographic-propinquity condition, should associations of states frequently labeled "sub-regional," associations like the Organization of Eastern Caribbean States, be seen as Chapter VIII organizations? Can propinquity be broken by water as in the case of the North Atlantic Treaty Organization? NATO itself was not a test case because it made clear its desire not to be considered a regional organization, but rather as a self-defense organization functioning under the aegis of Article 51.

The central issue, with which I am flirting, is whether any group of states can organize themselves on the basis of a collective or reciprocal right to intervene for whatever purposes they choose to enumerate. In other words, can states effectively cede to each other or a central authority they establish so substantial a part of their sovereignty as sovereignty has traditionally been conceived?

It would be interesting to see whether we have a consensus response to this question. I imagine that at least some of you will have reservations about an unqualified affirmative answer, fearing, perhaps, that it could result in the unintended legitimation of hegemonic relationships essentially like 19th Century protectorates. Perhaps you would feel comfortable with regional organizations simply because any association so perceived is almost certain to have a sufficiently large and diverse membership to preclude one member from practicing imperialism behind a facade of multilateralism. Or some may wish to draw distinctions on the basis of the precision with which intervention scenarios are defined in the governing treaty and / or the degree of consensus required to trigger the right to intervene. I presume, in any event, we would agree that an agreement to authorize intervention for ends or under circumstances in conflict with the purposes and principles of the United Nations Charter would be void.

The arrangement which, I suspect, is most likely to provoke unease among you is one in which states agree, apparently voluntarily, to cede a broad and largely undefined right of intervention and one of those states is far more powerful than all of the others combined. *Christian* expressed concern about pacts of this character, pacts with a hegemonic look to them. Of course you have ample reason for concern. Yet one can conceive of pacts guaranteeing, for example, human rights or democratic government, which, although incorporating a state with hegemonic capabilities, are nevertheless benign.

Naturally the hegemon will not enter the pact for wholly philanthropic reasons. Self-interest will be its guide. But if the hegemon is a liberal state, its broader interests are served by the survival, indeed by the proliferation of liberal regimes. To presume that such pacts are so inherently coercive as to make them legally ineffective as mandates for intervention on behalf of purposes and principles privileged by the UN Charter may prevent the formation of useful pacts. A number of leading theorists in the international relations field have argued, not unpersuasively, that enduring international regimes require a leader or hegemon able by its size to absorb short-term losses and to shrug off a certain degree of free-riding by smaller participants.

Stein:

I would like to come back briefly to some of the questions which I see linked to the limitations on the exercise of the right of self-defense under Article 51. Professor *Frowein* has identified, so to speak, two opposite poles: one being that if the Security Council adopts only recommendations under Article 39, the right under Article 51 would remain unaffected; and the second pole is that if the Security Council decides to take action under Article 42 of the Charter, then Article 51 ends. We reached agreement in the coffee break after the presentation that if the Security Council decides only to impose economic sanctions under Article 41, this would not affect the right of self-defense under Article 51.

The longer I think about it, the more I feel that it is probably not as easy as that. Article 51 gives a right to self-defense against an armed attack. An armed attack is, at the same time, an act of aggression, a breach of the peace; and in the case of an act of aggression or breach of the peace, Article 39 gives the Security Council the choice between, apart from recommendations, measures under Articles 41 or 42 in order to maintain or restore international peace and security. Article 51 uses the same terms "measures necessary to maintain international peace and security" for describing a situation in which the right of self-defense shall end if the Security Council has taken such measures. So it is probably not totally inconceivable that the Security Council decides that measures under Article 41 are all that is necessary at the moment, even *vis-à-vis* an armed attack. I still believe that the rule that measures under Article 41 do not preempt a state or coalition from using measures of self-defense is right, but we then have to find a reason for that, that is for saying that Article 41 measures may not be all that is "necessary" in a given situation. We would probably have to define the "necessary measures" in the sense of Article 51 as those which are likely to have the same effect as the self-defense options at hand in a given case.

Let me try to give an example: If in the Gulf crisis the coalition forces had been ready for combat much earlier than they actually were, at a stage where there was still some resistance in Kuwait and at a stage where the economic embargo imposed by the Security Council was in effect, would the coalition have been able to go on and move into Kuwait under Article 51, by saying, "Why should we sit here and wait until more territory is lost, until more lives are lost, facing an ongoing Iraqi aggression in Kuwait?" or would they have had to wait for a 678-type resolution? Or does it matter in that situation whether the Security Council has not yet authorized the use of force, because any such attempt has been vetoed so far? Or is the situation different if the Security Council has not authorized the use of force, because it deemed that authorization to be premature at the time? I also have certain doubts as to whether we can really strictly say that: once the Security Council has taken action under Article 42 — that is military measures — this preempts self-defense in all cases. If the Security Council decides to send in a battalion where one would reasonably expect two divisions to stop an ongoing attack, could one say that this battalion preempts self-defense?

Another rule, which Professor *Frowein* mentioned this morning, was that "authorization by the Security Council to use force takes away Article 51"; maybe my notes on this are too fragmentary, but it seems to me that even this rule is a relative one. What happens if the Security Council authorizes the use of force under Article 48 and then, for whatever political reasons, withdraws that authorization before the objectives named in the relevant decision have been achieved? Is the right of self-defense revived in that moment or not? Or is it revived if the objects which are named in the decision authorizing the use of force are achieved, but if it turns out that they have been framed too narrowly from the very beginning, and are therefore not sufficient to re-establish peace in that area?

I think maybe those rules are a bit relative in themselves. We probably have to say that states are preempted from exercising their individual or collective right of self-defense under Article 51 only if the Security Council takes or authorizes measures which can reasonably be deemed to be as effective as any proportionate self-defense options at hand in the given case ("proportionate self-defense options" means that, if the Security Council has taken, or authorized to take, the necessary conventional military measures, states which are prepared to do so may certainly not invoke Article 51 for saying, "We will use non-conventional weapons and do the job faster than the Security Council"). I think that is the way we have to define Article 51.

Wolfrum:

According to Mr. *Schreuer,* the more severe the enforcement measures are, the more they require a collective legitimization. This statement was not objected to by anyone so far, and I believe that the other speakers would be ready to accept it. However, it brings up a very crucial question: What really legitimizes an enforcement action? Mr. *Schreuer* referred to the parallel in national administrative law systems; police may only act on the basis of law. The respective law is to be found in Chapter VII of the United Nations Charter. When the United Nations Charter was drafted, especially the United States delegation argued that enforcement action should be decided on a purely political level, and therefore the legitimization should come from procedure rather than value judgments. This approach did not materialize to 100 per cent in the Charter, which represents a compromise. As far as the enforcement under Chapter VII is concerned, values as well as limitations are of relevance. Certain value judgments are frozen in Article 39 and can be derived from the Preamble as well as Articles 1 and 2 of the Charter. This applies to forcible as well as economic measures. However, Article 39 is, by referring to the "threat to the peace," open to a progressive interpretation. Therefore, it is possible that, by a decision of the Security Council, this notion can be given a far-reaching meaning.

This leads to the next question as to whether such progressive interpretation can be challenged either by a member state or the International Court of Justice. With respect to the member states, Article 25 is the relevant rule. Through it, member states have accepted Security Council decisions as binding. The words "in accordance with the Charter" as used in Article 25 do not open the possibility for member states to challenge the legality of a Security Council decision. Any other interpretation would seriously undermine the effectiveness of the system of collective security as provided by Chapter VII. The position of the International Court of Justice is different in this respect. Hence, the allegation that the Security Council has exceeded its functions can be brought before the Court.

What are the rules concerning peace-keeping? There are no rules in the UN Charter in this respect, and therefore one may ask for the legitimization of the respective measures. It is to be derived from the consent of the states or parties involved in the stationing of peace-keeping forces. Mr. *Frowein* raised the question whether this consent, as has been the case, can be withdrawn during action. I would tend to agree with him that, at least *de lege ferenda,* this consent should not be withdrawn after action has started so that the troops can pursue their functions until the mandate has been fulfilled.

May I draw attention to another aspect. Although this symposium might be in agreement that peace-keeping actions draw their legitimacy from the consent of the states concerned, developing countries have argued to the contrary on some occasions, by indicating that consent was not the only prerequisite. Some objections were voiced against calling in peace-keeping forces to Haiti, to have them involved in El Salvador, etc. Although this attitude did not prevail, one has to accept that at least some members of the community require further legitimation for peace-keeping operations, not only consent from the states concerned.

Let me now turn to the action on the regional, sub-global, or the contractual level. Certainly, the legitimacy of these actions lie in the contract or agreement providing for such regional agreements. Mr. *Tomuschat,* while drawing our attention to Article 103, has raised a very important point: What is the interrelationship between those sub-global or regional organizations on the one hand, and the United Nations on the other hand? One has to differentiate. The subsystem may function under the mandate of the Security Council. In this case, the legitimacy of such system is beyond doubt. It is another question whether a sub-global organization may function without such a mandate. In my view this question should be answered affirmatively; states may agree amongst themselves for a system which is similar to the United Nations system, in spite of Article 103 UN Charter. Unilateral forcible measures can be undertaken under the UN system, as has been pointed out by Mr. *Frowein,* under Article 48, a provision which has long been neglected. It is, however, questionable as to whether unilateral forcible measures can be undertaken on a unilateral basis without that mandate. I would not go into Article 51 again, but rather switch over to another issue focussed upon by Mr. *Simma,* namely, the *erga omnes* norms. In my view, *erga omnes* norms should be looked upon as a means of providing for unilateral non-forcible measures. They result in improving the enforcement mechanism. When it comes to the enforcement of *erga omnes* norms, third states, even those not directly involved, not only have a mandate, but may even be obliged to take a stand against the wrongdoer through economic means. Furthermore, states are under an obligation to provide aid for those states enforcing the *erga omnes* norms.

Riedel:

A lot of what I was going to comment upon has been said in a very erudite fashion by the speakers before. So I will try and be as short as possible. I should like to address myself to an issue that has been on our mind all the time both yesterday and today. It has not been mentioned very frequently, namely, the actual attempts of the enforcement measures in the recent Gulf War. It has been in the back of our minds but we have not dicussed it. That is really a test case in one of the most serious incidents where there have been acts of aggression and at least breaches of the peace.

If you look at what happened in that context, we find that at the United Nations system level the whole scale of possible actions were in fact utilized. If you look at Resolutions 660 right down to 678, you have the Article 39 or 40 approach with Resolutions 660 to 664; you have the Article 41 situations with blockades, assets freezing, boycotts, embargoes and the setting up of the Committee of the Security Council under Resolutions 661 to 665; and you have reference to the possibility of having recourse — if that does not work and if the Security Council would not work — to operate under Article 51 as the last resort; and, moreover, using the Secretary General under Resolution 677 as the good offices possibility. You had the whole array displayed before the Article 42 measures were actually put into effect. That, to my mind, was all an exercise of Chapter VI and "Chapter VI and a half" right up to January the 15th.

Then under Article 42 Mr. *Frowein* apparently seemed to be questioned by Mr. *Simma* with regard to his scale of recommendations under Article 39, decisions under Articles 49 and then 42 and 48, and the residual function of Article 51. Mr. *Simma,* I did not see exactly where your point of divergence was with Mr. *Frowein*'s analysis. I fully agree with Mr. *Frowein* when he pointed out that under Article 42 you have the Articles 43/47 situation under full UN control or the Articles 42/48 situation of either individual states' delegation under UN command or collective state delegation under the command of the coalition, and it was only in this last instance, the approach actually adopted under Resolution 678, that the difficulty arose whether there is in fact a clear mandate to keep it under the Security Council control or whether the residual function of Article 51 crept up just in different words.

In my opinion, as soon as you apply the *Schreuer*-formula — that the more severe the violation of the norm, the more necessary the collective action — if you apply that test here, as soon as you enter the Articles 42, 43 and 48 level, then there is no question that there is no room for Article 51. To that extent I would contradict Mr. *Stein*. However, I am not so sure, and I would like to know what Mr. *Simma,* Mr. *Schreuer,* and particularly Mr. *Frowein* think of Mr. *Stein*'s argument that if Article 41 does not work in a situation, or if in an individual situation self-defense it should be felt right, whether these are sufficient grounds to fall back on Article 51. To put it bluntly, it is a threshold problem. You can either say it is an Article 39 action or recommendation, or you can say it goes all the way through and whenever the Security Council is not up to scratch, then you can fall back on Article 51.

I suspect that Resolution 678 in fact tried to have it both ways and left it entirely open, because the language used "decides to remain seized," originally "*actively* seized of the matter," sounded as though this was under full control of the Security Council, which in fact it was not. Therefore, I think what we need here is a clear indication, and at least from a scholary point of view we should come out in favour of the collective UN-enforcement measures approach. As soon as you have an Article 42 situation, you must insist on the collective responses, and Article 51 with its individual self-defense or collective self-defense approach should not override that. This seems to me to be the only answer.

Delbrück:

Thank you very much. I should like to change roles, leave the chair symbolically and make an objection here. I think, legally speaking, the situation was quite clear: the Security Council did say it remained seized. Politically, it may have been difficult to do it otherwise, to remove the Gulf action from the agenda, or to have a new decision taken whether to stop it, or whether to continue or to broaden the mandate; but again legally speaking, it was a clear-cut situation: that the Security Council remained seized of the matter and perceived the actions taken as not falling under Article 51 without expressly saying so.

Bothe:

I would like to join in Prof. *Schreuer*'s appeal to see to it that the rule of law determines also the action taken by the Security Council. In this sense I would like to make a few comments on some of the issues which were raised and which have been debated in the afternoon. One of the fundamental issues in my view is whether there is anything in between collective self-defense on the one hand and enforcement actions taken by the Security Council, in the narrow sense, on the other. Both rapporteurs have said there is. The Security Council may choose an intermediate way of not running the whole enforcement action itself, but authorizing states to do the job. This was indeed the case in the Gulf-Kuwait crisis. If it is a correct interpretation of the Charter to consider this as legally admissible, you have to forget the first sentence of Article 42, which says that it is the Security Council who takes the military action; it is the Security Council who runs the show. I do not say that it is impossible, when interpreting the Charter, to forget one or the other sentence. It is done quite frequently, but you have to be clear about what you are doing: a non-literal interpretation of the Charter.

This stance was, for example, adopted by the International Court of Justice in the *Namibia* case, when it had to find some general powers of the Security

Council to justify the decisions actually taken by the Council, because the specific powers were of no help. However, it is necessary to think twice before we take such a stance, which, to a certain extent at least, is, I would perhaps not say in contradiction, but somewhat at odds with the text. Prof. *Frowein* rightly pointed to the precedent of Rhodesia, where indeed the same approach was taken, yet that was a very limited action. What we had in the Gulf case, however, showed all the possibilities which may ensue if this is accepted as a general possibility. It means that the Security Council can waive its control of the situation, just abdicate and say to a state or a group of states, "You can do what you like." Whether this is a desirable interpretation of the Charter, if we think of the rule of law, I have my doubts.

Along the same lines I have some problems with Prof. *Simma*'s thesis that a determination made under Article 39 may serve as a justification for action taken by states. True, a determination envisaged by Article 39 is a binding decision, binding according to Article 25, but you cannot extend that binding effect beyond the actual scope of Article 39. Article 39 is a determination of a certain situation. If the determination is that "that state is the aggressor," then it clearly follows from Article 51 that there is a right of individual and collective self-defense. If the determination just says, "there is a threat to peace, please will everybody behave," then that is all it says. The latter kind of determination, in my view, cannot justify any unilateral action. Thus, it is possible that a determination under Article 39 can serve as a justification for the use of force, but it really depends on the concrete content of that determination.

I have also some problems with the question of how far the right of individual and collective self-defense is maintained in the case of action being taken by the Security Council. If one takes Article 51 literally, any action taken by the Security Council, including Article 41 action, constitutes an exercise of the responsibility of the Security Council "measures necessary to maintain international peace and security" within the meaning of Article 51. If the Security Council then decides, "we first start with economic sanctions," there is an implicit judgment that this is what is necessary and appropriate at the time. So, in all logic, the right of individual and collective self-defense no longer works, the Security Council has taken over. Now, this is perhaps a little bit difficult to accept in terms of . . .

Stein:

Unrealistic!

Bothe:

Yes, but sometimes logic is unrealistic! If we interpret the Charter, I think the first thing is to try be logical and then we have to accomodate certain interests. I agree with that, but I want to be intellectually honest, which is why I take this as the starting point. The members of the Security Council in the Gulf crisis were aware of that logic, of course they were. This is why there is a formula in the preamble of the first resolution which can be understood and, I am told, was understood as constituting a waiver of that logic by the Security Council. It is an interesting question whether the Security Council is indeed empowered to waive that consequence which would follow from Article 51. If the Security Council may authorize the use of force without being limited to measures under Article 42, why should it not also waive the limitation on the use of force which would otherwise follow from Article 51?

I have a number of additional problems along these lines. I would like to concentrate, however, on the issue of enforcement of *erga omnes* norms. I still think they exist. Indeed, they exist in the field of human rights and in that of humanitarian law, where they can be deduced from the text of article 1 of the Geneva Conventions. They exist and are being developed in international environmental law. A similar situation exists in internal law where there are also problems concerning the choice of appropriate actors in the enforcement process. There we have, in a way, a different line of reasoning. Generally, it is government agencies who are in charge of enforcing *erga omnes* norms, norms which serve the public or general interests in contradistinction to individual interests. This applies especially to the field of environmental law, but to many other fields as well: competition law, consumer protection, etc. In these cases, there is a certain tendency towards decentralized enforcement by citizens' suits, associations' suits and similar procedures. I think what is desirable both in international and national law is a good mix of both. There is a lot of decentralized enforcement in international relations, there should be more central enforcement. There is too much emphasis on enforcement by states, there is a need for other actors, too. We have an example in the Geneva Conventions where there is a non-governmental organization in charge of some enforcement (or call it: implementation) functions, which is the International Committee of the Red Cross, a non-governmental organization in a certain sense at least. This is an example which could be followed in other fields of *erga omnes* norms as well.

Tomuschat:

It is suggested that the Basic Law of the Federal Republic of Germany be amended to allow action or contribution by German troops to enforcement action by the Security Council, second blue helmet actions, but not to actions authorized by the Security Council. I think this is interesting for the further debate.

Reisman:

May I join the other colleagues who have congratulated the speakers of this morning. This has been a feast of ideas, a stimulating review of the literature and a very provoking and useful examination of critical texts. It will take me quite some time to absorb it. I have a number of comments on some of the issues. I make them tentatively in the spirit of contributing to the debate and particularly to some of the questions *Bruno* raised toward the end of his discussion.

Christoph Schreuer put his finger on something critical when he said that we need a teleological interpretation. Chapter VII of the United Nations Charter is a constitution. A constitution is not, as *Oliver Wendell Holmes* said, a suicide pact. It has to be interpreted in a way that yields the results for which it was established. Chapter VII deals with maintaining security when there is a threat or an accomplished act that puts the community in jeopardy. As we move into the 21st century, we have to follow *Christoph*'s guide and look teleologically at the basic policies of Chapter VII. As a matter of preference, the Security Council should try to take control of the matter. It should try to use assets around the world, including those of regional organizations and of individual states or groups of states. It should use less rather than more coercion.

But we cannot establish rigid priorities between the series of policies and say, for example, that if the Security Council has seized itself of the matter, competences under Article 51 are always excluded. I agree with Prof. *Stein*. The issue is sensitivity to context while never losing sight of the basic goal, which is to restore the order that has been breached. This is best achieved by teleological interpretation in context, following the basic policies of the documents. It also requires us to acknowledge that in some cases for all purposes and in some cases for particular purposes, certain designs from 1945 may not work in 1992 or in the 21st century.

I have reservations as to *Christoph Schreuer*'s notion that, with regard to the use of coercion, the more intense the coercion, the more inclusive it should be and the more we would like the Council as a whole to conduct it. I think it depends on the situation. Bear in mind that in some circumstances economic sanctions, which we characterize as less injurious or less damaging, may in fact be more damaging than would be military action! I cite the economic sanctions taken by the United States against Panama, which reduced the economy to rubble, and the economic sanctions taken by the Organization of American States against Haiti, which turned a desperate situation for the people there into an impossible one. In some circumstances, as undesirable and as violent as military action may be, it may be less value consumptive than would be an economic sanctions program. Here again, context is very important.

With regard to context, I suggest that *Christian Tomuschat*'s notion should be subjected to contextual interpretation. A unilateral military intervention treaty, such as the one between the former Soviet Union and the former Empire of Iran, which gave Moscow a unilateral right to intervene, under circumstances that *it* would determine, for objectives that *it* would determine, would certainly raise serious questions under contemporary international law. However, a right of protection by one state over another state where the concerns of abuse are much less might pass muster if we knew what the goals were, had a juridical technique for scrutinizing options, and could minimize abuse. Under General Assembly Resolutions 1514 and 1541 of 1960, free associations may be established in which one state may sign over its foreign policy to another state. It can get awfully close to the example you are concerned with, indeed to the extreme example that *Tom Farer* raised and then dismissed as beyond the pale of consideration.

Prof. *Frowein*'s notion of general authorizations to regional or sub-global organizations could actually enhance the authority assigned to the Security Council, for it could be used more efficiently in future crises. In some circumstances, you may get more effective international action if the Council is *not* involved. I cite as an example Cambodia. The tragedy of Cambodia was moving towards a solution, pressed largely by Australia and a group of states in the region, until France insisted that the matter be brought into the Security Council. That, of course, brought China into things. China is the protector of the Khmer Rouge. So now we have a solution that includes the Khmer Rouge who are the spoilers. Under the Australian procedure, we were moving towards a solution that would have effectively quarantined the Khmer Rouge and substantially reduced their role.

In deciding whether or not the sub-global, or regional, or the Security Council is the appropriate level, we have to look at the type of problem, the context, the composition of the Security Council, and the interests of the Permanent Members in the problem. Professor *Frowein*'s notion of a general authorization that can be achieved at moments of international consensus, when, in particular, the five Permanent Members agree, has another advantage. It can act as a deterrent *pro futuro* to would-be aggressors who would assume, in the absence of such a general authorization, that once they have accomplished their own illicit objectives, one of the Permanent Members will block the Security Council.

There are already implicit patterns of this general authorization. I referred to ECOMOG in West Africa where a sub-sub-regional organization, which had no military components, found itself, in effect, regulating and gradually bringing under control a civil war, in a country in which incidentally there was no longer any government.

Bruno Simma raises the issue of *erga omnes* norms. I was not certain as to how various norms entered into the magic *erga omnes* circle. Some of the norms that he mentioned represent policies I agree with, but I think one would have a hard case in trying to establish that they are law. A norm is essentially a statement made in a subjunctive mood: "You ought to put your coat on when you go outside"; "You ought to take your hat off when you go into church." A normative statement is not necessarily law. A norm is lawful when, in addition to having authority, it also creates an expectation that there are a number of critical actors or the community as a whole who are willing to invest resources to make it effective. I fear that a lot of the *erga omnes* norms that *Bruno* was talking about may not achieve that status.

By the way, I do not understand why a theory that allows for *erga omnes* norms that are created by a general, diffused and complex law-making process, which includes CNN, CSPAN and BBC, does not also allow for a complex law-enforcing process, which may include unilateral action. If some of the *erga omnes* norms you are particularly concerned about do not have some unilateral enforcement, they will not be enforced.

Let me conclude these remarks by briefly commenting on military intervention, since it is a primary technique for enforcing some *erga omnes* norms concerned with human rights. No one in the world — with the exception of those of us who are convened here today — is altruistic. Everyone is motivated by self-interest. When there has been a humanitarian intervention to stop gross violations of human rights, the critical question is not the motive of the party that intervened. The question is the gravity of the evil that the intervenor has addressed and whether it is removed at that particular moment. The motive is not critical.

Panama is both a good and a bad example of this issue. In Panama, a government run violently by a dictator who had no popular authority was removed by a military intervention. It was messy, but the *Endara* government, now in place, was elected in a free election, certified by international observers. For a year and a half before the United States intervention, the Inter-American Commission of the Organization of American States routinely issued communiqués and reports lamenting the denial of democracy in Panama. After the intervention, it began to issue reports congratulating the Panamanian people on the restoration of democracy. It also issued several statements condemning the United States for intervening in Panama. Somehow, no one made the link between the fact that that intervention was the *sine qua non* factor that ended the dictatorship and restored a popularly elected government.

Rubin:

Fortunately, much of what I have to say has been said by *Jonathan Charney* and *Mike Reisman*. But there are some supplemental things worth mentioning.

I should like to emphasize a point made, I think, by *Bruno Simma* in passing, mentioned afterwards perhaps by *Christoph Schreuer*, that if the Security Council had the authority it might claim under a literal reading of parts of the Charter, it might begin to act in ways that are not consistent with our notion of when collective action is appropriate. It might act more in ways that the Holy Alliance used to act; assuming a supervisory responsibility for the forms of government internal to states. The dangers seem to me not only political but also legal; the Charter cannot properly be read in bits and pieces, but, like other legal documents, must be read as a whole. The great powers and other groupings have their own agendas; to allow the Security Council competence to determine the outer reaches of its own authority is to invite abuses of this competence as well as abuses of the authority derived from it.

There are ameliorating steps that could be taken without major changes in the institution. It is possible, for example, to provide that the Security Council cannot "decide" on enforcement measures that cost money without the equivalent of an appropriation by the General Assembly *via* the regular UN budget, or by voluntary contributions by members of the UN who are not in arrears in their regular assessments. The United States is nearly two years in arrears right now. It is also possible to require all states participating in an enforcement action to accept an obligation to pay for the injuries (beyond what the law of war permits) done by their troops. Alternatively, the Security Council could be required to accept that potential legal liability as a community cost; or a cost-sharing arrangement could be required, similar to the division of liability that has been part of the NATO Status of Forced Agreement, article VIII, for about forty years. Another idea would be to pre-position a tribunal with authority to measure the conformity of UN-sponsored enforcement action against the laws of war, including the justifiability of "collateral damage," and to evaluate the injuries that unlawful activities cause. It might be noted that the United States agreed to pay Iran for the accidental destruction by the USS Vincennes of an Iranian civil airliner during the Iran-Iraq war; although the offer was of an *ex gratia* payment and the American Congress has not yet appropriated the funds, the obligation was accepted in principle by President *Reagan* and there is no reason to believe that appropriate wording cannot be found for setting up an institution for evaluating similar situations to encourage similar *ex gratia* settlements.

As to obligations *erga omnes,* I believe I go even further than Prof. *Reisman.* I doubt that there are any such obligations in strict law. If there are any such, then I certainly do not believe that there is any evidence other than the wishful thinking of some publicists that they extend to the human rights area. I do not understand what other source there can be for the obligation than the consciences of publicists who have no money to spend, no troops to send, no children likely to die in a military action. It seems to me that we are reduced to publicists' consciences, a subsidiary means of determining the law under article 38, paragraph 1 (d), of the Statute of the ICJ and, in this case, not clearly consistent with any treaty obligations, practices of states accepted as law, or general principles recognized as applicable in the municipal laws of many states without eviscerating exceptions.

On the other hand, I can agree with Prof. *Charney* that in some cases, like pollution of the high seas, there is a legal problem and universal standing might be part of the evolving law. But not yet. I would not categorize pollution of the high seas as an *erga omnes* situation. No state is defending the rights of a third;

it is the acting state's right to equal access to the resources of the sea that is being protected on its own behalf. The usual citation to the universal condemnation of genocide is particularly enlightening. Under the Genocide Convention, the "crime" is clearly *removed* from the category of *erga omnes* offenses. The only legal order empowered under the Convention to act in the case of an accusation of genocide is the state with territorial authority over the place in which the alleged genocide occurred. I know nothing that has happened since the Convention was concluded to indicate a change in the position of the parties on the issue of standing. Who intervened to prevent "genocide" in Cambodia (if massive killings ostensibly for political and economic reform are genocide at all — another question that brings the "humanitarian" scope of the prohibition into doubt)? And were there no self-proclaimed "humanitarian" powers condemning the Vietnamese intervention? I am not satisfied that there is any treaty or practice to support the common assertions.

I also agree with *Bruno Simma* that before anything can be defined as *erga omnes* it is necessary to define the *"omnes"* — what group or individual can get the "standing" that is supposed to be universal? Can any individual, state, or organization enforce its version of the "universal" law against anybody? Can a third party from half-way around the world come in and rectify something in which it has no legally significant interest? I know of no actions *erga omnes* permitted in any municipal legal order, including the Roman Law that used the term in a rather special sense. The notion cannot rest on "general principles of law recognized by civilized nations." Nor is it based on practices accepted as law, nor on treaties.

I also have problems with the notion of *ius cogens*. The frequent assumption that any violation of a human rights norm of law is a violation of *ius cogens* seems to me exaggerated. There are many violations of norms of international law that have legal consequences, and it does not help the discussion of those consequences to insist that the applicable norms are part of the *ius cogens*, assuming there are any norms of international law that are *ius cogens*.

Finally, I would not want to leave my other American colleague, Prof. *Farer*, out. I have a lot of difficulty with the notion that some less-than-universal organization should have the legal authority to suppress revolutions that we do not like, whether or not anti-democratic. Since when is revolution illegal as a matter of public international law? Revolutions are always "illegal" under the municipal law of the country whose constitutional authorities they are trying to overthrow, but as a matter of public international law the argument was made seriously only between 1814 and 1848. With apologies to our Austrian colleagues, *Metternich* no longer sets the rules. The Holy Alliance can no longer determine the public order of Europe or the world, even when called the OECD or the Security Council of the United Nations. The United States, among many other countries, was founded in a revolution and our great revolutionary ancestors were called traitors and criminals by the defending British, as indeed they were by British law. *John Paul Jones*, our first Navy hero, was called a "pirate" by them and actually expelled from The Netherlands at British insistence; he went to Le Havre, where he fitted his ship out for battle with French blessing. I do not think that it is legally possible to make revolution illegal by treaty.

Can a ruling elite invite foreigners in to maintain their authority? If so, whom does that elite represent? Do they, the ruling elite, represent the state that they say adheres to that treaty, or do they represent themselves fighting against the will of the "state" that they purport to represent? It seems to me that there is a real distinction between governments and states. Most governments represent the states whose constitutions put them in positions of legal authority; some do not represent the state in any meaningful sense, although it would be much more convenient for lawyers if they did. I conclude that the kind of treaty that Prof. *Farer* suggests, under which third party intervention would be appropriate to preserve what we elites agree to be fundamental principles, in disregard of what the people being ruled by those principles might believe, itself violates a fundamental principle of the international legal order. Such a treaty would probably be void. One could say that it violates *ius cogens*.

Farer:

Prof. *Rubin* asked for municipal law analogies with respect to standing. If I walk down the street and I see my friend *Bruno* being beaten to a pulp by someone, I am certainly authorized to intervene and use appropriate force to terminate the threat to his life. That is to mention one municipal law . . .

Reisman:

You run a risk when you do that.

Farer:

You asked for the municipal law analogies. There it is.

Rubin:

Municipal law occasionally gives standing to a passerby; it does not give standing to people who have no knowledge of the facts in adequate detail. If you intervene and then discover that *Bruno* is the mugger, you will be in some jeopardy under the applicable municipal law. All systems that I know of place such limits on the competence of third parties to authorize themselves to intervene in matters that only peripherally concern them. And when they are authorized to intervene, they act for the community under strict rules limiting their authority to judge for themselves the propriety of their intervention.

Morrison:

I want to thank all the speakers of today and yesterday. Yesterday we began with some elegant presentations about the background structure of things that had to be considered in establishing the law. Today we have gone much more deeply into the law itself and my commentary may go even beyond that down to the practical level. To some degree that takes me back to some of the questions of the first day, because the practical level is the use of the intermediate level of text to achieve the goals that were talked about in the first day.

One of the things that has disturbed me in a way is a mixing of Chapter VII as all one thing. But Chapter VII is clearly protecting two rather distinct interests which overlap. One of them is the interest of the community in the reduction of the use of hostilities, and the other is the interest of the individual state in the preservation of itself from hostile attacks. Those are the two anchors for Articles 49 and 51. These interests are a quite different and, I think, balanced. This is one of the reasons I would disagree with Prof. *Schreuer* that necessarily, as the use of force increases, the central authority increases, because the use of force in the Article 51 situation is the use of force which concentrates upon the interests of the particular attacked state, while the use of force in an Article 39/42 situation is the use of force which concentrates upon the interest of the community as a whole in the reduction of hostilities within the community.

In this regard it seems to me that, of course, our biggest concern and our biggest problem is the possibility under the Security Council practice and under the veto that there will be no decision at all coming out of the Security Council. And what happens in this circumstance? But it is also a problem of what will happen if there is only a partial decision. This is a problem but is not one which we are really willing to solve. One which we will look at and say, "Yes this is too bad, we are sorry, Austria will be swallowed up." Just to take one example where we will only impose minor economic sanctions. Does Austria in that example have the right or not to respond?

I think one of the things that has been omitted today in the use of the words "maintain international peace and security" is that some of the adjectives and some of the tenses are different, as you move between Articles 51 and 42. The adjectives that I will refer to are "inherent" and "necessary," and the tense I will take with that. First, Article 51 talks about an inherent right, not just a right. That seems to give it a particular strength and it seems to me that the particular strength of the inherent right would require at least an explicit action to limit it, not an implicit negation because an action has or has not been taken under another article. Secondly, if you look at that language about "maintain international peace and security," it appears in Article 39, but that is simply determining the existence of a threat to peace. The Security Council shall determine the existence of a threat to peace; there is no physical action called for in Article 39. The language does not appear in Article 41. It does appear in Article 42, in a subjunctive future tense, whether action "may be necessary." It appears again in Article 51 in a present perfect tense "has taken." The existence of a resolution that something "may be necessary" is not the same as "having taken action." It is a step towards action, but it is not "having taken" action. It is the initiation of the process towards that, but it is not the perfect tense "taken." It is very difficult to argue from the language alone that simply Article 41 or 42 or some resolution under Articles 41 and 42 are automatically *per se* enough to limit Article 51 self-defense rights until the action has in fact been taken and succeeded. This is particularly so because of the different interest that is being protected.

Finally, I was going to comment about the words "actively seized." I have always assumed that the language "actively seized" in those resolutions is Article 12 language to keep the General Assembly out. It means nothing more whatsoever.

Schreuer:

I will try to be brief and also selective, something I abhor in the context of human rights, but which is necessary here.

Mary Ellen raised the interesting question to what extent states are under an obligation to aid in the enforcement of obligations *erga omnes*. I think there must be a differentiated answer. Certain reactions would be obligatory, for instance, non-recognition of situations created by such a violation or the obligation of not aiding a violator. When it comes to more coercive reaction, it is rather difficult to argue in favour of an obligation. For instance, I would be rather hesitant to argue that there is a general obligation to join in economic sanctions unless there is an institutional framework for such an obligation. That, in a sense, underlines the necessity of such an institutional framework to create a prospective obligation in situations of this kind.

Mary Ellen also raised the question as to the limits of economic sanctions. Are states, or for that matter even international institutions, free to take any economic sanction, any non-military sanction? My answer very clearly is "No." I think it was a tacit assumption when we spoke this morning that economic sanctions too have to be appropriate and proportionate. This leads to the next question. I am not a great believer in the strict dichotomy between military and non-military coercion. In fact, as *Michael Reisman* pointed out, non-military reactions can be extremely coercive, perhaps just as coercive as military sanctions. Therefore, some economic sanctions like strangling an economy to starvation should fall under community or inclusive competence. This is not to shift military action away from the coercive end of the spectrum and hence open them up for unilateral actions.

Mr. *Tomuschat* has raised the question of a "European Security Council" and any limitations on such a regional body. Obviously, the first answer is that there need to be checks and balances on the regional as well as on the universal level.

The question, of course, is: Do we absolutely need the UN Security Council to check such a regional body? If there are appropriate regional checks and balances, perhaps not. On the other hand, it would be highly undesirable to establish divergent practices and standards on the regional and on the universal levels for questions as important and basic as the use of force. In terms of the UN Charter we have Article 103, which clearly tells us what to do in case of conflict with other treaty obligations.

Tom Farer has presented us a complex matrix. This matrix seems to be dominated by the criterion of formal authorization by the territorial states. You were talking about various forms of intervention by invitation. However, I am wondering whether that is the only relevant or even the most relevant question. The obvious answer may be to look to what extent these invitations conform or conflict with obligations *erga omnes*.

This leads me directly to Mr. *Wolfrum*'s remarks about consent. He asked rethorically, "Is consent enough for blue helmet activities?" Again, I cannot give a simple "Yes" or "No" answer. Consent may be an important element. We also have to ask ourselves what we mean by consent. Does it only mean *ad hoc* consent to the particular activity when the situation arises? Or does it include consent that may have been expressed historically in a treaty twenty or thirty years ago? Does the consent continue to be valid after the state that has given *ad hoc* consent changes its mind and no longer wants the blue helmets or whoever acts externally on its territory? Again, this may be a formal perspective which should not be decisive. For example, if action is necessary to counter violations for which the local government is responsible, consent is obviously not decisive. If the intervention by the Security Council or by a regional organization has been initiated to stop human rights violations by the local government, consent is clearly not relevant. Again, we have to adopt a more value-oriented approach to these questions.

Torsten Stein has raised the very interesting problem of ineffective Security Council action. Mr. *Morrison* has also raised that problem. In other words, what happens if the Security Council seems to act, at least formally, but is acting ineffectively, for instance by imposing an ineffective blockade under Article 42, which has no noticeable impact? If you read Article 51, you may get the answer. Article 51 refers to "measures necessary to maintain international peace and security." Again, we should not opt for a formal answer. The fact that the Security Council has acted in one way or another should not mean that this is the end of Article 51. Also, the difference between Article 41 and Article 42 should not be seen too rigidly. The question is whether the Security Council really has dealt with the question effectively, not whether it has been seized or whether it has cited any particular article in one of its resolutions.

Bothe:

Is the decision of the Security Council implying a holding that the action taken is the one which is necessary not binding?

Schreuer:

It depends for what. It is certainly binding in operative terms. If the Security Council says that a blockade should be maintained, that is binding. However, that should not necessarily preclude the state that has been attacked from exercising self-defense. Action by the Security Council merely creates a strong presumption of illegality for forcible unilateral action, especially by a third state.

Mr. *Wolfrum* has briefly spoken about procedural legitimacy. I have already pointed out that procedural legitimacy in terms of inclusive action is an important element. However, it is not enough. As *Michael Reisman* has pointed out, there are values in the Charter. We have to find these values but not only in historical terms but also in the way they change over time.

Alfred Rubin has raised a number of questions. Let me just address one of them. He said that the Security Council should not be allowed to act unless it has clarified the question of financing. No doubt, financing is an important technical problem. It must be resolved, but I rather doubt whether it is best resolved in terms of a limitation of essential action by the Security Council. This reminds me of horror stories we sometimes get in the European press about American hospitals, withholding essential treatment from patients until they come up with a guarantee that they are able to foot the hospital bill. This is not the kind of alternative that I would cherish.

In reply to Mr. *Morrison*'s remark concerning my preference for inclusive action when it comes to more coercive situations: My statement was not one of fact or necessarily of existing law, but a policy preference derived from the general structure of the Charter. For me, Article 51 is simply a sign of imperfection. It is necessary as a residual authority for unilateral action but still a sign of imperfection.

Finally to Mr. *Bothe,* who was unhappy about the way we interpret Articles 42 and 51 and accept intermediate solutions. It has been mentioned several times that the Charter is a living body. We cannot address it only in terms of what the founding fathers had in mind in San Francisco in 1945. Mr. *Bothe* also pointed to the dangers of giving too much discretion to the Security Council and to states authorized to act by the Security Council. Perhaps we can encapsule our entire discussion in the sentiment that on the one hand we want a maximum of effectiveness of protection for obligations *erga omnes* (or to some other obligations for those who do not believe in obligations *erga omnes),* but on the other hand we are rather worried about unilateral abuse. Some of us are even worried about excesses that might originate from international bodies. In other words, we want a maximum of effectiveness with optimum legal protection. Obviously, there is no simple answer to that. This epitomizes the dilemma of the *Rechtsstaat*, of the state under the rule of law, the dilemma between effectiveness and legal protection.

Simma:

I will also be very brief. With regard to *Mary*'s first question as to whether there is an obligation, I can subscribe to every word which *Christoph* has just said. Your second question was whether humanitarian interventions undertaken by the Security Council could really be considered legal. And I remember you said you could not discern a rule. But I think here you have to distinguish between the legality of humanitarian intervention undertaken by individual states or groups of states and that of humanitarian intervention undertaken and authorized by the Security Council. With regard to action by individual states or groups of states, I agree with you that I cannot discern a pattern of practice or a pattern of *opinio iuris* that would lead to, let us say, a rule of customary law. All the instances have been very controversial. With regard to the Security Council I do not need to find another rule in general international law, because for me the rule is right there, in the words "threat to the peace," and I personally would not subscribe to a view that the Security Council would act *ultra vires* if it subsumed things under this notion that *prima facie* have nothing to do with (negative) "peace" as understood in 1945. I think the whole legislative history, among other things, as well as a teleological interpretation of the Charter speak out in favour of opening up, let us say, the ambit of action available to the Council. I think the notion of a threat to the peace is a very apt key to do so.

O'Connell:

Article 39 says that the Security Council can determine the existence of a threat to the peace, but it takes action under Article 41 and 42 to maintain or restore only international peace.

Simma:

I would have no problem to subsume grave breaches of human rights under the notion of a threat to international peace.

O'Connell:

Even if no border is crossed? You want to expand the rule ...

Simma:

I simply do not have your problem, but time is running out. With regard to *Christian Tomuschat*'s idea of a European Security Council: I cannot get around

Article 103 as easily as he seemed to do, because I think there is a clear limitation here. Of course, a "Security Council" does not mean anything as long as security is being talked about and so on. But if you want to establish a "European Security Council" with the competence to engage in, let us say, "European Chapter VII" action without calling for UN Security Council authorization, you are in clear breach of Articles 53 and 103, and states engaging in such actions would be under conflicting obligations. In such a situation, one would have to give precedencc to the Charter. In fact, I am happy to recall that we actually needed the Chinese to do peace-keeping in Yugoslavia, whereas we did not need — and we did not have — a European Security Council. The universal Security Council did a good job. UN people are marching into Yugoslavia. Europe did not accomplish this.

With regard to *Jonathan,* who has difficulties finding obligations *erga omnes.* I have good news for you: According to my jurisprudential view — *Al,* you are going to really explode now — obligations *erga omnes* exist because we international lawyers think that they exist. Not just professors, but people with, let us say, a little more authority, like the legal advisors which we have had around us. Who else are we waiting for? *Jonathan,* I think there is a right but certainly not a duty to help. As to details, I refer you to the answer which *Christoph* just gave to *Mary*'s respective question. With regard to non-military responses to violations of *erga omnes* norms, I would like to read out a sentence in my paper, which I probably read out too fast the first time. I said, "As long as the UN Charter is recognized as the higher law of the international community, any regional enforcement action employing military force, or, as in the case of economic sanctions, affecting the rights of third parties will require an (express) authorization by the Security Council." What I meant by this was that, if a group of states engaged in non-military reprisals, let us say, in a blockade or embargo, and by doing so affected the rights of third states that decided not to go along with the group of obligations *erga omnes* enforcers, that would be a problem. Assume, for instance, Yugoslavia getting oil from state A, and the EEC starting to blockade Yugoslavia and thereby infringing a treaty right of A to get the oil into Yugoslavia. I think the EEC countries would not be justified in doing so and, if I read the newspapers correctly, something like that was expressly stated as a reason for the EEC sanctions not encompassing an oil embargo against Yugoslavia. For that we would need a Security Council authorization — which is in exact conformity with my view.

With regard to Mr. *Wolfrum*'s question of consent to peace-keeping: I think, first we have to apply the differentiations which *Christoph* just developed. Then we also have to apply differentations with regard to what consent means. By that I refer to the "hardness" of consent. I think nobody has ever said that there is a treaty obligation on states suffering or enjoying peace-keeping operations on their territory to let the "blue helmets" just march into their territory. There is consent — embodied in the word "agreement" — but the agreement which existed, for instance, between Egypt and the United Nations with regard to UNEF I was not an agreement as hard and as binding, so to say, as a treaty. Egypt had the right to come up and say, "Would you please leave." In such an instance you can, of course, like in our *Mietrecht,* ask for another month or two. But there was no right of the United Nations to say, "No, we are going to stay because you are obliged by treaty to let us sit there on the Suez-Canal." Consent means different things in different circumstances.

Mr. *Riedel* inquired what the difference was between my view of a trichotomy of Chapter VII action *vis-à-vis* the dichotomy advocated by others. Well, the difference is that I do not do what *Michael Bothe* accused Prof. *Frowein* of doing, namely of leaving out sentences from Charter articles; something that *Michael Bothe* then did himself. I, for my part, read Article 39 without omitting anything . . .

O'Connell:

You left out "international" from the last line.

Simma:

I omitted "international" because I did not think it was relevant. Article 39 says that the Security Council "shall determine," and for me the determination actually has a lot of effects. It is addressed to the violator and says, "Listen, you are in breach of an obligation and you stop it." So the determination has, if you want, a certain aggressive function. The determination is also addressed to the other states: they are no longer allowed to aid or to assist the state in breach. But in my view the other states would also be justified to engage in countermeasures if, and now I come to the point which you omitted, if the Security Council makes a recommendation, because Article 39 says that the Security Council determines and shall make recommendations, or decides what measures shall be taken. I know, of course, that in the legislative history of the words "shall make recommendations" there is a strong view which says that these recommendations were designed to be recommendations to the parties to a conflict to finally stop the shooting before the Security Council really gets serious. But again, this refers us to Articles 31 and 32 of the Vienna Convention, and I read the rules on interpretation, especially the rules on interpretation of constitutive instruments of international organizations, in the sense that legislative history really does not play a role as long as the body actually "lives," which in the case of the UN it certainly does.

With regard to the question of the relationship between Security Council action and Article 51: I subscribe to *Torsten Stein*'s and to *Fred*'s view. I think you really have to be contextual here and you cannot say that, as soon as the Security

Council has done anything, Article 51 is out of the question. That will be a too formalistic view.

Michael, how does a rule enter the magic circle of "OEO"? I am happy to report that people like you are shoving these norms into the magic circle by what you say and what you write. For me it is not decisive whether these norms are capable of being enforced on a regular basis. What is decisive for me is that there is a community consensus according to which these obligations have a special force and a special status. Enforcement is a *cura posterior* and, of course, there is always the possibility of unilateral as well as collective enforcement.

With regard to what you said on humanitarian intervention: first, I refer to my answer to *Mary*. As to Panama, I really do not know what the people there might be enjoying. I am sure that Mr. *Endara* is enjoying his honeymoon, but from what my Committee has had before it as evidence on, let us say, problems of housing and the like in Panama, the enjoyment of democracy as an idea might be one of the few pleasures left to the majority of the population in Panama. I do not want to go as far as excluding any morally justified instance of unilateral intervention. But in such cases I would really prefer what I think *Ian Brownlie* has called the euthanasia approach: Let us not make a rule out of that, for instance a rule in the books which says in cases of somebody hopelessly sick you may turn off the oxygen! Let us not make such a rule, let us maintain the prohibition! If there is a case in which action of a doctor — or action by the U.S. — is really strongly justified, all right, public condemnation will be hesitant accordingly.

With regard to *Al*'s point about limitations on Security Council action — no action without money — I would humbly submit that this would be a good idea to consider also if states decide to engage in unilateral action. No action without money, please.

Frowein:

"Den letzten beißen die Hunde", as the Germans say. It is difficult, when time is running, to say anything. Let me pick up three points and apologize to those whom I am not going to mention expressly.

First point: obligations *erga omnes,* although that was really *Bruno Simma*'s main story. I find it somehow astonishing, I must admit, that there seems to be a sort of cleavage between the Americans and the Europeans on that point. It is very difficult to circumvent the fact that the ICJ has used the term "obligations erga omnes" clearly in a premeditated way and has to a certain extent tried to explain what it means. We have a very important treaty in force which acknowledges the notion of *ius cogens,* the Vienna Convention of the Law of Treaties. Only France has voted against the draft in that respect, but France has now clearly moved away from its earlier position. There are important statements by acting state-officials concerning the notion of *ius cogens* in the Vienna Convention. The United States' legal advisor said in 1979 if there should really be a treaty justifying Soviet Union intervention in Afghanistan, it would be a treaty violating *ius cogens* and therefore null and void. Although Afghanistan would be bound by the procedural aspects of the Vienna Convention, assuming for the moment both parties are bound by it, a third party or an international organization is not bound by that and can in fact take up the nullity right away. This was accepted by the international community. I find it somehow backward-looking and not really keeping pace with development of public international law not to recognize that we have reached that point where a hierarchy of norms in public international law is well recognized and entrenched. Although I would never go as far as saying that there is an obligation for all states to enforce, there is a possibility to act in order to restore the international order under those circumstances, normally, of course, without forcible action. Forcible action is only lawful in the Article 51 context and under Security Council authorization.

Second point: the relationship between Security Council action on the one hand and Article 51 on the other. I was too short on that and I apologize. I think it is rather clear that Article 41 can never exclude Article 51. The textual arguments which were made are important. One should not overestimate the text of the United Nations Charter as some people have said, but one should not underestimate it either. One should read it carefully, and if you look to Article 51 it is really telling that for the limiting phrase in the first sentence you find: "until the Security Council has taken measures to maintain" and only maintain. What does it mean? In all the other versions you have "maintain and restore." Must it not mean that here the measures must have had some success already? It is certainly not by accident that in Articles 39 in 42 you find "maintain and restore" as you do in Article 51's last sentence. But there it makes good sense because it says: As long as an Article 51 unilateral measure is in process, the Security Council may nevertheless act. The unilateral action is foreclosed only where you have "has taken to maintain." It would mean in my opinion that economic sanctions under Article 41 can never foreclose unilateral action.

As to Mr. *Stein*'s position: where the Security Council takes action using the force of arms, the whole idea of the system is that there the Council's monopoly in that respect prevails. That is a difficult point. I think one should not underestimate practical difficulties which would arise with parallel forcible action by the use of arms on one hand under the Security Council authority, on the other hand under unilateral authority of some states. The matter came up in the Gulf context. It is not by accident that the United States felt pressured, maybe by the other partners in the coalition, maybe by the political forces working in a context of that sort, not to argue that one should occupy Baghdad. Rather as soon as one had accomplished what was the clear purpose of the United Nations authorization, fighting was stopped.

My last point: regional agencies. I was not willing to argue that under public international law in general intervening in a civil war does not mean intervening against the territorial state. The question was: Can a state, by entering into a regional agency system, give the consent beforehand which would be a valid consent also at the time of intervention? That would mean that this is not enforcement action in the sense which needs specific authorization by the Security Council. I remain convinced, and I was very happy to hear *Tom Farer*'s and *Michael Reisman*'s comments, that this is really a road to be investigated further. I personally feel that the borderline between a valid and binding consent given beforehand on the one hand, and the right unilaterally to withdraw what you have committed yourself to, is something of great importance. Public international law was never based on the idea that you can withdraw at any moment a consent validly given. To pick up that UNEF problem again, a lot can be said for *Bruno Simma*'s comment that there was not a formally binding obligation. But the position was taken by some within the United Nations system later, that the exchange of notes should have binding effect. Assuming for the moment that this was the correct interpretation, then I would not go as far as saying because of the situation of troops stationed on the territory of a state, there must be an inherent sovereign right to withdraw consent at every moment. That is going clearly too far.

Now to *Tom Farer*'s different scenarios: I am not going into them all. But what I would like to say is this: We should not overlook that we have practiced treaty law implemented in several cases where many of these different alternatives have been tested. France has intervened on the basis of treaty commitments on the request of African governments where *coups d'état* had already taken place or were about to take place. The French practice in that respect is very relevant. This is something where we as international lawyers should do more than we have done so far. Giving authority to a clearly structured regional system may involve use of police power, to put it in this way. Of course, revolution as such is not unlawful under public international law, but that is really begging the issue.

The question is: Is it possible to set up a regional system with a specific value system enshrined which would be valid regional law? We are not far from that. The CSCE system has, as you all know, formally proscribed, not only for Europe but for vast parts of the world, democracy as a general commitment. The CSCE so far is not a legally binding treaty, but maybe we are not so far from a legally binding one. With the European Community, machinery is in force to operate against *coups d'état,* against revolutionary changes. It has operated in the Greek Colonels revolution in 1967-1974, in the Turkish *coup d'état* by the army in 1980, not only within the system of the European Convention of Human Rights but also within the EEC by freezing the association agreements.

What is the position of the Security Council of the United Nations under those circumstances? It is the idea of the Charter that the Council must have the monopoly in enforcement action against any state which has not given its consent. There I would read it very literally: no enforcement action shall be taken under regional arrangements or by regional agencies without the authorization of the Security Council. The question is: What sort of action is enforcement action in that respect? Can the Council give that authorization in a general way under a specific system, under a specific structure, as long as that structure exists?

I thank you very much for all your remarks. I have learned a lot this afternoon. Since I am the last speaker here, I think what I should do just before terminating is to thank the organizers of that colloquy for the beautiful idea to assemble us all here and run the thing so beautifully well. Thank you very much!

Delbrück:

We have reached the end of this symposium. I shall just take the liberty of adding a few remarks. I shall not attempt to summarize, co-comment or super-comment what has been commented so ably just now. But I want to express the organizer's deep satisfaction with the outcome of the symposium which we planned as a first start for further transatlantic scholarly exchanges. My conclusion from the discussions is that this American-European / German dialogue really should be continued. I think, the discussions have fully borne out our assumptions about divergent approaches on either side of the Atlantic to the issues under consideration, but it has also become clear that there are no irreconcilable divisions between the several approaches. In fact, there has been a rather fruitful tension between the different positions taken and these were not confined to the transatlantic dimensions of our meeting, but rather these challenging differences of positions were also visible within the American and the European groups of participants. This is a very encouraging sign and proves us to be an "open society," not a closed one, which should make it worthwhile to pursue these kinds of exchanges based on concrete issues, but with the different methodological and basic orientations in mind, as we have conducted our symposium during the last two days.

With this in mind, I like again to thank you all, first, for coming, secondly, for contributing so substantially to our common effort. I hope, the publication of the papers and proceedings will be out within less than twelve months, and I am sure that it will fully bear out my first impressions of the quality of this meeting. Again, thanks to all the participants!

Next, I feel urged to express my sincere thanks to the staff of the Institute, who provided such excellent service making the symposium so enjoyable. First of all, thanks go to Dr. *Dicke,* who has carried the brunt of the administrative and planning work, starting with the applications for the financial support of the symposium and ending up with taking care of the various individual needs of participants. The staff has to be congratulated again for an excellent work, dedication, and friendliness. There seems to be a special spirit around the Institute which makes it such a pleasure to work with the Institute. Some of the participants have mentioned the special atmosphere at this and earlier symposia held here in Kiel, and I gladly pass this mentioning on to the staff.

We very much hope that we shall be able to organize future symposia in the same spirit, and I sincerely hope that among these future conferences there will be a number of additional transatlantic meetings, possibly with the help of Professor *O'Connell* also in the United States. Thank you very much again! Let me close our meeting with an up-beat note: the sun has come out this afternoon — an indication that there will be a bright future for establishing ever closer contacts among the international legal communities here and abroad. Good bye!

List of Participants

Prof. Dr. *Michael Bothe,* Universität Frankfurt

Prof. Dr. *Lucius Caflisch,* Institut universitaire de hautes études, Genève

Prof. *Jonathan I. Charney,* Vanderbilt University, Nashville, Tenn.

Prof. Dr. *Jost Delbrück,* Universität Kiel

Priv.-Doz. Dr. *Klaus Dicke,* Universität Kiel

Prof. Dr. *Antonius Eitel,* Auswärtiges Amt, Bonn; Universität Bochum

Prof. *Tom Farer,* The American University, Washington, D.C.

Prof. *Luigi Ferrari Bravo,* Università di Roma

Prof. Dr. *Jochen Abr. Frowein,* Max-Planck-Institut für ausländisches öffentliches Recht und Völkerrecht, Heidelberg

Prof. Dr. *Konrad Ginther,* Universität Graz

Dr. *Reinhard Hilger,* Auswärtiges Amt, Bonn

Dr. *Winrich Kühne,* Stiftung Wissenschaft und Politik, Ebenhausen

Prof. *Fred L. Morrison,* University of Minnesota, Minneapolis

Ass. Prof. *Mary Ellen O'Connell,* Indiana University, Bloomington

Prof. Dr. *Albrecht Randelzhofer,* Freie Universität Berlin

Prof. *W. Michael Reisman,* Yale Law School, New Haven, Conn.

Prof. Dr. *Eibe H. Riedel,* Universität Marburg

Prof. *Alfred P. Rubin,* Tufts University, Medford, Mass.

Prof. Dr. *Christoph Schreuer,* Universität Salzburg

Prof. Dr. *Bruno Simma,* Universität München

Prof. Dr. *Torsten Stein,* Universität des Saarlandes, Saarbrücken

Prof. Dr. *Christian Tomuschat,* Universität Bonn

Sir *Arthur Watts,* London

Prof. Dr. *Rüdiger Wolfrum*, Universität Kiel

Prof. *Elisabeth Zoller*, Université Robert Schuman, Strasbourg

MIX
Papier aus verantwortungsvollen Quellen
Paper from responsible sources
FSC® C105338

Printed by Libri Plureos GmbH
in Hamburg, Germany